D0874008

JAZZ IN SEARCH OF ITSELF

LARRY KART

Jazz in Search of Itself

Yale University Press   NEW HAVEN AND LONDON

FOR JACOB

Published with assistance from the Louis Stern Memorial Fund.

Set in Minion type by Binghamton Valley Composition.

Printed in the United States of America.

Library of Congress Cataloging-in-Publication Data

Kart, Larry, 1942–
  Jazz in search of itself / Larry Kart.
    p.   cm.
  Includes index.
  ISBN 0-300-10420-0 (cloth : alk. paper)
  1. Jazz—History and criticism. I. Title.
  ML3506.K37 2004
  781.65'09—dc22   2004041413

A catalogue record for this book is available from the British Library.

The paper in this book meets the guidelines for permanence and durability of the Committee on Production Guidelines for Book Longevity of the Council on Library Resources.

10 9 8 7 6 5 4 3 2 1

The following pieces were first published in the Chicago Tribune and appear here by permission: Johnny Griffin; Ira Sullivan; Louis Armstrong; Black Beauty, White Heat; Earl Hines; Count Basie; Duke Ellington; Arthur Rollini; Arnett Cobb; Artie Shaw; Louis Bellson; Ruby Braff; Dizzy Gillespie; Thelonious Monk; Herbie Nichols; Oscar Peterson; Stan Getz; Woody Herman and Stan Getz; Al Cohn; Art Pepper; Sonny Stitt; Jackie McLean; Clifford Brown and Max Roach; Philly Joe Jones; Horace Silver; Bill Evans; Keith Jarrett; Gary Burton; Pat Metheny; McCoy Tyner; Wayne Shorter; Ornette Coleman; Cecil Taylor; Roscoe Mitchell; Evan Parker; Village Vanguard Jazz Orchestra; Milestones; Miles Returns; Lee Konitz; Marsalis at Twenty-One; The Death of Jazz?; "The Death of Jazz?" Revisited; The Marsalis Brothers Further On; The Sound-Alikes; Gershwin Musicals; Hoagy Carmichael; Smithsonian Pop; Billie Holiday; Sarah Vaughan; Cabaret Music; Chris Connor; Tony Bennett; The Jazzman as Rebel; Anita O'Day; Jazz Goes to College.

The following pieces were first published in Down Beat magazine and appear here by permission: Notes and Memories of the New Music; Lee Morgan, Donald Byrd, Blue Mitchell; Frank Zappa; Miles in the Sky; In a Silent Way; The Lost Quintet; Jazz in the Global Village; Raiders of the Lost Art.

An excerpt from The Oxford Companion to Jazz appears here by permission of Oxford University Press.

Jazz and Jack Kerouac first appeared in The Review of Contemporary Fiction.

CONTENTS

PART FOUR **Moderns and After**

PART FIVE **Miles Davis**

PART SIX **Tristano-ites**

PART SEVEN **The Neo-Con Game**

PART EIGHT **Singers and Songmakers**

PART NINE **Alone Together**

PREFACE

In every case the pieces collected here came to be written because other people asked for them. But that is no excuse. Long before I put myself in a position to be asked to write regularly about jazz—first, in 1968–69, for a magazine (*Down Beat*) and then, from 1977 to 1988, for a newspaper (the *Chicago Tribune*)—I wanted to be put there, in part because of a notion I'd begun to have about the role that someone who writes about jazz necessarily occupies.

Unlike the two other chief new arts—photography and motion pictures—that arose or coalesced at some point during the nineteenth century, jazz does not have a primarily technological basis, though it would come to benefit greatly from technological means of dissemination (the phonograph record and radio). Instead, jazz's primary "material" is the quintessentially historical set of human circumstances under which it arose—the collision/interpenetration of particular peoples under particular conditions in a new and expanding nation that had a form of government based on particular principles. And perhaps it is that inaugural immersion in the flux of history that has made jazz's further artistic development so immediate, visible, and intense—as though this art were compelled to give us a running account of its need to be made and the needs its making served. Of course, the same could be said of any other burst of novel artistic activity—say, painting and sculpture in fifteenth-century

Florence. And the wonder is that in relation to jazz we are in effect a bunch of fifteenth-century Florentines. Unavoidably implicated in what the artists make, we can, if we are alert and self-aware, quiz ourselves as to what necessities their various makings might fulfill, in us and in themselves. It was that realization, that sense of at once grasping and being in the grip of this music's perpetual intimate narrative, that made me eager to talk about it.

I have called this collection *Jazz in Search of Itself* for two reasons. First, the frequent unity in jazz of performer and composer, and the typical jazz circumstance of composition/performance in the moment, seems to me to place the ongoing expression of individual instrumental and vocal personality at or near the heart of the music. Second, there is the matter of the music's own "self" or "selves," the shapes its collective expression has taken and will go on to take. In the first decade of jazz's second century, it would seem that "search" and "self" are terms that fit.

My thanks to colleagues, friends, and mentors Bob Chatain, Harriet Choice, the late Ross Feld, Bill Kirchner, John Litweiler, Terry Martin, Doug Mitchell, Dan Morgenstern, Chuck Nessa, and the late Martin Williams, and, of course, to the musicmakers.

INTRODUCTION: ENACTMENT IN SOUND

It seems clear that when Ernest Ansermet wrote "I couldn't say if these artists make it a duty to be sincere" in his famous 1919 article about Will Marion Cook's Southern Syncopated Orchestra and its "extraordinary clarinet virtuoso," Sidney Bechet, he meant that sincerity of some special sort was among the virtues he found there. This was shrewd, even prescient, as was the comparison Ansermet drew between those musicians, especially Bechet, and the "men of the seventeenth and eighteenth centuries" who cleared the way for Haydn and Mozart by making "expressive works [out] of dance airs."

That the creation of "dance airs" was the literal role, socially and economically, of much jazz up through the end of the Swing Era almost goes without saying. And yet this was not the only role the music had to play, as Ansermet's emphasis on sincerity and expressiveness may suggest. Draw a line as early as the mid-1920s, and in the large body of remarkable music that already exists a strikingly individual personality is at work in almost every case—Bechet, King Oliver, Jelly Roll Morton, Louis Armstrong, Bix Beiderbecke, Johnny Dodds, Frank Teschemacher, Ma Rainey, Bessie Smith, James P. Johnson, Fats Waller, Earl Hines, et al. It could be argued that many of these musicians (certainly Armstrong and Smith) were inherently self-dramatizing, larger-than-life entertainers working in and for a marketplace that urged them to aggressively develop their skills

1

along individual lines. But the weight of biographical and recorded evidence suggests that the dramatized selves these artists
projected to the public were very much in tune with the selves
they actually possessed, while other jazz artists who were not of
a bold, demonstrative stripe (Beiderbecke, for one) also placed
a definite personal stamp on their work and were, like their less
reticent counterparts, valued for doing so.

Valued by whom and in what ways, to what ends and to
what effect? Valued by their colleagues, first and foremost. Allowing for considerable differences in role and temperament
among the mid-1920s stalwarts mentioned above, there is a
strong sense of a common project being worked upon, of technical and expressive resources being vigorously explored and
shared. To take the most obvious example, there was the immediate and lasting impact of Armstrong's innovations in rhythmic detail and formally coherent, overtly dramatic solo construction. From a practical, how-to-do-it point of view, these
achievements struck other musicians the way power tools did
the building trades—as Coleman Hawkins said in 1937, "About
ten or fifteen years ago Louis was so much ahead of everybody
that he became the inspiration for all of us." And Armstrong was
not alone in proclaiming that jazz's intensely attractive rhythmic
compulsiveness was allied to individual expressive impulses,
that this music was, among other things, a form of self-enactment in sound.

That is not to say that the music was simply autobiographical, nor should self-enactment be confused with self-exposure.
As Carl Dahlhaus says in his *Esthetics of Music*, "Musical expression is not to be immediately related to a composer as a real
person. Even the extreme 'expressionists' of the eighteenth century, Daniel Shubart and Carl Philipp Emanuel Bach, when they
'expressed themselves through music' were showing not their
empirical person in private life, but their 'intelligible I,' the an-
alogue of a poet's 'lyric ego.'" At one end of jazz's expressive
spectrum, then, stands a compositional thinker like Jelly Roll
Morton. While he is certainly among the most colorful figures
of any jazz era, even in his most striking solo piano perfor-

mances Morton does not thrust a dramatized self before us, in the manner of Louis Armstrong (or Bessie Smith or Sidney Bechet); rather, the composer-performer is present but at one remove—we focus on the way the game is being played and at the end salute the skill with which we have been stirred, diverted, and satisfied. But especially when other players, other voices, are involved, as in his famous Red Hot Peppers recordings of 1926–28, Morton's gift for shaping surprise-reward formal structures also extends to the realm of dramatic discourse.

The Red Hot Peppers' "Dead Man Blues" "undertakes a touchy combination of sprightliness and seriousness," as Martin Williams put it, and there and on "Sidewalk Blues" one feels that Morton the composer-bandleader is precisely, almost cinematically, grading the distance and angle of our emotional vantage point. On "Sidewalk" the gentility of the "Liebestraum" theme, already mocked the first time through, is further guyed on its reappearance by a tart voicing for clarinet trio (as Morton's piano dances at its heels); then it's virtually elbowed off the sidewalk, as it were, by the piece's final freewheeling trumpet-trombone-clarinet stomp. Hurly-burly urban reality meets and defeats lace-curtain respectability in this sly pocket drama, the musical counterpart to a George Herriman Krazy Kat cartoon or a Buster Keaton two-reeler.

On "Dead Man," with its New Orleans funeral framework, the byplay between the clarinet trio's homogeneous flow and the trumpet-trombone-clarinet heterophony has a very different effect. That the former's undertow of release and regret and the latter's life-force swing are shown throughout in the same even light and are found formally and dramatically to be of equal weight is the piece's expressive program—marvelously realized, remarkably mature. If cornetist George Mitchell's solemn, graceful solo on "Dead Man" does not strike us as a self-portrait, as any number of Armstrong's solos do, that is largely because Morton's three-minute drama requires Mitchell to at once be himself and play a semi-choral role—a messenger bearing news from Corinth to Chicago.

At what point can we say of this rapidly evolving music that it too has a self—that is, an identity of which it is conscious and that shapes its sense of what it can and should do next? Perhaps that is a question for which there can be no definitive answer; one might as well ask when, if ever, the citizens of fifteenth-century Florence thought they were living in the Renaissance. But if we think of Armstrong, for one, as an actor writing his own script and doing so on the run, it is not hard to find jazz works of the 1920s in which a self-reflective strain is very much present, is even of the essence. "Dead Man Blues" and "Sidewalk Blues" implicitly set up a dialogue between a "here" and one or more "theres" (urban and rural, present and past, man and machine, North and South), while exploring and expressing such criss-crossing states of consciousness is the explicit goal of Duke Ellington's "Creole Rhapsody" and "Black and Tan Fantasy" (both from 1927)—a pattern that would remain prominent throughout Ellington's career.

The audience for this music was of course not confined to the men and women who were making it, nor did it consist (if musicmakers are set aside) solely of those for whom it served as airs for dancing. Jazz is a meaning-making activity; its acts ask to be read, and have even come to be at various times and places hungered for. (In his essay "Remembering Jimmy," Ralph Ellison wrote: "Jimmy Rushing was not simply a local entertainer—he expressed a value, an attitude toward the world for which our lives afforded no other definition.") And those acts of reading inevitably alter the curious, meaning- and pleasure-seeking listener—whose responses to the music, especially if they are made in a public forum, tend to become part of the process whereby jazz discovers, shapes, and thinks about itself.

I am, of course, one of those hungry-curious listeners, and this book consists of a little less than forty years of in-public responses on my part. While I have corrected errors of fact and in a few cases have combined two or more pieces that deal with the same topic, latter-day second thoughts have been kept separate from the original material. Just as the "who plays what, when" circumstances of jazz performance are more than circumstantial, the "who thinks and says what, when" aspects of how we respond to jazz have evidentiary value and should not be disguised. In fact, a commitment to lack of disguise, the "duty to be sincere" that Ansermet heard in the music of Bechet, has been part of jazz from the first. Modifying the title of José Ortega y Gasset's famous tract *The Dehumanization of Art*, "the rehumanization of art" is among the key roles this music has had to play; and its ability to do so probably accounts for the speed and depth with which it affected audiences and musicians around the world.

It is common for those who can recall their own earliest encounters with jazz to describe what took place then as an act of recognition—or as Bechet rather dramatically put it in his autobiography, *Treat It Gentle*, "That's what the music is . . . a lost thing finding itself." In Bechet's account, the advent of jazz is firmly linked to the aftermath of Emancipation: "All those people who had been slaves, they needed the music more than ever now; it was like they were trying to find out in this music what they were supposed to do with this freedom; playing the music and listening to it—waiting for it to express what they needed to learn." The "lost thing" is said to be "like a man with no place of his own . . . a stranger right in the place where he was born" who eventually "finds a place, his place," having been schooled to do so by the music's journey "all the way up from what it had been in the beginning to the place where it could be itself."

If those remarks have an air of fable to them, they are at the very least a fable that one of jazz's primal creators chose to entertain. Nor does it seem accidental that one of the music's key mysteries is touched upon here with such precision. "Playing the music and listening to it," Bechet says, "[the people were] waiting for it to express what they needed to learn." Where, then, does the tutelage and the consciousness that underlies it reside? In a separate class of courageously individualistic, expressive artists? (Bechet describes his perhaps semi-mythical grandfather Omar in such terms, and he himself would seem to fit the model.) Yet it is both listeners and players who "needed to learn" and who were, over time, taught. So is the music itself a third

place or force? And is it there, or through its agency, that tutelage occurs?

The short answer to those latter two questions is, yes. Tempered by the fact or the aura of improvisation, the direct or
alluded to presence of swing, the potentially literal identity of
composer and performer, and the participation on all sides of
selves that are not counterfeit, jazz involves the active passage
through time of specific individuals at specific moments—or at
least that is the ground-base situation from which possible var-
iants spring. Thus one aspect of the mutually dependent
expression-learning/playing-listening process whose importance
Bechet emphasizes. Provided they survive—on recordings, in
memories, in the work of other musicians—jazz's acts of occupied, speaking, self-reflective presentness continue to speak in
the present tense. For example, when Coleman Hawkins's solo
on "If I Could Be With You One Hour Tonight" (1929) is placed
alongside his "Donegal Cradle Song" (1933), his "Body and Soul"
(1939), his "Picasso" (1946–47), his "Until the Real Thing Comes
Along"(1958), and so forth, a virtual artistic autobiography begins to emerge, one in which each chapter comments on and
modifies the whole. That Hawkins, as critic Terry Martin has
explained, found a way to evoke romantic moods yet handle
them objectively, "with the ease and cunning of a great dramatist," is an aesthetic-historical-spiritual discovery that continues
to reverberate—not only in the music of Sonny Rollins, Wayne
Shorter, and others but also in the sensibilities of a host of listeners.

A further example of jazz's learning curve at work, one that
seems to me revealing in its youthful waywardness of how and
what expression teaches. The first live jazz performance I heard
was a Jazz at the Philharmonic concert that took place at the
Chicago Opera House on October 2, 1955, with a lineup that
included Roy Eldridge, Dizzy Gillespie, Flip Phillips, Illinois Jacquet, Lester Young, Oscar Peterson, Herb Ellis, Ray Brown, and
Buddy Rich. Aware of the music for just five months, at age
thirteen I knew the names of most of these musicians. And one
of them, Eldridge, was a particular favorite because he seemed

to speak so personally and openly through his horn, with such passion, genuineness, strength, and grit. (By contrast, I thought that Jacquet and Phillips's tenor saxophone battles were exciting but mostly for show, not to be taken at face value.)

Lester Young, however, was only a name to me; I'd yet to hear a note of his music. And partly because of that lack of context, much of what he played that afternoon struck me as very strange. (As it happens, the concert was recorded, and eventually released on the album *Blues in Chicago 1955*, so I can place memories alongside what actually occurred.) Young was not in good shape on the 1955 JATP tour, physically or emotionally. He would be hospitalized for several weeks that winter, suffering from alcoholism and depression, though he would recover sufficiently to make two of his best latter-day recordings, *Jazz Giants '56* and *Pres and Teddy*, in mid-January 1956. But in the gladiatorial arena of Jazz at the Philharmonic, the wan, watery-toned Young I heard seemed to speak mostly of weakness, even of an alarming inability or unwillingness to defend himself. And yet this state of being was undeniably, painfully being expressed, though at times perhaps only out of dire necessity; the brisk tempo Gillespie set for the piece the two of them shared was one that Young could barely make.

Then toward the end came a ballad medley, which began with Young's slow-motion restatement of "I Didn't Know What Time It Was." That he seemed to be more in his element here was about all I realized at the time, though even that fact was provocative. And the recorded evidence confirms this, as Young bends a bare minimum of resources to the task—as though he were saying, "This is all I have," and asking, "Is this not enough?" Admittedly, that is largely an adult response to a performance that now seems remarkable to me. Yet something of that sort must have been crystallizing back then, because I was immediately eager to find out more about Lester Young. And when I did—an album of vintage Basie material that included "Taxi War Dance" and the arrival of *Jazz Giants '56* were crucial—any number of doors began to open.

First, it was clear that quite a few tenor saxophonists of the

day—Stan Getz, Zoot Sims, Al Cohn, Bill Perkins, Richie Kamuca, et al.—had been inspired by Young, though in each case
there was an individual strain, a personal translation of Young's
techniques and sensibility. Second, these networks of affinity ran
all through jazz and were continuing to run through it—sometimes in concert, sometimes divergently or even in apparent conflict. What, for example, to make of the fact that so many of
Young's disciples were white, while the most striking young
tenor saxophonist of the day, Sonny Rollins, was African-
American and seemed to come at the music from a very different
angle? Any thought that jazz could be viewed from a safe, mu-
seumlike distance now seemed absurd; this was an art in which
history was always happening, and it was happening to *us*.

Almost fifty years further on, is that still the case? The first
of the pieces that follow, "Notes and Memories of the New Music," is a response made in 1969 to what had been a decade of
remarkable artistic upheaval in jazz—a "history is always happening" time to be sure. But such a rate of change could not
continue unabated, and one result is that jazz now has what
might be called a permanent avant-garde. Perhaps that sounds
paradoxical, even absurd—how, after all, can the latest thing of
several yesterdays ago still be avant-garde? But artistic avant-
gardism in general and the jazz avant-garde in particular are
not merely timeline affairs. In the words of music historian Carl
Dahlhaus: "Newness is also an aesthetic factor, which for example is inextricably bound up with the earliest atonal works,
Schoenberg's Op. 11 Piano Pieces and the final movement of the
Second String Quartet. What is seemingly most transient—the
quality of incipient beginning, of 'for the first time'—acquires a
paradoxical permanence. Even half a century later it can be felt
in almost undiminished form, and as an immediate aesthetic
quality at that." The same could be said of the music of Ornette
Coleman, Cecil Taylor, Albert Ayler, Evan Parker, Derek Bailey,
et al.—the sense of language upheaval is inherent and does not
become normalized.

Transforming tradition into an immediate aesthetic virtue
has been the goal of Wynton Marsalis and others of his ilk, and

the pieces gathered here under the heading "The Neo-Con Game" argue that, except in the realm of publicity, this attempt has failed. Not because the jazz past is or should be a closed book; the possibility always exists that living musicians will be driven to make contact with what has come before them and make something vital and new out of it. But when tradition is being brandished in the name of order, stability, or status, direct, language-level contact with the music tends drastically to diminish—or so the course of Marsalis's career suggests.

The term "mainstream" is in jazz parlance not merely descriptive. Coined in the mid-1950s, reportedly by English critic Stanley Dance, it arose from the belief in some quarters that bop, and modern jazz in general, was something of an artistic wrong turn, and that a number of still vigorous swing musicians (for example, trombonist Dicky Wells, trumpeter Joe Thomas, and tenor saxophonist Buddy Tate) were far less visible on the jazz landscape than they ought to be. Thus the labeling of such musicians as mainstream was at once an expression of aesthetic preferences and an attempt to translate those preferences into permanent values. But even though the style of music that led to the coining of "mainstream" has now edged over into revivalism, if only because almost all the original swing stylists are no longer with us, when the term is used today it retains some of its original ideological wishfulness. The belief or the hope is that within shifting stylistic boundaries a majority of musicians still agree on how the music can and should be played, that it is within this area of language agreement that the music's most genuinely creative figures are at work, and that the course of the music will and should flow along in this manner. In fact, things are a bit more complicated than that.

Leaving Marsalis's wax museum aside, the mainstream of contemporary majority practice does share a common language—a mélange of the mid-1960s Miles Davis Quintet, the Bill Evans Trio of the Village Vanguard recordings (made in 1961), and the early- to mid-1960s John Coltrane Quartet. That doesn't account for everyone in today's majority-practice, common-language mainstream. Bop and hard bop devotees and musi-

cians who incorporate aspects of such avant-garde figures as
Eric Dolphy and Ornette Coleman can be found there as well.
But the point is that some forty years have elapsed since the
sources of this shifting common language emerged—a remarkably long stretch of time when one recalls that only nineteen
years separate the broadly influential first recordings of Louis
Armstrong (1926) and those of Charlie Parker (1945). Of course
jazz was almost irresistibly drawn to rush down the lines of its
initial language inventions; and it could be argued, in the words
of critic Max Harrison, that an "excessive rate of stylistic change
. . . forced jazz to bypass areas of possible major growth." But if
Armstrong's "Cornet Chop Suey" (1926) and Parker's "Ko-Ko"
(1945) do not stand in opposition to each other, the stylistic distance between them seems much greater than that between the
Davis Quintet's *E.S.P.* (1965) or the Coltrane Quartet's *Crescent*
(1964) and any representative common-language mainstream
recording of today.

That the rate of language innovation in jazz has slowed or
even stabilized over the last forty years seems undeniable. Thus
the notion of repertory performance is seen as attractive, even
necessary, while shifts in style increasingly come in response to
aspects of the surrounding musical or extramusical terrain.
There is the omnipresence of rock in its various guises
(standard-era popular songs and rhythm and blues, formerly
part of the common cultural backdrop, have not played that role
for decades); the distinctive sensibilities of the non-American
regions of the world in which jazz has taken root and flourished
(for example, the Netherlands, Scandinavia, Central Europe);
the desire to assert and explore social, spiritual, or political identities (John Zorn's "radical Jewish culture" music, Uri Caine's
game-playing with Mahler, Bach, and Wagner), and so forth.

Underlying jazz's current oscillating, semi-steady state are
the vicissitudes of a specific element of the music's language. Up
to and including Charlie Parker, jazz's rhythmic discourse has
depended on the presence of relatively stable metrical frameworks. But the ability to make meaningful microsubdivisions of
the beat within such frameworks may have reached a physical/

perceptual barrier in Parker's music, and in the four decades since his death, it would seem that that barrier has remained unbreached. As a result, such first- and second-generation avant-gardists as Cecil Taylor, Roscoe Mitchell, Evan Parker, and Derek Bailey have more or less abandoned metrical frameworks in order to continue their modernist pursuit of extremes of sensibility and technique, of near-atomistic levels of nuance. If those pursuits are not divorced from the world of Armstrong, Ellington, Young, and Parker—as I and many other listeners believe—the majority of the jazz audience seems to feel otherwise. And so do a good many, perhaps most, jazz musicians, if only because the highly individual languages that Taylor et al. speak necessarily cut across the grain of the music's communal craft professionalism.

The premise with which I began—the one that drew many of us to the music in the first place—was that jazz is, among other things, "a form of self-enactment in sound." And the music presents us with any number of instances of the need to keep writing openly and honestly in the book of life—not only from musicians whose inventiveness simply refused or refuses to quit (Earl Hines, Coleman Hawkins, Benny Carter, Lee Konitz, Ruby Braff, Von Freeman, Steve Lacy, Martial Solal), but also from those whose music spoke of and from states of personal distress that might well have reduced them to silence (Lester Young, Billie Holiday, Bud Powell, Serge Chaloff, Jackie McLean, Hank Mobley, Chet Baker, Art Pepper). One doesn't want to be sentimental or unworldly about this; some artists eventually say all that they have to say, after which they may choose to earn a living by repeating themselves with slight modifications. But if Johnny Hodges, for example, did not wear his heart on his sleeve each time he played "Day Dream," his ability to animate his personal presence was crucial to his art; an uninhabited Hodges "Day Dream" would have been no "Day Dream" at all.

Is the expression of individual instrumental personality still the norm in jazz? The facelessness of so many technically adept younger jazz musicians is often remarked upon ("The soloists have become so generic," in the words of veteran composer–

valve trombonist Bob Brookmeyer), and this is commonly attributed to the homogeneity of the jazz education system, the
long-lasting, pervasive influences of John Coltrane and Bill
Evans, the sheer weight of the music's past, and so forth. But
perhaps it also is a kind of revolt or protest from within, a way
of saying that the role openly expressed, ongoing individuality
has played in jazz no longer matches up well with the habits of
the rest of the world or that it now comes at a price that is too
high to be paid.

And yet Sonny Rollins and Wayne Shorter already were
stepping back from the direct expression of self some forty years
ago—guided, especially in Rollins's case, by Coleman Hawkins's
example. The rich complexity of Rollins's musical thought, and
his ability to at once dramatize and ironically comment upon
virtually any emotional impulse that came to mind, led him to
express multiple points of view—one could even say summon
up multiple selves or characters—within a single solo. This was,
however, not an approach that Rollins could sustain during the
1960s, in the face of rapid stylistic change in the surrounding
jazz landscape. Responding to those changes in his own work,
as he did quite strikingly up to a point, also meant that the
broadly shared musical-emotional language of romantic sign
and sentiment that had so deeply stirred Rollins's own sentiments and wit was now becoming historical. It was a language
that could still be referred to and played off of, but for him
apparently not with sufficient immediacy.

Shorter's temperament—also deeply, even subversively
ironic—led him at first to toy brilliantly with the idea that any
soloistic gesture could or should be taken at face value. In the
typical Shorter solo of the early- to mid-1960s, seemingly forthright, "heated" musical-emotional gestures are disrupted, even
mocked, by oblique, wide-eyed shifts to other levels of speech
(cool, chess-master complexity, blatantly comic tonal and rhythmic distortions, and so forth). Rollins had said, in effect: "There
are many selves at work here, and I am present in all of them."
Shorter took the next step: "Why assume that any of these selves
is a self, that any of them is me?" Significantly, this aspect of

Shorter's music emerged at the same time that Coltrane was plunging headfirst into the expressionistic sublime, although Shorter's seemingly innate distancing diffidence also seems to have played a role. In any case, after he left the Miles Davis Quintet, Shorter increasingly withdrew from the solo arena (from 1970 to 1985 he was a member of the jazz-rock group Weather Report), and on the rare occasions when he has returned there, it is his diffidence that he essentially expresses. (That Shorter returned to the concert stage and the recording studio beginning in 2002 is a hopeful sign, though the rather studied elegance of the results so far suggests something less than full engagement.)

In the music of Rollins and Shorter, humorous or ironic speech turns into doubt about the act of speaking, about the ongoing integrity of the language itself. Here, it would seem, the scrim of postmodernism begins to descend upon jazz, perhaps before the concept was even formulated. From that point of view, the peculiar course of jazz in the Netherlands is revealing. As Kevin Whitehead's book *New Dutch Swing* explains in intriguing detail, from the mid-1960s on, jazz in this small, economically and culturally dependent nation came to be marked by an aggressively playful slyness. When pianist-composer-bandleader Misha Mengelberg first heard Charlie Parker, on a 1947 recording, he immediately recognized "that nobody was able to do what Parker was doing. There are generations after him who tried but nobody succeeded." Thus, to Mengelberg and others, the need to take apart and manipulate the given external language was obvious. "Because jazz . . . came [to them] second-hand," Whitehead notes, "the Dutch feel no impulse to preserve it in pure form. . . . The heritage is all available." But in what sense? Distance (historical, cultural, geographical) is both acknowledged in this music and built into it, at times to striking effect. On Ab Baars's *Songs*, the saxophonist-clarinetist responds to a series of Native-American melodies with intense inventiveness and no hint of guilt or travelogue sentiment; the breadth of the cultural gap Baars chose to jump must have been a large part of what enabled him to do it. And yet the liveliness of Dutch jazz is so firmly linked to its quirkiness (Mengelberg speaks of wanting "to put sticks into spokes of all the wheels") that the results can seem a bit wistful, even elegiac—a case of fun and games before the fall. Perhaps, like Frost's oven bird, "The question [it] frames in all but words / Is what to make of a diminished thing."

Is that a question that jazz as a whole should be asking itself? In the face of a thousand more young tenor saxophonists who sound just like each other and/or Michael Brecker, one might think so. But just beginning to list the musicians I find myself turning to these days as a matter of course—Tim Armacost, Bill Carrothers, Harold Danko, Billy Drewes, Jason Moran, Joe Morris, Mark Shim, Christophe Schweizer, Wadada Leo Smith, Henry Threadgill, Walt Weiskopf, Edward Wilkerson Jr.—I find variety, individuality, and signs of continuing growth. Besides, jazz's sense of active speech, its gift for personal address, is not confined to this or any other present. The other day I found myself listening to the Fats Waller pieces that his mentor James P. Johnson recorded in April 1944, four months after Waller's untimely death at age thirty-nine. Full of crystalline detail and buoyant swing, these wonderful performances are not heart-on-the-sleeve affairs. And yet the sense that Johnson is almost literally communicating with Waller is overwhelming, as the elder statesman lays out his most intimate, subtle, "inside" inventions—one pianist to another, so to speak—and leaves the rest of us to eavesdrop as best we can.

Obviously, I can't prove that what I think I hear there is the case, any more than I can prove that Lester Young's "I Didn't Know What Time It Was" solo was more than an assemblage of figures that felt comfortable to him, that the selves of Sonny Rollins or Wayne Shorter or Roy Eldridge are present in their music to the degree and in the way I believe they are, and so forth. But I do know that such "conversations" have been part of this music from the first and that without them jazz would not have the meaning it does.

"What has the beauty of music to do with that melting mood it may produce in me?" asks Ortega y Gasset in *The Dehuman-*

ization of Art. "Is this not a thorough confusion. . . . Seeing requires distance. Each art operates a magic lantern that removes and transfigures its objects. . . . When this derealization is lacking, an awkward perplexity arises; we do not know whether to 'live' the things or observe them." In jazz, something like the opposite is true. Seeing demands presence; Ortega's "thorough confusion" is a chimera; to live and to observe are one; Bechet's "lost thing" finds itself. Or at least that, by and large, has been our experience.

PART I

Notes and Memories of the New Music, 1969

People put all these labels on the music, but actually all it is is cats playing.

—LESTER BOWIE

A ND cats listening, too. When *Something Else,* Ornette Coleman's first record, came out in early 1959, I was a seventeen-year-old high school student living in a Chicago suburb. I'd been listening to jazz for about four years.

The first jazz record I'd bought, back in the spring of 1955, was a 45 EP by Lu Watters's Yerba Buena Jazz Band, entrancing not only for the music (its calculated rusticity sounded unlike anything I'd ever heard) but also for the liner notes (which proclaimed that this was "the only *real* jazz band in America"). Early in the next school year, my eighth-grade homeroom teacher, hearing that I was interested in jazz (he was a fan himself), recommended that I buy a Charlie Parker record and took me and a friend to a Jazz at the Philharmonic concert at the Chicago Opera House that featured Roy Eldridge, Dizzy Gillespie, Lester Young, Flip Phillips, and Illinois Jacquet, among others. That was it. From then on, all the money I could spare went into records.

I found others who shared my enthusiasm—that aforementioned friend, with whom I engineered what seemed to us monumental record trades (a ten-inch Ellington LP that contained

"Ko-Ko" and "Concerto for Cootie" once brought ten less desirable albums in exchange), and, later on, an astonishingly good fifteen-year-old drummer, who had practiced for two years to Max Roach records in his attic before playing in public. I'm sure that his necessarily practical approach to listening—a quest to discover in other musicians virtues that he himself could put to use—helped to deepen and ground my own understanding.

Eldridge, Young, Miles Davis, Clifford Brown, Sonny Rollins, Roach, and Philly Joe Jones were my gods, and their records were the texts of a religion. We were still too young to hear these men in clubs unless we brought a parent along, so we went to off-night, all-ages-welcome sessions run by Joe Segal and discovered a host of local deities—multi-instrumentalist Ira Sullivan, tenor saxophonist Johnny Griffin, pianist Jodie Christian, bassists Victor Sproles and Donald Garrett, and drummer Wilbur Campbell.

Then came John Coltrane's *Blue Train* album, with the leader's galvanic solo on the title track. This, to me, was the first sign that the music could and would change. Perhaps because I had come to jazz during a period of musical consolidation, it hadn't occurred to me that the music might once again undergo an upheaval comparable to that of the 1940s. But Coltrane's playing made it clear that, as far as he was concerned, something new was happening. Listening to *Blue Train* again, I realize that, beyond Coltrane's stylistic innovations, it was his music's emotional aura of intense and unceasing search that was the clue. Today it appears that Sonny Rollins will have a deeper musical effect on the new music, but Coltrane was the herald for me.

Fortunately, at about the same time, I heard Chico Hamilton's quintet, and, amid the polite thumping, the group's reedman picked up a strange-looking ebony horn and played a solo that sounded like Coltrane translated for the human voice. Of course this was Eric Dolphy on bass clarinet, and now my belief that change was occurring had a second point of reference.

Ornette Coleman was the third, and the leap in understanding that *Something Else* required was more than I could manage at first. In fact, *Something Else* remains a weird record. Pianist Walter Norris attempts to accompany Ornette with pertinent harmonies, creating "advanced" harmonic patterns that clash with Ornette's homemade, and ultimately downhome, tonal, rhythmic, and melodic concerns. The record is a perfect example of Ornette's distance from the conventions of the forties and fifties, but the emotional tone of the music is bizarre—as though Johnny Dodds had recorded with a Red Nichols group.

The next Coleman record I heard, *The Shape of Jazz to Come* (with Don Cherry, Charlie Haden, and Billy Higgins), had a more homogeneous atmosphere. "Peace" and "Lonely Woman" were such direct and intense emotional statements that I found myself listening to them constantly, even though I had little understanding of what Ornette was up to in purely musical terms. I felt that the music was beautiful, but my fifties-trained ears told me that it was exotic and "outside."

That barrier finally fell when I heard "R.P.D.D." from the *Ornette* album under rather unusual circumstances. As I played it for the second time, late one night, I drifted off to sleep and dreamed that, in a pastoral setting, I was hearing a music more warmly human and natural than any I'd heard before. I awoke to discover that Coleman's "R.P.D.D." solo was what I'd been hearing in the dream, and that the quality I'd given it there was one it actually possessed. In no emotional sense was this music "far out" or abstract. Instead, I found that I had to turn to blues and early jazz to find music that conveyed human personality as directly.

The next beneficent shock to my ears was administered by Coltrane (by this time, the summer of 1960, I was about to become a student at the University of Chicago). Ever since *Blue Train*, my drummer friend and I had listened to every Coltrane recording we could find. The then most recent one, *Giant Steps*, sounded to us like it might be the end of the musical road he had been traveling for the past several years. Still, when Coltrane came to the Sutherland Lounge in mid-August, we went expecting to hear those qualities which had marked most of *Giant Steps* (recorded in May 1959 and released early in 1960)—

dense harmonic patterns negotiated with a brilliantly hard and even tone. Instead, we heard something quite different.

This was the group with pianist Steve Kuhn, bassist Steve Davis, and drummer Pete LaRoca (the direct predecessor of the group that would record the album *My Favorite Things* two months later), and the difference between *Giant Steps* and the manner and matter of Coltrane's current playing seemed immense. The tunes on tenor were mostly up-tempo blues with the harmonies stripped down toward modality, and the keening, granite-hard tone now exploded into growls and honks. The tunes on soprano saxophone, a horn we had some difficulty in recognizing, used harmonic change to form hypnotically circular rhythm patterns, over which Coltrane wailed like a blues-possessed snake charmer. To say the least, we were astonished and moved. As Coleman had done in his way, Coltrane unearthed a degree of passion rare in any music. [I also recall Coltrane conversing between sets with the visiting Johnny Hodges, his former boss, and passing his soprano sax on to Hodges for examination. Hodges had played the instrument himself in the late twenties and early thirties.]

From then on, Coltrane's Chicago visits were essential experiences. I remember in particular an engagement at McKie's Disc Jockey Show Lounge, during which a tune from *Giant Steps*, "Mr. P.C.," became a nightly challenge. "My Favorite Things" and the other soprano tunes would be dealt with in the first two sets, and by 1 a.m. he would be playing "Mr. P.C." on tenor with an intensity that seemed to demand in response all the volume Elvin Jones could muster. The tune would be played for at least forty minutes, and some performances lasted well over an hour. As novelist Jerry Figi wrote of a later Coltrane group: "What they did prove was just how *hard* they could try. That they could beat themselves bloody pounding at the farthest reaches of experience and come back with only their effort as an answer."

But there were other answers, or their beginnings, in the music of Coleman's *Free Jazz* and Cecil Taylor. I see that, so far, my memories have centered on the emotional freedom that Col-

trane and Coleman won for the individual improviser. The group
settings seemed basically to be springboards for their solo efforts, although the wholeness of performances like "Lonely
Woman" and "Ramblin'" should have been clues that Coleman,
at least, had something else in mind.

Free Jazz made it clear that the relative liberation of the soloist was only the beginning of this music. The discovery that
one soloist, using emotion as a determining force to an unprecedented degree, could produce music of great power led quickly
to the thought of what might come from a *group* of musicians
who simultaneously played in this way. The musical risks in
such an approach are obvious. But *Free Jazz* overcame them to
an amazing extent. Here were four hornmen, only two of them
having much in common stylistically (Coleman and Cherry),
producing a collective music that multiplied the power of Ornette's playing without sacrificing its order.

I had heard Cecil Taylor's music before this, but *Free Jazz*
made me aware that he had an alternative and personal approach to the same situation. Taylor's orchestral approach to the
piano determined the nature of his groups' creations. His recordings show that, given reasonably sympathetic musicians, he
could enclose and order their playing from the keyboard, in one
moment overseeing both rhythm section and front line. Still, as
Taylor grew in solo power, or perhaps revealed more of what
was always there, his virtuosity became overwhelming, and
none of the hornmen he recorded with could function on a similar level. Taylor plays more brilliantly on *Live at the Café Mont-
martre* and *Unit Structures* than on *Looking Ahead,* but the group
interaction on the earlier album is more satisfying. Perhaps, like
Tatum, Taylor would fare best as a solo performer.

But I seem to be getting ahead of myself, because by 1963
I had heard local musicians who were playing the new music.
I've never been able to pinpoint the different effects produced
by live and recorded music, but the difference is a real one.
Therefore, hearing in person the bass playing of Russell Thorne
with the Joe Daley Trio was a revelation. Thorne was the first
bass player I know of who could create an instantaneous com-

bination of passion and order out of the new music's materials. The quality of his *arco* playing has not yet been approached in jazz, and if the kind of order he created owed something to modern classical composition (he had symphony orchestra experience and knew his Boulez, Cage, and Barraqué), it never had the sterility of so-called third-stream jazz.

His music and his acquaintance also made me aware of a source for the new music that is gradually being acknowledged—the innovations of Lennie Tristano, Lee Konitz, and Warne Marsh. I suspect that their music, with its unique rhythmic and harmonic qualities, and its emphasis on group creation, has already had an effect on a number of young musicians. Thorne no longer seems to be active as a musician (he works in a bookshop), but I doubt that music could ever be far from his mind. I hope that once again he will give some of it to us.

The second Chicago-based player of the new music I heard was Roscoe Mitchell. Coltrane was in town, and Elvin Jones was appearing at an off-night session. As Jerry Figi once put it, Elvin was laying about "with a vengeance, one of those prehistoric movie-monsters crashing through a city"—in the process wiping out a James Moody-like tenor player. Suddenly, in the middle of a tune, a young alto saxophonist climbed on the stand and played a solo that met Jones more than halfway. What he played, a version of the birdlike cries that Dolphy used, was inseparable from the way he played it. His raw, piercing sound was powerful enough to cut through the drums, and Elvin found himself playing with and against someone. When the saxophonist had finished, he climbed down and disappeared into the audience. Someone was able to answer my question with the name Roscoe Mitchell, and I filed it for future reference.

Another in-person listening experience occurred during a New York visit in the spring of 1964, when I went to a loft session featuring the Roswell Rudd–John Tchicai group, with, as I recall, bassist Louis Worrell and drummer Milford Graves. They were playing well when one of those incidents happened that helps me understand the antagonism many older musicians and listeners feel toward the new music. A tenor player sat in and played the same note, spaced out with much "significant" silence, for about ten minutes. In between notes, he screwed up his face in dramatic indecision, as though he were considering and rejecting countless musical possibilities. It would have been funny if it hadn't been so sad.

After this performance, another man borrowed the tenor player's horn, and joined Rudd and Tchicai. His remarkably broad sound bristled with overtones, and his melodies moved from a groaning, funereal lyricism to jaunty, anthemlike marches. The group fell into a joyous New Orleans polyphony (aided by Rudd's Dixieland experience), but the effect was of the 1941 Ellington band in full flight—Rudd the whole trombone section, Tchicai the trumpets, and the tenorman capturing perfectly the overtone-rich sound of the Ellington reeds. As you may have guessed, he was Albert Ayler, whom I'd read about but never heard.

That fall I returned to the University of Chicago after a two-year absence to discover that the Hyde Park–Woodlawn area in which the school is located was the scene of burgeoning new music activity. At first, my ears and my mind were in conflict, because I'd been trained to think that New York City must be the center of artistic endeavor in this country. These local musicians, both in conception and performance, seemed to be going beyond anything I'd heard before, but surely this couldn't be so. But a few months of listening to Joseph Jarman, Roscoe Mitchell, et al. convinced me that my ears (and emotions) were correct.

The first Roscoe Mitchell album, *Sound,* was probably all the evidence I needed, for here in three performances ("Ornette," "Sound," and "The Little Suite") were the past, present, and future of the new music. "Ornette" was the new music's past, i.e., Coleman to 1966. Over a dense but swinging pulse set up by drummer Alvin Fielder and bassist Malachi Favors, the horns played excellent solos (tenor saxophonist Maurice McIntyre, at once downhome and abstract, was especially impressive). But the jolly, Coleman-like theme that began and ended the performance was phrased with a savagery that implied that this kind of enclosure was no longer sufficient. "Sound" was the present answer—a blank canvas upon which each soloist in turn was free to determine melody and rhythm for himself, without reference to a stated theme or a steady pulse. Whether it was planned that way or not, the actual performance did have a constant point of reference—an evolving mood of melancholy that each soloist extended.

While "Sound" was perhaps bolder in conception than "Ornette," the latter's mercurial leaps of energy were a more direct link to "The Little Suite" and the future. My first reaction to this piece was that it was primarily fun and games. The absence of separate solos, the use of harmonica, slide whistle, etc., and the overall tone of dramatic satire seemed unserious. After all, wasn't solo prowess the final test of a musician's worth?

But as I relaxed and let the music work on me, I heard the beginnings of a new kind of musical form. In a sense, the piece was composed (there were prearranged sections, like the little march), but how such sections would be reached and where they would lead seemed as freely determined as the playing of any soloist. The form was dramatic, for, as in "Sound," mood was the dominant force in every passage, but the shifts between moods were kaleidoscopic, and the opening theme's return seemed spontaneous rather than preordained.

Shortly after *Sound* appeared, I heard a live performance by Mitchell that confirmed and elaborated on the direction of "The Little Suite." At the time, Mitchell's regular group included trumpeter Lester Bowie, bassist Favors, and drummer Phillip Wilson, but Favors was absent for this miniature concert, held in a darkened lounge on the Chicago campus. In fact, for most of the evening the group was a duo of Mitchell and Wilson, because Bowie chose to offer only occasional comments.

Perhaps it was the darkness of the room, the absence of a stage, or the quiet participation of the listeners, but for whatever reasons the music was relaxed and serene in a way that had been largely foreign to the new music. What had been lost with the disappearance of swing was regained, for both sound *and* silence were filled with music. The feeling of a man moving through time with grace and power was once again as vivid as it had been in the music of Louis Armstrong, Sidney Bechet, Lester Young, and so many others. With this, the new music no longer seemed imprisoned in the intensities of the moment, like so much of modern, energy-determined art. The force of memory in music was rediscovered, both as procedure and historical reference, and the music's past was now a living part of the present—e.g., Bowie's statement which began this article.

With the mention of memory, I find that I've come to the end of my own, since what I've heard in the past year feels as if it has all occurred yesterday. As Roscoe Mitchell has said, "Jazz is young, it's not like other types of music. . . . It's broad but not as broad as it's going to be as it matures, as the musician matures." It will happen.

PART II

A Way of Living

One of the words to which jazz gives a special tilt is "scene"—"the place where an action is carried on, business is being done, or events are happening . . . where people of common interests meet . . . also, loosely, an activity or pursuit; a situation; an experience; a way of life." A "scene," in jazz, is all of those things, but especially a way of life—or rather, a way of living. And while the music that jazz musicians play is not always fruitfully linked to the nature of the places in which they play and the tastes and expectations of the audiences that come to hear them, a good deal of circumstantial connectedness is inevitable. Indeed, the flavor—not to mention the very existence—of a particular scene in a particular geographical area at a particular time can be crucially related to the kind and quality of the music that is produced, which then may go on to have a more or less independent existence, touching the hearts and minds of musicians and listeners who don't necessarily know what the "scene" was like in New Orleans in 1915, in Chicago in 1925, in Kansas City in 1935, in New York in 1945, and so forth.

Re-creating the realities of as many significant jazz scenes as possible is a vital scholarly task, one that calls for a blend of hard work in the area of source-hunting and source-sifting, a good deal of sociological-historical savvy, and a sound sense of aesthetic issues and values. While that is not a task that I am about to undertake here, as this book's initial piece suggests, early on I was a witness-

participant in at least three interrelated jazz scenes—a network of
high school- and college-age fans and players who lived in Chicago's northern suburbs in the late 1950s; Chicago's artistically vigorous hard bop scene of the time, whose key figures included tenor
saxophonist Johnny Griffin, multi-instrumentalist Ira Sullivan, and
drummer Wilbur Campbell; and, in the mid-1960s, the scenes that
nurtured Chicago's versions of the avant-garde, most notably the
one formed by the players associated with the Association for the
Advancement of Creative Musicians. Thus, in an attempt to clarify
the role that the knots and whorls of the scene play in jazz—and
to emphasize the extent to which every figure in this book, including its author, is shaped by the scene's contingencies—I have
grouped together several pieces in which Griffin, Sullivan, and
Campbell speak directly about their Chicago roots.

JOHNNY GRIFFIN
[1978]

JOE Segal masquerades as the impresario of the Jazz Showcase, but in real life he is "Mr. Keane, Tracer of Lost Persons."
Last September he engineered the return of multi-instrumentalist Ira Sullivan, who left Chicago for Florida fifteen years ago.
And now he has brought back tenor saxophonist Johnny Griffin—a Chicago legend who hasn't set foot in the United States
since May 19, 1963. On that date, Griffin sailed for Holland,
turning his back on a jazz scene that he felt had gone sour, even
though his work with Thelonious Monk, Art Blakey, and Eddie
"Lockjaw" Davis had earned him considerable acclaim.

"I left because I had to get out of America," Griffin says.
"Everything had gone wrong for me—my family life was all
messed up and so were my finances. I was drinking too much,

and I really felt bad. I had been to Europe the year before, and the people really liked my music. Why stay in America and go through this mess, I thought, when I can go over there and enjoy myself."

Griffin's decision to emigrate turned out to be fruitful. Well received in Paris, where he played with Bud Powell and Kenny Clarke, he remained in France until 1973 and then relocated to a small Dutch village about thirty miles from Rotterdam. There he found peace. "I calmed down considerably," Griffin says, "after about three years of being frantic. In Europe, it's not so much the quantity of life as the quality of life that's important. The people really know how to relax. But I don't feel European, even though I've been over there fifteen years. Man, I still feel South Side Chicago."

In fact, few if any jazz artists are more "South Side Chicago" than Johnny Griffin. Not only is Chicago's South Side his home turf but if, as novelist Richard Wright once said, this city has at its core "an open and raw beauty that seems either to kill or endow one with the spirit of life," then Griffin's music captures Chicago's contradictory soul as surely as any art that has sprung from our streets. In fact "street music" is Griffin's favorite term for the urgently swinging style of jazz he has been perfecting since the early 1940s when, like so many fine musicians, he studied at DuSable High School under the late Capt. Walter Dyett. And to this day one can detect a "Chicago sound" (the "open raw beauty" Wright spoke of) in most of the South Side saxophonists of that era. "About ten years ago," Griffin recalls, "I was taking a blindfold test, where they play a record and ask you to say who it is. I listened to this saxophonist, and for the first few bars I thought it was me. So I took a guess and said 'Von Freeman' [a fellow DuSable graduate]. And I was right. Then a few months ago I was listening to the radio in my manager's office and she said, 'Isn't that you playing?' It turned out to be Red Holloway, who also went through school with me."

Vital to the Chicago saxophone style of the 1940s are two other virtues that Griffin has in abundance—a big, bristling tone and a zealous sense of musical competitiveness. "We were always striving to get a big tone," Griffin recalls. "We'd practice in the park, figuring if you could be heard there, you could be heard anywhere. The competitiveness, that was because of all the jam sessions. The club owners would come, and the guys they thought were the best were the ones who would get the gigs. Now I've learned how to relax, how to pace myself and use space a little better. But for a long time trying to *prove* that I could play as well as my contemporaries was always uppermost in my mind. Sonny Stitt really made me study my horn. He used to come to sessions and drive everybody crazy. When I was in the service and had plenty of time to practice, I would stand in the corner and play, thinking about Stitt. I'd imagine I was back in the States, working in a club, and he would walk in, and I'd invite him up on the stand and hold my own. It worked out like that, too."

The creation of Johnny Griffin, South Side Chicago jazz musician par excellence, probably began at his grammar school graduation dance in 1941—an event at which tenorman Gene Ammons, still a teenager himself, was featured with the King Kolax Orchestra. "I saw that cat," Griffin recalls, "and knew I wanted to be a tenor saxophonist. But when I got to DuSable, Capt. Dyett said, 'That's no good—play the clarinet.' After about a year I worked up to first clarinet and asked if I could play the sax now. And he said, 'No, you play oboe and English horn because the oboist is graduating.' Finally, he let me play alto."

Alto saxophone was still Griffin's horn in 1945 when he was called to join Lionel Hampton's orchestra in Toledo, Ohio, three days after his high school graduation. He was walking on stage for the first show when Hampton's wife Gladys said, "Where's your tenor saxophone? You're playing tenor in this band." Griffin since has unraveled the chain of circumstance that led to this misunderstanding, but at the time all he could do was catch a train back to Chicago, buy the required horn, and return to the gig as quickly as possible. "Immediately, I was in trouble," he says, "because Hamp wanted me to do these tenor battles with Arnett Cobb. And that cat had a huge sound. I had been doing all right with my alto; I could make a lot of noise there. But with the tenor I had to change everything around, and for a while I was in a panic."

Although Griffin soon mastered the larger horn, his playing retains an alto-saxophone quality. Johnny Hodges was his initial inspiration, and he refers to Charlie Parker as "the greatest influence in my life." In between Hodges and Parker, the young Griffin was particularly moved by the music of Lester Young, Ben Webster, and Don Byas. Others who played key roles in shaping Griffin's style were three giants of modern jazz piano who also were close friends—Bud Powell, Thelonious Monk, and Elmo Hope.

"When I was in New York in the late forties with the Joe Morris band," Griffin recalls, "Elmo joined our rhythm section, and through him I met Bud and Thelonious. We were together almost every day, playing and listening. It was music twenty-four hours. Monk would have a band that would rehearse for three months and then go to a gig and get fired the first night. Yet ten years later, when I was working with Monk, those same people who fired him wanted to hire him and couldn't afford to pay his price." The paradoxical "ugly beauty" of Griffin's sound and his acute ear for dissonance made him a logical partner for Monk, and the albums on which he appears with the pianist include some of his best recorded work, particularly *Thelonious Monk at the Five Spot* and *Art Blakey With Thelonious Monk*.

Early on Griffin was dubbed "the Little Giant"—little because he is five feet five inches tall, giant because of that huge, fierce tone and his kaleidoscopic skills as an improviser. And what does improvisation mean to a master of the art? "The excitement of not knowing," Griffin says, "that's what I like. Certain parts of a solo you can think about beforehand, maybe plan an entrance. But the fun is not knowing what you're going to do next and then having the wherewithal and the vocabulary to really pull it off. Jazz has always been a twenty-four-hour thing for me. Not only is it my livelihood, it's my hobby also—a whole philosophy of living. It's like I sometimes say on the stand before we play: 'This music comes from people who have decided to feel good in spite of'—meaning 'in spite of conditions.'

"I don't think my playing has changed much over the years, but I do feel a little more relaxed. But then I never was that relaxed in the first place. Music always excited me so much that it was all I could do to keep from exploding. And now that I'm back it's hard to keep cool—especially the way I was received at the Monterey Jazz Festival and at the Keystone Korner in San Francisco. Dexter Gordon was always telling me it would be like that if I returned, because it happened that way with him. 'Griff,' he said, 'I'm a pop star now. I was at the Village Vanguard and people were lined up around the corner. You wouldn't believe it.' So I'm really looking forward to getting back to Chicago. I've wanted to come back before to see my family—I have a ninety-seven-year-old grandmother, and I haven't seen my father and mother and kids in fifteen years. But I didn't want to come unless I could come playing, and I wasn't ready for that. Now I am. I'm staying as calm as possible, but the excitement is wow. The atmosphere is crackling around me."

[1983]

"BEAUTY will be convulsive, or it will not be at all." Those ominously prophetic words, which conclude André Breton's surrealist novel *Nadja,* are a good way to approach the music of tenor saxophonist Johnny Griffin. The sound Griffin gets—so rich in overtones that it can seem internally dissonant—the splintered logic of his lines, the jagged rhythmic thrusts in the midst of gentle ballads, the blatant tonal distortions all proclaim that beauty no longer can be met in isolation, that instead it can arise only when the artist confronts the radical discontinuities of the modern world. Indeed, if a representative Griffin solo were to be transformed into a work of visual art, one envisions a structure shaped from various pieces of cultural-physical debris—a cracked jukebox, a smoking truck tire, and some buzzing neon tubing fused to a 1953 Buick Skylark grille and bumper. The title? "Ugly Beauty"—a composition by Griffin's former employer Thelonious Monk.

Notable in this regard is one of Griffin's key traits, his taste for musical quotation. A lot of players insert quotes in their solos, but Griffin's quotes have a unique flavor because they are so highly distorted, not only in the way he jams them into seemingly impossible places in the harmonic fabric of a piece but also because the quotes tend to be outrageous in themselves— sea chanteys, "Dixie," "Morning Song" from Grieg's *Peer Gynt Suite*, "Buttons and Bows," "The Donkey Serenade," and "Popeye, the Sailor Man," to name just a few of his favorites. But, then, Griffin once recorded Saxie Dowell's nagging "School Days" of his own free will, and I have even heard him make something lovely and strong out of "Happy Birthday."

Griffin's chief models are Johnny Hodges and Coleman Hawkins, and while Hodges was one of jazz's genuine romantics, Hawkins, despite the lush tonal surface of his solos, was not a romantic but a man who strove to surmount self-erected technical barriers. Blending those two styles and adding a dash of Charlie Parker's rhythmic agitation, Griffin came up with a music in which romantic emotions were present but constantly beleaguered, a way of playing that had to test each tender impulse by running it through an acid bath. So even though the notes that finally emerge from Griffin's horn may not be beautiful in any ordinary sense, they are a kind of beauty that urban America permits and inspires.

IRA SULLIVAN
[1977]

THE Living Legend. It's one of the stalest hypes around, rivaled only by its first cousin, The Comeback. From sports to politics and throughout the arts, at least one of them comes down the pike every year—a person who is supposed to be of interest not so much because he does something well but because he's doing it at all.

At first glance, jazzman Ira Sullivan would seem to be The Living Legend par excellence. Beloved by knowledgeable fans for his brilliant trumpet and saxophone playing, Sullivan has labored in semi-obscurity during most of his career. He has had a troubled past, struggling with and finally exorcising the demons of drug use. And when he appears at the Jazz Showcase this week and next, it will be the first time he has performed in his hometown in fifteen years (since 1962 Sullivan has been living in Miami). There's one catch, though. Ira Sullivan is a musician first, last, and always. Turn him into another human interest story and you rob him of his most precious possession— his art. Still, it's unavoidable that Sullivan's return to Chicago will be surrounded by an aura of romance. Absence gilds memories, but so many of the ones he left behind were golden from the first.

Born in Washington, D.C., in 1931 and reared in Chicago, Sullivan started playing trumpet at the tender age of four, picking up the horn that his father noodled on as a form of relaxation, "the way other men play golf." "Dad played straight melody," Sullivan recalls. " 'Show me those notes you put in there,' he would ask. 'I don't see that on the music.' 'No,' I'd say, 'but you bend this note here, add a little triplet there.' 'OK,' he said, 'put those extra notes in. I'll just play the melody, and you embellish it.' "

Aside from his father, and two uncles who were in John Philip Sousa's band, Sullivan's early influences were a pair of rather corny trumpeters on the periphery of jazz, Henry Busse and Clyde McCoy. "I liked to hear the trumpet player cry through his horn—like Busse with his wah-wah style—and I dug McCoy's lip slurs on 'Sugar Blues.' Then Harry James became one of my big favorites. From about eleven to fifteen, there wasn't a record he made that I didn't have."

Even though Sullivan never had a formal lesson ("I thought that if I found out what I was doing I might not be able to do it anymore"), in his mid-teens he was powerfully affected by the informal teachings of Dizzy Gillespie and Charlie Parker, the masters of the new music called bebop. Sullivan became an instant disciple, palling around with such like-minded young musicians as pianist Lou Levy and bass trumpeter Cy Touff.

Soon the trumpet prodigy had added the alto and tenor saxophones and the drums to his arsenal, and the legend began to grow. There didn't seem to be an instrument made that Sullivan couldn't play. More important, Sullivan was beginning to forge an individual style. The first recording to bring him national attention, made in 1955 with trumpeter Red Rodney, features him on tenor saxophone, where he shows signs of being influenced by Sonny Stitt. But on one track Rodney allows him to play trumpet, and Sullivan proves that he already could excel in very fast company. (Rodney, a prodigy himself, had spent two years in Charlie Parker's band.)

Sullivan's wry sense of humor surfaces as he recalls that recording session and a later date with Rodney that also included one trumpet duet: "Red was always telling me, 'Play your tenor, man, so we can get that blend.' Then, about two or three hours into the session, he'd say, 'Why don't we do one on trumpet?' 'Man,' I'd say, 'I got no chops now!' [The utterly different embouchures that the tenor saxophone and trumpet require make the switch very difficult.] That's when I realized I had to get my shit together because these cats were going to whip game on me."

But too many jazz musicians in those days were playing another, sometimes deadly game—the Russian roulette of narcotics addiction. The list of Chicago artists whose lives were cut short by drug use includes a number of Sullivan's friends, and he too might have succumbed to what he calls the "bust-out lifestyle" if he hadn't abruptly moved to Florida in 1962. "The best way to explain it," he says, "is that God told me, 'Don't do that anymore.' It wasn't a voice from on high, but you know the line 'Death is nature's way of telling you to slow down'—it was that kind of thing. The Creator came in and said, 'It's all over for you; you're going to change.' I didn't have a special discipline, didn't go through any program. It was a very painful way to do it—painful not only for me but also for my family. But it worked. A lot of people say I'd be good at warning others of the evils of that life, but I wouldn't know what I was talking about. I'm not hiding my head in the sand, but I remember only the positive aspects of those days. The world has evolved. We don't have musicians today who accept the stereotypes—you know, this is what I'm supposed to be if I'm a jazz musician or a rock musician. I've got a group of students from the University of Miami that I play with, and you tell them to be there at 8 and they're there at 7:30. They don't smoke, and they don't drink; they're just out to play music."

Sullivan's approach to jazz has changed since he moved to Miami, evolving from hard bop to a personal version of the avant-garde. It's likely, though, that during his Jazz Showcase engagement Sullivan will be shifting back and forth from the "free" bag into his older style, because impresario Joe Segal will be pairing him with a number of musical friends from the fifties. The lineup includes saxophonists Von Freeman and Joe Daley, pianists Jodie Christian and John Young, and drummers Wilbur Campbell and Vernel Fournier.

To the Chicago jazz community, the return of Sullivan is an inescapably dramatic event. But the man at the center wants things to be as unsentimental as possible. "As far as I'm concerned," he says, "I'm just going to come back and play. The real reason I stayed away so long is that I just don't like to travel; if you've seen one hotel room, you've seen 'em all. I suppose I've missed the city, but so much has been going on down here that I haven't had any time for sentimentality. From what I read in the Bible, the Lord frowns on that anyway. Love is one thing, but sentimentality gets into the maudlin. The human mind can't help thinking about yesterday and tomorrow, but that's a fallacy and a trick bag. Because you can't experience anything except what you see in front of you."

Not a bad piece of advice from a man who knows a "trick bag" when he sees one. Ira Sullivan has come back to play, so forget about living legends and check your rose-colored glasses at the door. As the title of Charlie Parker's famous blues puts it, "Now's the Time."

WILBUR CAMPBELL

Johnny Griffin is an acknowledged master who has performed around the world and made hundreds of recordings. Ira Sullivan, while not obscure, is known to far fewer listeners and had performed primarily in Chicago and the Miami area until he co-led a quintet with Red Rodney in the early 1980s, and Sullivan's recorded legacy is less extensive than one would wish. Even less well-known is drummer Wilbur Campbell (1926–1999), although he is one of the most remarkable percussionists in the history of jazz. The following interview, done in 1969, was not published then; in Catch-22 fashion, Campbell, recently released from state prison after a conviction for drug possession and with almost none of the few recordings he had made by that time still in print, was not felt to be enough of a "name" to merit a profile in a national jazz magazine. But while fame would never come to Campbell, the remaining thirty years of his life were rewarding. The house drummer at Chicago's Jazz Showcase for much of that time, he earned the admiration of the hundreds of artists with whom he performed; pianist Stu Katz, a frequent partner, has aptly described his "gentle but completely assured dominance of the rhythm section." In one sense, Campbell typifies the fate of jazz's thousands of local heroes—the men and women who for one reason or another did not make much of an impact beyond the scenes they were part of, even though their talents were large. Campbell can be heard at his best on these recordings: Ira Sullivan's *Bird Lives!* (Koch), *Blue Stroll,* and *Nicky's Tune* (both Delmark), Von Freeman's *Serenade and Blues* and *Have No Fear* (both Nessa), Wilbur Ware's *The Chicago*

Sound (OJC), and Pete and Conte Candoli's *Two Brothers* (Hindsight).

[1969]

I was born July 30, 1926, a Leo, the second of six sons. The brother next to me was a musician, and I guess I was inspired by him. He played bass and violin, and guitar. I studied piano. I went to DuSable [High School] and studied under Capt. [Walter] Dyett. I went to school with Johnny Griffin, [tenor saxophonist] Gene Ammons, [trombonist] Benny Green, [tenor saxophonist] John "Flap" Dungee, who played with Eckstine, [tenor saxophonist] Von Freeman and [guitarist] George Freeman, [alto saxophonist] John Jenkins, [tenor saxophonist] John Gilmore. We had a very good teacher. He's turned out quite a slew of musicians, from [trumpeter-violinist] Ray Nance on.

We had to play weekly assignments and there was competition for your seats, for your chair in the band. Each week you had to play your assignments, and if you fell down, then you played fourth chair. I was playing drums and tympani and bells in the marching band. We had a regular jazz orchestra, we had a concert band two periods a day and a jazz band one period. On drums we had Wesley Landers, Lindell Marshall (who used to play with Pres). I got him that job with Pres in '46. I was working at the Hurricane and had just started school under the GI Bill. I was studying under Frank Rullo and José Betancourt at the Bobby Christian School, the Western Conservatory of Music. I didn't want to leave town. I had worked with Pres before, so he asked me 'Who can I get?' and I told him Lindell.

I stayed at Western for three-and-a-half years. At the same time I was playing with Jesse Miller at the Hurricane. He's dead now. Johnny Board was in the band and playing alto, and Clarence "Sleepy" Anderson, who was a fine organist, was playing piano. We were there for about a year, and during that time we used to have some awful sessions. When Diz's band would come to town, [drummer] Joe Harris came and played and Bags [vi-braphonist Milt Jackson] came and played. At that time I played vibes too, and I had a set on the stand. We just had a ball.

I went to school until my scholarship ran out, and then I dropped out. I was in the Navy from January 1945 to July 1946. I got to hear some of the famous bands at Great Lakes [Naval Air Station]—[alto saxophonist] Willie Smith's group, [trum-peter] Clark Terry was up there, [trumpeter] Jimmy Nottingham. I was in a band that shipped out to California; we played for guys going out and ships coming in. I had a pretty sweet tour of duty.

After you learn to read and learn your rudiments, all a teacher can do is watch your flaws and weaknesses. The first thing I learned to do was use the wrist, drum corps style. It all comes from the wrist. Betancourt was my vibes and marimba teacher. I studied with the church organist, when I was about nine or ten. Every tune I play I know the changes. It helps in this respect—you know where the vacant spots are, and you know what you can put in there.

I freelanced at the Savoy Ballroom with [tenor saxophonist] Claude McLinn for six months—that's when I first met Bird and Max [Roach]. The second time, I was with [trumpeter] Roy Eld-ridge at a place called the Tailspin, and it was right down the street from the Argyle Lounge, where Bird was working. And I knew Max and Miles (Miles was a youngster then), [pianist] Duke Jordan, [bassist] Tommy Potter. This was '47 or '48. That was one of the greatest times in my life. I remember I got in a little hassle with Roy. I was going to hear Max and them, and he was playing that thing, that new thing, and it was *fine*. So I heard it, and I was trying to cop. I'd come back from the set and try to play what I'd heard, and one night Roy got mad. He said, "You're not playing over with Charlie Parker—he's playing down there and you're playing with me. I want you to just play some titty-boom." So I said OK and I just played a little titty-boom for a while, but then I'd come back and go on *into* it. I said, 'To heck with it—this is just one job, but this is the opportunity of a lifetime, to be hearing Bird and Miles and Max every night. I got the advantage that no other dude has—I can run next set and try it, try what I hear. I could never play it exactly as [Max] played it, but it would stimulate ideas, and by me trying to play what I *thought* I heard, I would get my own conception, my own voice. And it did; it helped me develop my style. It mostly was a case of listening. As far as talking drums [with Max], I didn't do that because I just wanted to build a friendship, I didn't want to be a bug and keep saying, "Look, how did you do so and so?" Then you make yourself unwelcome; the guy feels that you're picking his brain or trying to get free lessons. Where we did exchange [information] was about vibes. After Bird and Max, then I was on my way. I was playing the new thing.

Ike Day was about my age, might have been a little older. A thin guy. A truly amazing drummer. Max and Art [Blakey] and everybody had respect for Ike. Ike was the kind of cat—it'd be zero outside, and he'd walk up to the stand and beat off some way up tempo and never miss a beat, clear and precise. He was more out of the Sid Catlett school because that was his era. He was established with his own voice and his own style before I'd ever heard of Max or any of them. He'd come by the house and we'd practice. He sort of brought me along and showed me a lot of things. Just listening to him was a lesson in itself. He could take two pieces—a cymbal and a bass drum—and make it swing. He was a natural drummer. He had fast hands, and he used both feet and both hands. If the tempo was up there, he'd be on the bass drum and it wouldn't be loud—you felt it more than you heard it. Next to old man Jo Jones and Big Sid, Ike could do more with a pair of sock cymbals. He could make them breathe. Dorrel [Anderson] was like that too. A hell of a natural drummer. We all came up together—Dorrel, Ike, and myself—but Ike was the older, more experienced one and could play better.

The first time I played with Bird was in '49—I got to sit in at the Pershing [Ballroom]. The last time I played with him was the last time he was in Chicago, at the Beehive, about two months before he died. Playing with him was a treat within itself, because I was trying so hard to listen and still play, because he was playing such fascinating things. To play with him and listen and accompany without taking away from the other things was quite an experience. It's a pity that a lot of guys today never got to hear Bird. I don't think there was hardly any other direction anybody else could have taken that line. The guy who was most qualified to do that was Sonny Rollins, and he had to go off in another direction.

[Beehive engagement with Thelonious Monk, Johnny Griffin, and bassist Wilbur Ware]: That was one of my most profound experiences. It was intriguing musically and a challenge. That's why I'm so glad that I've always been the type of guy who listens to everything and everybody. I happened to have liked Monk before I ever met him, liked the things he was doing, so I was sort of familiar with his style. His rhythmic structures are beautiful, especially for a drummer—he inspires you, inspires your thoughts. It swings so beautifully, and it's so rhythmic that all you've got to do is swing, listen, and speak back. I almost played the Little Red Wagon date [*Monk's Music*—the album, recorded in June 1957, has a picture on the cover of Monk sitting in a child's wagon]. Art [Blakey] didn't show up, almost, and we were ready to record.

I worked with Miles briefly when I was in New York. We got off to a bad thing. I was supposed to work in Philly Joe's place, and something happened to the subway, and I was late on the job. I played the rest of the night (Kenny Dennis sat in for me), but Miles was drugged with me, and through that incident word—badmouth—sort of got out on me.

[Ira Sullivan]: Ira is a fantastic musician. His old man was a trumpet player too. They had that myth that Ira couldn't read, and that's bullshit.

[Wilbur Ware]: He's a little older. I first met him in '43. Wilbur's what you'd call a natural bass player. He was a humdinger. We've played together many a time. We buddied up onstage as well as off, so I guess it's natural that it would show up in our playing.

The free jazz music style that has come out of Chicago—I was playing that style but I sort of had a setback when I went to the penitentiary for a period of time. It came at a crucial time.

I did what they call eight years; in actual time it was four years. I did two years, was on the street for seven months and went back and did two more. It happened at a time just when the movement was coming. At the time that I left we were pioneering in that movement. Nicky [tenor saxophonist Nicky Hill] and Donald [bassist Donald Garrett] and myself were playing things like [Ornette Coleman's] "When Will the Blues Leave." Then after I came out the first time I was a member of the AACM [the Association for the Advancement of Creative Musicians]. We gave a few concerts, and the movement was just starting out. Then I went into something else personal and I got sidetracked. I don't know—I just never did get to expand too far. I guess I was out of the environment. Perhaps if I'd stayed in the environment I would have been one of the "old" new-timers. I know that according to certain thoughts I'm playing dated somewhat, but I believe that if I was in that environment say for a month, I think I could be playing things that would fit. As it is now, to an extent I'm isolated. The gigs I've been working, like with Don Patterson, playing with the organ, there's no freedom there because you have to help carry the time.

I think [the drummer's] role should be that of an accompanist, embellishing an instrumentalist, keeping time. I've never been one to dominate a conversation. It's a case of communication to me—venturing maybe a sentence, listening to a paragraph in return, and just adding little marks of punctuation and comment. I guess at times I tend to command the environment, but that's exceptional and generally when something has to be done.

I've been on methadone for maybe five months. Methadone is one phase of the program. I've become pretty involved with it, and they seem quite pleased with my actions so far. I'm being trained to counsel other addicts. Its something like AA. Alcoholics are able to work with alcoholics. [Drug use] seemed like it was part of the times, whereas today it is not. Then it was part of social acceptance. When I started, it was just a normal accepted thing; I didn't get started by other musicians, for the purpose of playing. I got started through the environment outside of music, kids on the block. And when I got into it, I found out that other musicians were into it, and that's where the blame eventually ended up, on musicians. Sure, some of the other musicians were using it who were popular at that time, and the blame went out on their influence, but basically, as for myself and for other musicians I know, it didn't stem from that, it was an outside scene. The way it started was some of the guys, we all hung together, would say, "Now I got something I want you to try." And you do it. Then you get together tomorrow and the next day and do the same thing. Look up and you got a Jones [drug habit]. Then I might get picked up, and they say, "Oh, you're a musician, on the stuff." And music gets the blame when actually it had nothing to do with it. I guess the musicians today, they've seen the dues that we've paid, seeing us run around to get money to cop, having to borrow their horns. And then some of the older musicians have told them to stay away from it. And so many good musicians have died from overdoses and things.

The older musicians have had a great influence, at least by their actions, which is a great price. They find out that it is not necessary to have something to play. It's not that drugs make you play any better, they just relax you more. Myself, I think it relaxes me to the point that I can function with less inhibitions. But I found out now that I don't have to do it. I remember when I first came out of the penitentiary, I had this hang-up that I couldn't play anymore. Guys were expecting me to play like I was before I went in—better, because they thought I had been practicing every day in the pen, and it wasn't near about like that. Something took place in my mind where I actually damn near couldn't play—until I went and got high. Then I forgot all about that and played as if nothing had happened. Then I told myself, "Oh, you have the habit." Then I stopped again and I found out that I was able to play and I found out that it was all anxiety, it was all mental.

[Duke Ellington's] "Jack the Bear, "Pitter Panther Patter"— I heard them and I wanted to play the bass. But then right before I was starting school, the show changed and Basie's band came on, and I heard old man Jo Jones. Then I wanted to play drums.

They played "Ol' Man River." He used to make the sock cymbals breathe.

[Chick Webb]: I heard him, but not when I knew I wanted to play drums. He was quite flashy, quite a drummer, a good pair of hands. But I didn't hear him like I got to hear old man Jo and Sonny Greer. Sonny Greer to me is the father of the single-stick beat. Sonny Greer used to sit up there and move that whole band playing "tink-tink-tink-bop." And the band would be *swinging*. He'd be sitting up there surrounded by chimes, tympani, gongs—he used to play all of them. He kept time like a metronome and *moved* that band. I got to see Sid Catlett and Gene Krupa. Sid sat in with Gene's band at the Savoy one time, and he really swung that band—he was playing much more modern than Gene. Sid got up there and swung that band with a pair of brushes. I always liked Louis Bellson. To me he always swung a band much better than Buddy Rich. Buddy doesn't have that looseness that Louis has.

Every drummer who's been playing can play anything he thinks of; the trouble is thinking of things to play. Lots of cats can play what they think, but they don't think it.

PART III

The Generators

There is only one generation of men and women (Jelly Roll Morton, born 1890; Bessie Smith, born 1894; Sidney Bechet, born 1897; Duke Ellington, born 1899; Louis Armstrong, born 1901; Earl Hines, born 1903; Bix Beiderbecke, born 1903; Coleman Hawkins and Fats Waller, both born 1904, and so forth) who were key participants in and witnesses to the process whereby jazz came to be, and came to be regarded as, a self-sustaining form of music. And while one could disagree about where and how to draw the line, there is a relatively distinct second generation, too, which includes such figures as Count Basie (born 1904), Johnny Hodges (born 1906), Red Norvo (born 1908), Art Tatum, Benny Goodman, and Lester Young (all born 1909), Mary Lou Williams (born 1910), Roy Eldridge (born 1911), and so forth. Dates of birth are not the sole factor here; Basie and Hodges, for example, arguably belong to the second generation, while Waller (born in the same year as Basie) and Bechet belong to the first, because Waller and Bechet were fully formed figures when Basie and Hodges were not, and Basie was directly inspired by Waller and Hodges by Bechet. That is, one of the hallmarks of the second generation was that it knew of and was reacting to the first; a historical continuum was undeniably at work.

With the third generation, another line needs to be drawn, because there are, in fact, at least two third generations. One is made up of those musicians—Dizzy Gillespie and Thelonious Monk (both born 1917), Lennie Tristano (born 1919), Charlie Parker (born 1920), Bud Powell (born 1924), Miles Davis (born 1926), and so forth—who not only came after the second generation but also found themselves making a music that virtually had to be called modern jazz in relation to what had come before. As for the other third generation, it consists of musicians who came after the second but did not for various reasons cross the temperamental/stylistic divide into forthright, self-conscious modernism. For example, pieces about such figures as tenor saxophonist Arnett Cobb (born 1918), drummer Louis Bellson (born 1924), and cornetist Ruby Braff (born 1927) appear here because their music is stylistically continuous with that of the second generation, while Gillespie, Monk, et al. belong in the next section, Moderns and After, or, in the cases of Tristano and Davis, they have sections to themselves.

The point here is not to place undeniably individual musicians into neat little boxes but to emphasize what ought to be obvious: that jazz is a music whose nature and growth has been crucially shaped by the ways in which musicians who think of themselves as jazz musicians react to the music of other musicians who play jazz. Other things matter, too, but that is what matters most.

LOUIS ARMSTRONG
[1983]

Perhaps the most remarkable thing about Louis Armstrong is that the power and glory of his music have not diminished one bit with the passage of time. Listen to any of the vast number of great Armstrong recordings ("Potato Head Blues," "Struttin' With Some Barbecue," "Sweethearts on Parade," "West End Blues," "Weather Bird," "Tight Like This," "Beau Koo Jack," the list goes on and on), and the liberating shock of his trumpet playing is felt anew every time. Overflowing the normal boundaries of art, each of these marvels of shaped majesty is an object that can and should be contemplated, but each is also a living deed, an event whose "nowness" remains unmistakable.

What, then, of the man who created this magic? How can one stand back and explain Louis Armstrong, when, more than a decade after his death, his art continues to dance before us, redefining who and what we are? In his new Armstrong biography, *Louis Armstrong: An American Genius,* which claims to be far more thorough and scholarly than previous efforts, James Lincoln Collier tries to explain the man away.

Beginning with the idea that Armstrong was "the preeminent musical genius of his era," Collier apparently can't believe that this claim is true, for he indulges in a good deal of irritating, wrongheaded condescension, including some truly outrageous armchair psychoanalysis. In addition to "obsessing publicly about his bowels" (although "we have to bear in mind that Armstrong grew up in a culture where the crude basics of life were, after all, public matters"), it seems that our hero had a "problem with self-assertion, not to mention an "insatiable, visceral hunger for applause." A man "clearly afflicted with deep and well-entrenched insecurity, a sense of his own worthlessness so thoroughly fixed that he was never to shake it off," Armstrong could "quench that relentless, sickening, interior assault on his self-respect by performing . . . which for a moment pushed away the feeling that nobody liked him, that he was basically no good."

The best response to such drivel is Armstrong's music, for if the flaming virtuosity of "Swing That Music" or the joyful complexities of "Weather Bird" were produced by an "afflicted" insecure human being who never shook off "a sense of his own worthlessness," then we are in the presence of a mystery far greater than the one this book attempts to investigate. The real mystery, it would seem, is where Collier is coming from, and eventually he supplies the necessary evidence.

"The pioneer New Orleans jazz musicians," Collier writes,

"were ill-educated people from a subculture most middle-class Americans of today would find foreign. We cannot perceive Louis Armstrong as we might Ralph Ellison, James Baldwin. He was, by the standards of middle-class America, rough, uncivilized, naive, and ignorant." Leaving aside the dubious idea that Ellison and Baldwin are readily perceived from the vantage point of "middle-class America," what is the sense in setting up this opposition between "our" (that is, Collier's) supposedly civilized "middle class" standards and Armstrong's "rough, uncivilized" naïveté? Smugly ensconced in what he believes to be the mainstream of American life, Collier apparently thinks that Armstrong would have been better off if he had resided there too, for he writes, "There is no question but that his lack of insight into the nature of show business and wholly unanalytic approach to his craft hampered the development of his music."

Again, the music is the best answer. By what standards, "middle class" or otherwise, is "Tight Like This" or "Sweethearts on Parade" unsophisticated? And what entertainer does Collier have in mind when he says that Armstrong, one of the most artistically and financially successful performers of our time, lacked "insight into the nature of show business"?

Dealing with a figure such as Armstrong, who largely and triumphantly invented his own standards, the least one can expect from a biographer is some acceptance of what is there, a willingness to grant to genius the terms by which it lives. Collier, however, seems to want a Louis Armstrong who could first create "West End Blues" and then coolly analyze what he had done while sipping a dry martini in a suburb-bound commuter train. As Armstrong himself might have put it, it's enough to give you the heebie jeebies.

BLACK BEAUTY, WHITE HEAT
[1982]

FRANK Driggs has devoted most of his adult life to accumulating the world's largest collection of jazz memorabilia, and he and coauthor Harris Lewine have packaged the best of this treasure trove with all the love and attention to detail it deserves. Indeed, *Black Beauty, White Heat: A Pictorial History of Classic Jazz, 1920–1950* is such a superb piece of bookmaking that one needn't be a jazz devotee to be fascinated by its more than fifteen hundred photographs, advertisements, sheet-music covers, and record labels (many of them quite rare). Jazz, after all, is America's major native art form, and on page after large-sized page, there are images here that should draw any onlooker into the half-secret history of this country's culture—specifically the rich, turbulent exchange of social and artistic information that has always gone on between black and white Americans.

If jazz is about anything, other than the beauty of the sounds its artists create, it is a music about America—about what it means to grow up, live, and die in a country that speaks of hope and denial, transcendence and limitation in one and the same breath. For instance, the photographs of Louis Armstrong—there are more than fifty of them here, each deserving its place—can be read in any number of different ways. Most of the images of Armstrong are flamboyant and "showbizzy," though this aspect of the man usually was an offshoot of his extrovert personality rather than a concession on his part to "Uncle Tom" stereotypes. But there are at least two Armstrong photos here that should stop the reader dead in his or her tracks. The first comes from 1949 and shows Armstrong dressed up as the King of the Zulus for that year's Mardi Gras celebration. Wearing a long, flowing wig and a plumed headdress, he has his face covered by inky black makeup, except for the cartoonish white circles around his mouth and eyes. That image may sound like an ugly racial caricature, yet it is anything but that, for there can be no doubt that Armstrong's expression is radiantly tri-umphant. He is King Zulu, after all, the first black New Orlean-ian to have been granted that honor (though the photo makes it clear that, in fact, he has *claimed* the title). The costume and the makeup have their origins in racial caricature, but they are Armstrong's property now, transformed by him into the trap-pings of an intense, joyful power.

Startling in a different sense is an Armstrong photo, circa 1933, at the bottom of page 216. Gazing a little to the right of the camera, his face is in complete repose, enabling us, for once, to see the private man, not the public performer. Exactly what this photograph expresses I would be hard pressed to say. But I do know that it is one of the essential icons of American life, an image that can draw anyone who contemplates it into a dialogue with the man it so calmly and beautifully depicts. No less pow-erful in its similarly quiet way is the image of Coleman Hawkins one encounters a few pages later on. On tour in England during the 1930s, and clearly very much at ease, the great tenor saxo-phonist meets our eyes over a cup of tea—suave and aristocrat-ically reserved yet with an undercurrent of leonine aggressive-ness that brooks no contradiction.

A book as pictorially rich as this hardly needs words, but there are additional delights in the succinct, informative, and often witty captions that Driggs and Lewine provide. A snapshot of a figure in a natty three-piece suit who stands in what seems to be a railroad yard, holding a wine bottle to the light as he inexplicably squints at its underside, leads to these remarks: "Eccentric Indiana trumpeter-trombonist Jack Purvis had played and recorded with Hal Kemp and the California Ram-blers in 1929–31, set fire to hotel rooms, flown as a mercenary in South America, written suites for a 110-piece orchestra and returned to New York to play 52d Street briefly in 1935. Three years later, he made headlines when he was discovered leading a prison band in Texas. His bravura trumpet style is heard on 'Mental Strain at Dawn' on Okeh."

Then there are discoveries that the reader is left to make for himself, such as this inscription, which adorns a photograph of

Thelma Terry, a Chicago bassist and bandleader of the 1920s: "Dear Jack—You're sweet. Please, always reserve your 'wise cracks' for a Bass Viol woman. Thelma." Who Jack was or why Terry enclosed "wise cracks" in quotation marks, I don't know. But surely what we have here are the makings of "The Bass Viol Woman," an unwritten Ring Lardner vignette. So it goes throughout this book of wonders.

EARL HINES
[1983]

THE passing of pianist/bandleader Earl "Fatha" Hines—who died April 22 in Oakland, California, at age 79 after suffering a heart attack—was an event whose sad significance it would be difficult to exaggerate. A true pioneer ("No musician," wrote critic Dick Hadlock, "has exerted more influence over the course of piano jazz history"), Hines also was a remarkably vigorous artist who reached his first creative peak in the mid-1920s and continued to develop almost until his death. (The best of the many recordings he made during the last two decades of his life at least equaled, and may have surpassed, any that he had made before.)

Most important of all, Hines was, as fate would have it, one of the last of jazz's first men—a key figure among the generation of primal giants (Louis Armstrong, Duke Ellington, Sidney Bechet, Coleman Hawkins, et al.) who decisively shaped America's chief native art music, transforming it from a neo-folk form into a music that was at once mature, sophisticated, self-reflective, and destined to ceaselessly, aggressively develop. Indeed, listening to the still-astonishing group of recordings that Hines made in 1928, on his own and with various Armstrong-led ensembles, maturity and sophistication are the first words that come to mind. On "Weatherbird Rag," "Skip the Gutter," "Caution Blues," and "West End Blues" (to name a few of these masterpieces), there is no hesitancy whatever, but rather a sense that Hines's and Armstrong's music was at once radically new and wholly ripe.

Born in the Pittsburgh suburb of Duquesne, Pennsylvania, on December 28, 1903, Hines turned to the piano after early experiments with the cornet (his father was an amateur brassman). Classically trained, Hines was performing professionally while still in his teens, having been hired as an accompanist by singer Lois Deppe. In the early 1920s, Hines was based at Pittsburgh's Collins Cafe, a club whose owner also operated the Elite Club No. 2 in Chicago. Then, in 1925, a dispute arose with the Elite Club's band, and Hines was sent to Chicago to take its place—a crucial move because it soon brought him in contact with Armstrong, perhaps the one man who could adequately respond to Hines's concepts. "When I met Louis," Hines once said, "he was playing the same style that I wanted to play. We'd sit there and use each other's ideas."

What was most striking (and prophetic) about the Hines-Armstrong collaborations was their exceptional rhythmic freedom. For these men the beat was not a thing of rigid regularity but a springboard to be used for joyous play—an extension of the concept of "breaks," in which the band would pause for several bars while the soloist soared in baroque arabesques, implying the beat rather than stating it. In fact, one of the secrets of Hines's style was his ability to infuse entire solos with the break feeling. In a typical chorus he would outline the beat with oblique, stabbing left-hand figures and then place against them a series of swirling right-hand variations, creating a unique rhythmic counterpoint that allowed him to expand or compress the listener's sense of the passage of time at will and with startling suddenness. As Hadlock put it: "Hines never lost the pulse, even when it was out of sight." Inseparable from those virtues was Hines's crystal-clear technique and his sense of keyboard layout, his ability to place each idea so it "sounded" to maximum effect.

A star sideman with Armstrong in Carroll Dickerson's Orchestra at Chicago's Sunset Cafe and then a featured soloist with clarinetist Jimmie Noone's quintet at the Apex Club, Hines inevitably became a bandleader himself, assembling a group that settled in at the Grand Terrace Ballroom in 1928, where it remained for more than a decade. By the early 1930s, Hines was leading one of the country's finest jazz ensembles, featuring trumpeter Walter Fuller, trombonist Trummy Young, reedmen Darnell Howard and Omer Simeon, and drummer Wallace Bishop, with adventurous arrangements being supplied by Cecil Irwin, Jimmy Mundy, and Quinn Wilson. It was during this period that Hines wrote his most famous composition, "Rosetta." The Grand Terrace band was regularly heard on a nationwide radio hookup, and it was during one such broadcast that a supposedly inebriated announcer gave the leader his nickname, signaling the arrival of the band's theme song, "Deep Forest," with the words, "Here comes Father Hines through the deep forest with his children."

The first Hines band gradually evolved into a different and equally exciting late-thirties crew that was sparked by the superb drumming of Alvin Burroughs and the writing and solos of tenor saxophonist Budd Johnson. But perhaps the most famous Hines band was one that never recorded because of the 1942–44 recording ban. Always a modernist (if that term has any meaning in his case), Hines welcomed into the ranks the two key figures of the music that soon would be known as bebop, Charlie Parker and Dizzy Gillespie, along with vocalists Billy Eckstine and Sarah Vaughan. Taken over almost wholesale by Eckstine when Hines quixotically chose to disband and surround himself with an all-female string section, this band was, by all reports, one of jazz's great ensembles.

Hines joined Louis Armstrong's All-Stars in 1948, beginning a phase in which some mistakenly began to regard him as a "traditionalist." Later he settled in the San Francisco area and was increasingly heard in neo-Dixieland formats until 1964, when he came to New York for a series of solo and small-group concerts. If "genius" is a word that still has meaning, Earl Hines was just that—a man whose music not only tested the rules but left us in doubt as to whether there are any rules, other than the ones his inspiration managed to create.

COUNT BASIE
[1986]

A MONG the glories of the big-band era are the albums of "air-checks" that have emerged in recent years, radio broadcasts from dance halls or nightclubs that dedicated listeners managed to capture and preserve. Playing for an audience, the bands often sound more relaxed than they did in the recording studio—the only drawbacks being the sometimes less than ideal sound quality and the network announcers, who tend to introduce each tune with a grotesque blend of condescension and smarminess. Yet I've always had a soft spot for the unnamed announcer who adorns one of my favorite Count Basie airchecks. Broadcasting from the Savoy Ballroom in 1937, Basie and the band have just done a marvelous job on "I'll Always Be in Love With You." Then as the final chords die away, this fellow chimes in with, "and once again the fields of gloom are adroitly plowed under."

A bit fanciful, perhaps, but otherwise just right. While Basie and his band have in effect always played the blues, even on pop tunes, their blues were songs of triumph and joy—celebrations of the very adroitness with which they were able to swing through a sometimes recalcitrant world. And the same could be said of Basie's autobiography, *Good Morning Blues*, which may be the finest book of its kind since Sidney Bechet's *Treat It Gen-*

tle. Told to novelist Albert Murray (who functions as a kind of literary orchestrator-accompanist), *Good Morning Blues* handsomely conveys the essence of Basie's life and times. And that, it should be said, is a rather surprising development, for Basie (who died in April 1984 at age 79) was a deeply reticent man who admits that he "never did have a lot of words." But perhaps because this book was Basie's idea (he and Murray collaborated on it for seven years), his words have the same leanly swinging eloquence that marked his keyboard and bandleading styles; it's as though one were listening to a top-notch tap dancer whose structures are built upon silence as much as upon sound.

Early on in Basie's narrative there are some verbal flourishes that recall his youthful piano work, which took off from the decorative stride playing of such Harlem masters as Fats Waller and James P. Johnson. Consider this childhood recollection of his mother's kitchen at Christmastime in Red Bank, New Jersey, "when there was all that nutmeg and vanilla and cinnamon and chocolate in the air. My mouth still waters when I remember those cakes with all that coconut icing and those jelly layer cakes and those potato pies and custard pies. And all mixed in with all that, you could also smell the celery and sage and black pepper in the chicken or turkey stuffing, and when my mother baked ham, there were the cloves and the pineapple glaze." The things Basie names are part of the effect, of course. But notice the clean-limbed rhythmic flow of this naming, which not only evokes each sensuous moment but also forms them into a chain of downhome ecstasies.

Again, the connection between Basie's verbal and musical craft seems obvious. But later on, as in his mature piano style, Basie achieves still deeper effects through a striking use of silence—an isolation of the essential that makes it reverberate with meaning.

A theme that recurs throughout the book is Basie's love of his wife, Catherine. He first sees her when she is sixteen, one of the three "Snakehips Queens" who danced with May Whitman's vaudeville troupe. And when they finally wed (or, as Basie puts it, become "boy and girl"), his profound sense of satisfaction is almost palpable. Then, toward the end of *Good Morning Blues*, Catherine Basie dies, and this is how the narrator presents it: "That album turned out to be the last one I made while Katy was alive, and she didn't get to hear it because we lost her last April while I was up in Toronto. She was at home in Freeport, where she had been since late fall because her doctor had advised her to stay home and take it easy and watch her weight. So I knew she was not in the best of health, but all during the time while I was at home during the Christmas break, she didn't seem to be having serious problems either. She was just her usual self, and that's the way she was when I came back to work in January, and that's how she sounded on the telephone every day. Then all of sudden she was gone. My Katy, my baby." That stark, four-word coda, with its double, falling cadence. Anyone, I suppose, can tell that only in this way could Basie express a weight of feeling that otherwise might have overwhelmed him— although in doing so he threatens to overwhelm us.

Full of accurate historical detail, *Good Morning Blues* is most illuminating when it deals with Basie's early career—in particular his encounter in Kansas City with the music of Walter Page's Blue Devils, the band that virtually changed his life. "At the time," Basie explains (he was then on the road with a vaudeville revue), "I didn't really think of myself as a jazz musician. I was a ragtime or a stride piano player, to be sure, but I really thought of that as being an entertainer, just another way of being in show business."

But then Basie joins the urgently swinging Blue Devils for a while and finds that "without being really aware of it, I was becoming more and more tied up with music itself and less and less concerned with show business and entertainment in general. Of course, it was all a part of the same world, but after playing with those Blue Devils, being a musician was where it was really at for me."

One has read so much nonsense on the subject of art versus commerce in jazz, especially from those who claim that jazz musicians in the "good old days" were content to think of themselves as entertainers pure and simple, that Basie's carefully measured words carry much weight. Yes, it is (or was) "all a part of the same world." But to choose to play jazz, as Basie did, meant that one had found within the music a kind of spiritual-artistic conscience that buoyed the soul and that one trifled with at one's peril. That is, the music always knows. And perhaps the best way to explain Basie's achievement is that he managed to blend what the music knows and what he knew into a single, seamless entity.

"It's the way you play it that makes it," he says toward the end of *Good Morning Blues*. "What I say is, for Christ's sake, you don't have to kill yourself to swing. Play like you play. Play like you think, and then you've got it, if you're going to get it. And whatever you get, that's you, that's your story. You don't have to play anything loud until you need it, and you don't need it until you really feel it. Then it's you."

DUKE ELLINGTON
[1984]

JAZZ used to be, and in many ways still is, a form of popular entertainment—a music so linked to the expectations of its audience it may seem unlikely that any performance would deserve the close attention given to masterworks of the classical repertoire. But quite a few jazz artists have managed to have it both ways, entertaining the public while satisfying their own imaginations and meeting the highest standards of musical creativity. Chief among them was the late Duke Ellington, "the most masterful of all blues idiom arranger-composers," in the words of critic Albert Murray, who went on to say that "a literary equivalent [of Ellington] would be beyond Melville, Henry James, and Faulkner." If that claim sounds extreme, it is backed up by any

number of Ellington performances; for within his best pieces the
sheer density of events and the emotional richness of the whole
are a never-ending joy to contemplate—even though, until the
advent of the long-playing record, most Ellington recordings
lasted less than three minutes.

One of those Ellington masterworks, recorded on August 28,
1939, is "The Sergeant Was Shy," a portrait, according to the
composer, of a "tough fighting man" who is "real shy in private
life." "The Sergeant Was Shy" is a variation on "Bugle Call Rag,"
which Elmer Schoebel composed in 1923 for the New Orleans
Rhythm Kings. Not a genuine rag, "Bugle Call" is a series of
twelve-bar blues choruses, each of which begins with a four-bar,
bugle-call "break," a passage during which the rest of the ensemble remains silent while the soloist soars on his own. "Reveille,"
the bugle call that originally began the piece, soon was replaced
by "Assembly," an equally familiar but more musically attractive
bugle call; and a strain from W. C. Handy's "Ole Miss" (sixteen
bars in length and without breaks) is added to most performances of "Bugle Call Rag" for the sake of variety.

With those materials to work with, Ellington could have
given his audience a straightforward version of the piece, which
is what he did when he recorded "Bugle Call Rag" in 1932, and
which is what Benny Goodman did when he made a very popular recording of "Bugle Call" in 1937. "The Sergeant Was Shy,"
however, is a remarkably oblique, subtle work—a fantasy-
variation on "Bugle Call Rag" that is so full of fascinating musical detail and so rich in dramatic wit that one hardly can believe it lasts only two minutes, thirty-six seconds.

Ellington begins not with the familiar bugle-call break but
with a sixteen-bar introduction, dividing the orchestra into four
separate instrumental units (five if we count the rhythm section)
that enter at four-bar intervals, with one layer of sound placed
atop another until one feels that the entire rhythmic-tonal canvas has been charged with meaning. First, we hear either two
or three woodsy-toned, lower-register clarinets playing a figure
whose rhythmic shape, rendered onomatopoeically, is "Dee-
doodle-*doo* . . . dee-doodle-*doo*." After four bars pass, three trom-

bones (one of them Juan Tizol's valve trombone) enter with "Bop
. . . *boo*-bop, boo-bop-boo-bop," followed four bars later by three
cup-muted   trumpets   playing   "Boop-bee-doodly-*boop-boop*,
boop-bee-doodly-*boop-boop*." And in the next four bars, clarinetist Barney Bigard adds to all this an upper-register trill that
sounds like a continuous *"Wheeeeee!"* Perfectly lucid to the ear,
this passage is remarkable from a rhythmic point of view, for as
"Dee-doodle-*doo*" and the rest should indicate, the figures played
by each of the four layers of instruments emphasize a different
beat (or subdivision of the beat) within the four-beats-to-the-bar
pulse—perhaps, as one critic has suggested, to evoke the sounds
of four different military drill teams passing in review.

The instrumentation itself is a typically Ellingtonian tapestry of tone colors, although the sensuous appeal of each layer
of sound is inseparable from the rest of its musical meaning.
The tangolike glide of the trombone figures, for instance, would
have a very different impact if played on a different group of
instruments. Clearly this is not a brass-saxophone-and-rhythm
dance band, although the Ellington orchestra could function in
that way, but a flexible, fourteen-man "instrument" from which
Ellington was able to summon up just about any combination
of sounds that came to mind.

But back to "The Sergeant Was Shy," for almost nine-tenths
of the piece lies ahead, including that obligatory bugle call,
which surely ought to arrive rather soon. When it comes,
though, Ellington has tucked it away slyly—at the end, not at
the beginning, of the next chorus. Played by four saxophones
instead of by the solo trumpet one expects, and without a
"break" feeling, the familiar melody sounds dogged and trudg-
ing, without the aura of exuberant release the bugle call nor-
mally evokes. Exuberance emerges at the beginning of the third
chorus, however, which is launched by four bars of chattering
muted trumpets—a coy, almost rickety-tick sound that is answered four bars later by a suave saxophone-section counter-
melody, which continues for sixteen bars while the trumpets
stick to their pattern. Here is a fine example of Ellington's
musical-dramatic counterpoint, for in addition to the perfect

rhythmic fit between the trumpets' brisk but essentially static figures and the saxophones' sinuous glides, the trumpet line seems mocking and puckish, while the saxophone counter-melody has a stately, aristocratic aura to it that, in effect, chastens the trumpets' nose-thumbing sprightliness.

Now, from the fourth chorus through the eighth chorus, Ellington launches into the standard twelve-bar "Bugle Call Rag" pattern, with the breaks being played in succession by Bigard, cornetist Rex Stewart, the saxophones, the trombones, and the unmuted trumpets. Chorus six is very intense, with Stewart insisting on repeated high notes until his relationship to the shifting saxophone harmonies beneath him becomes quite dissonant. Then at the beginning of chorus eight there is a moment of pure glory, as the golden-toned trumpets play a break that is all celebration and joyful release.

But there is one further act to this drama. (By this time, one has no doubt that Ellington is thinking in dramatic terms.) The rest of the eighth chorus finds the trumpets returning to their sassy, mocking mode, and, as before, this cannot remain unchallenged. The "elder" chosen to wag his musical finger at the trumpets in the ninth and final chorus is trombonist Tricky Sam Nanton, but in the marvelous sixteen bars that end "The Sergeant Was Shy," no one really gets the upper hand. Darting in and out of the orchestral texture, Nanton's "wah-wah/yah-yah" figures swing so hard that he and the irrepressible trumpets finally inhabit the same emotional world, and his final talking phrase seems to say, "Oh yeah, you were right," just before baritone saxophonist Harry Carney seals off the performance with a virile, thudding "Whomp."

In purely musical terms, much more could be said about "The Sergeant Was Shy." There is, for example, another striking dissonance in chorus nine, as the end of Nanton's break clashes with the trumpets' flaring figures in a passage that brings to mind the reaction of the young Charles Mingus to his first live Ellington performance: "Someplace, something he did, I screamed." But if the piece is so dramatic, what is it about, in addition to that "tough fighting man" who is "shy in private life"?

And where, aside from "Bugle Call Rag," did it come from? One guess would be that "The Sergeant Was Shy" is a celebration of one of the many ways in which black Americans have transformed the "givens" of American life—in this case, the military drill patterns that were taught to many black high school students of Ellington's age by black instructors who had served in the Spanish-American War. The idea, as novelist Ralph Ellison once said, was to make those drill patterns swing, to infuse the jazz spirit into every corner of experience. But perhaps that is just another way of saying that "The Sergeant Was Shy" is a joyfully triumphant celebration of itself.

The above piece was written to coincide with a conference on Ellington's music that was held at the University of Illinois at Chicago. I returned to "The Sergeant Was Shy" thirteen years later for a *Village Voice* jazz supplement—the task being to describe a favorite Ellington recording in two hundred words or less.

[1997]

KNOWING the emotional etymology of almost every sound a man could make and what those sounds said about the men who made them, Ellington built into some of his best works (and, of course, into the orchestra that cocreated them) a special sort of musical self-awareness. "The Sergeant Was Shy," from June 1939, is lovely that way, a kind of glorious, golden jest about how many ways there might be to feel about bits and pieces of "Bugle Call Rag"—marchingly mysterioso, Frenchified tangoish, parade-ground earnest, and "Here comes the band!" gleeful (all in the first sixteen bars alone). And yes, this two-minute, thirty-six second kaleidoscope of moods is about being such a kaleidoscope, about the ways we inevitably place ourselves by the way we sound. In fact, I think that among the most central points of celebration that Ellington ever allowed himself is the blaze-of-sunlight break with which the trumpet section

begins chorus eight, after which the master chastens their sas-
siness with the finger-wagging of Tricky Sam Nanton (this leads
to fierce dissonance) and then asks Harry Carney to smack his
basso seal of sobriety on a seriocomic masterpiece.

ARTHUR ROLLINI
[1987]

ARTHUR Rollini's name does not loom large in the history of
jazz, even though he was the younger brother of a major
artist (bass saxophonist and mallet percussionist Adrian Rollini)
and a member of Benny Goodman's saxophone section from the
inception of Goodman's band until 1939. But perhaps because
of his cog-in-the-wheel status, Rollini has written a very moving
autobiography, *Thirty Years With the Big Bands*—a book that captures the feel of the Swing Era from a sideman's point of view
with an attractive blend of stoicism and wit.

Rollini's tale also is suffused with a casual, peculiarly American grace, as though, like one of Sherwood Anderson's narra-
tors, the seeming innocence with which he addresses us were
essential to his message. Rollini records that an early childhood
memory was of "the brass and crystal Ansonia clock on our
mantel, which never ceased functioning as long as it was wound
every eighth day. It was always wound on time, and its little
mercury pendulum kept beating back and forth and intrigued
me. I would view it for hours." Nothing more than nostalgia,
one thinks, until, several pages and a decade or so further on,
Rollini's father dies and "the only sound in the living room was
the little clock on the mantel, which ticked away and gonged
softly on the hour and half hour, its little pendulum still beating
back and forth in perfect rhythm."

Following in his older brother's footsteps, Rollini was a professional musician at age seventeen—traveling to London to work with Fred Elizade's orchestra at the Savoy Hotel, where the Prince of Wales often sat in on drums. ("He was, let us put it this way, not too good," Rollini says.) Jazz fans will be most interested in Rollini's account of his time with Benny Goodman, which confirms the widely held belief that Goodman was a difficult man to get along with. "Inconsiderate Benny, the best jazz clarinetist in the world!"—Rollini uses that tag, and variations thereof, time after time, even when a harsher adjective than "inconsiderate" might apply. Rollini and Dick Clark were Goodman's initial tenor saxophonists, and "even at this stage," Rollini says, "Benny would look at Dick's bald head with disdain. He wanted a youthful looking band. 'Fickle Benny,' I thought, 'the best jazz clarinetist in the world!' Dick was a good player."

Quietly authoritative, Rollini's tales of the sideman's happy-sad life have a cumulative power. And two of them, when placed side by side, virtually define the big-band musician's paradoxical role. In the first, Rollini is playing a dance with Goodman when he meets an old high school friend, one Johnny Baker, who requests that the band play "Always," on the recording of which Rollini had a solo. At the dance, Rollini deliberately plays "something entirely different from what was on our recording, and after it was over Johnny Baker said to me, 'What did you change it for?' " Then, in the mid-1940s, when Rollini was an NBC Radio staff musician, he stops in a Manhattan bar after work and notices that "two young men were playing the jukebox and had selected Will Bradley's 'Request for a Rhumba,' which we had recorded in 1941. Finally I stepped off the bar stool and asked, 'Boys, why are you playing that record over and over?' One replied, 'We like the tenor sax solo.' I felt elated, but did not tell them that it was I who played it."

Arthur Rollini died in 1993.

ARNETT COBB
[1980]

THERE could be no better proof of the importance of sound in jazz, the tone or timbre one gets out of an instrument, than the music of tenor saxophonist Arnett Cobb. A native of Houston and one of the great Southwestern tenormen, along with Buddy Tate, Ben Webster, the late Herschel Evans, and Illinois Jacquet (who preceded Cobb in the Lionel Hampton band), this sixty-two-year-old master has a sound that no recording studio is equipped to reproduce.

It is, to begin with, simply huge, perhaps the darkest, most imposingly rich tenor saxophone tone of all. And what Cobb does with it—the range of chortles, whoops, cries, trills, swells, slurs, shouts, and just plain honks that he has at his command is such that he could say, with Walt Whitman, "I am vast, I contain multitudes."

Not that Cobb is limited merely to purveying that sound. He is, by any standard, a rhythmically agile, harmonically sophisticated player who shapes his melodic lines with surprising delicacy. But because the significance of sound per se is so often overlooked in jazz, as though it were a seasoning rather than an essential ingredient, it is his sound that I want to concentrate on for the time being.

When a man has a tone like Cobb's and can manipulate it so freely, he has at hand an almost literal musical language, a collection of timbres that each take on a specific emotional meaning. And that specificity of emotional tone-color—which any listener can hear, even if one doesn't wish to analyze it— also ranges outward to affect every other aspect of the music: rhythm, harmony, melody, etc. For example, during Cobb's solo on "Just a Closer Walk With Thee," he began a chorus with a seemingly simple two-note phrase, which might be rendered onomatopoeically as "*Yah*-duh." Now I suppose you had to be there to hear what that "*Yah*-duh" did, but let me assure you that within its apparent simplicity there was more musical meaning than words could exhaust. Aside from the way he attacked the first note, creating a catapulting sense of swing, there was the way its relative density—its heavy, centered sound—contrasted with the grainier, more oblique tonal texture of the second note. The effect of this might be compared to a gymnast's second, more easeful bounce on a trampoline. And listening to it one could feel a literal loosening in the knees, an invitation to enter a realm of sensuous physicality.

The creation and control of such effects, in which the abstract and the emotional aspects of jazz become one thing, is what Cobb's music is all about. And if the principles at work in that "*Yah*-duh," which must have lasted no more than a second, are expanded to cover an entire performance, it is easy to imagine just how richly varied this master's language can be.

Arnett Cobb died in 1985.

ARTIE SHAW
[1984]

ARTIE Shaw is back, even if he's not playing the clarinet. (Shaw hasn't done that since 1955, and he says he never will again.) Instead, Shaw is leading a new big band of such startling quality that one has to think again about the nature of the big-band tradition, the role Shaw played in it, and, perhaps most important, the reasons the so-called Swing Era captured the nation's soul in the late 1930s and early 1940s.

Assembled last fall at the behest of agent Willard Alexander, with Dick Johnson taking the clarinet solos, Shaw's new crew might seem at first to be an attempt to stir the embers of nostalgia—a "ghost band," à la the various orchestras that have been playing Glenn Miller's music for the past forty years. Yet Shaw hasn't taken that route, even though his band plays "Begin the Beguine," "Frenesi," "Back Bay Shuffle," and the rest of the old hits that have, as he says, "paid my rent." Instead, he has instilled in this group of mostly young players the virtues of lyrical perfectionism that have always marked his music, and the result is a band that doesn't sound like any other large jazz ensemble around today.

The simplest way to explain the difference is that every section of this band seems to sing. With Shaw out front, molding every phrase with his hands (and with, one feels sure, many hours of rehearsal to back up those emphatic but subtle gestures), the band has a command of dynamics and rhythmic flow that one seldom hears anymore. It's a caressingly sweet sound (the trumpets, though without a hint of schmaltz, almost sound like violins) as well as a swinging one, and the sheer romanticism of that swinging sweetness helps to explain why the Swing Era was more than just another blip on the chart of America's taste in popular music.

Epitomized by Shaw as much as by anyone else, the Swing Era was both a musical and emotional phenomenon, a period when a generation of American youth expressed its coming of age in sound. Sandwiched between the Depression and World War II, this music was a blend of gawky hopefulness and new-found sophistication, though at times it also had a poignant undertone to it, especially in Shaw's hands. From that point of view, it is no accident that such Shaw hits as "Frenesi," "Temptation," and his theme song, "Nightmare," were minor-key pieces, very romantic in mood in one sense but with an edge of stark, brooding realism to them. They wear very well, particularly the way Shaw's new band plays them, because the leader has made Johnson and everyone else feel their still-vital emotional force.

LOUIS BELLSON
[1982]

L ouis Bellson is so much a product of the latter days of the big-band era that he ought to have "1942" stamped on his forehead. That was the year Bellson, already the winner of a Gene Krupa sponsored contest for young drummers, turned eighteen and the year that bebop's invigorating rhythmic asymmetries were beginning to take shape. But the music Bellson played then (and the music he plays now) was one in which rhythmic evenness always prevailed, and speed, polish, and showmanship were the key virtues.

A dazzling technician who is rivaled in that area only by Buddy Rich, Bellson is a very different drummer, and not only because his basic geniality is alien to Rich's fierce, at times even brutal aggressiveness. Seven years older than Bellson, Rich came up when some big bands (such as the 1938 Bunny Berigan crew he drove so hard) still could proceed along rough-and-tumble lines. And even today, for all his whiz-bang flash, there is a guttural, woody undertone to Rich's playing.

Bellson, by contrast, is all chrome and stainless steel—unfailingly elegant and as streamlined as a P-51 fighter plane. Gliding along with apparent effortlessness, even though one knows that he has just produced something that borders on the impossible, Bellson plays as though effort ought to be concealed. In the midst of his dazzling and almost always musical percussion displays, he seems to be saying, "I'd just as soon be one of the guys," which may be why Bellson-led big bands and small groups tend to be as genial as their leader.

His current quartet certainly sounds happy. The only horn is saxophonist Ted Nash, twenty-two, nephew of the Ted Nash who starred with Les Brown, and son of trombonist Dick Nash. Unlike his smooth-toned uncle, Nash comes on like an academic John Coltrane disciple—of whom there are so many these days that one imagines them being turned out on an assembly line.

But Nash has an alert ear and played well on the only Coltrane-style tune of the night. More interesting was the rhythm section, which includes local stalwart Larry Novak on piano and George Duvivier, a suavely aristocratic, discreetly astonishing bass player.

Reacting to Bellson's bubbly sense of swing, Novak rode on top of the beat in an almost giddy fashion. At first, given the sheer speed of his trebly, multinoted lines, he seemed to be rushing. But, in fact, everything was locked into place, with the zeal of Novak's rhythmic and harmonic imagination suggesting a blend of early Bill Evans and the flashier side of Art Tatum. As for Duvivier, if Milt Hinton is "The Judge," he must be the Chief Justice. His walking lines are so rich in harmonic and rhythmic meaning (and so perfectly in tune) that it's a pleasure to listen to him in a supporting role. And as a soloist . . . well, there are few horn players of any era who make as much sense on their instruments as Duvivier does on his. Indeed, with the exception of the late Jimmy Blanton, Duvivier's true peers are such master saxophonists as Coleman Hawkins and Benny Carter.

Nice guy that he is, Bellson didn't hog the spotlight, featuring himself at length only on "Caravan." But when it's time for a Bellson percussion display, jaws tend to drop—at least mine did when Bellson matched an impossibly rapid and even snare-drum press roll to an equally smooth double-bass-drum pattern. But amidst all these wow-the-crowd devices, one noticed that Bellson's entire solo was built around a central rhythmic motif, which was varied with a rare orderliness and sobriety. A musician as well as a drummer.

RUBY BRAFF
[1985]

THE most glorious anachronism in jazz, cornetist Ruby Braff really shouldn't exist—for he may be the only man who has successfully stepped outside of the otherwise swift-running stream of jazz history, although Braff doesn't quite see himself that way. But that is more than appropriate, because Braff has always been a one-of-a-kind guy whose gleefully combative attitude toward life recalls Groucho Marx's famous quip that he "wouldn't belong to any club that would have me as a member." Suggest, for instance, that there is anything unlikely about what he has managed to do—build a truly individual style that nonetheless pays handsome tribute to the genius of Louis Armstrong—and the fifty-eight-year-old Braff bridles at the thought.

"Hey," he says, "I was playing in joints when I was still in grade school, and by the time bebop came along, in 1945 and '46, I already was deeply into music. So there wasn't anything odd about what I was doing. You know what they say, 'You are what you eat,' and I was just playing the way I heard people play."

But there is something unusual about Braff's achievement. Even though he was, back then, not the only young player who felt himself to be more in tune with the music of Armstrong et al. than with the music of Charlie Parker and Dizzy Gillespie, he was almost alone in his ability to steer clear of the tricky waters of re-creation and revivalism. Inspired by the past, Braff has always been a musician of the present, and his love of what might be called "the great jazz tradition" has only increased the individuality of his plush, throbbing tone and the gracefully soaring phrases with which, as one critic put it, Braff "adores the melody." So at a time when the virtues of the great tradition are seldom to be found, Braff not only presents them with all of their original force but also puts them to very personal use— creating his own music with a passion that transcends the boundaries of style.

Born in the Boston suburb of Roxbury, Massachusetts, the son of Russian-Jewish immigrants, Braff knew early on that he was destined to be "a performing animal." "Were I not playing the horn," he claims, "I'd be in vaudeville—a magician, a comic, something on the stage. And the reason I know that is that I know how I responded to performers, even when I was a baby. I'd hear something on the radio, even [boy tenor] Bobby Breen [here Braff does a choice takeoff on Breen singing "When My Dreamboat Comes Home"], and it would just stir things in me, drive me crazy. I, too, wanted to make noises like that and excite somebody the way those noises excited me."

The noisemaker Braff had his heart set on was a tenor saxophone, but when his parents took their rather diminutive son to a music store, they felt a trumpet would be more his size—a choice for which the jazz world has reason to be grateful. Switching from trumpet to cornet "because it looks better for shorter people" (Braff now stands five feet four inches tall) and also because "it has a mellower sound," Braff continued to think in saxophone terms—"which is good," he explains, "because if you think of another instrument, you can't help but sound a little different."

Braff found himself in good musical company early on—his compatriots included such older masters as clarinetist Edmond Hall, trombonist Vic Dickenson, and drummer Sid Catlett—and by the time Braff made his first recording, under Dickenson's leadership in 1953, he was a remarkably mature player. A number of fine Braff recordings were made in the wake of that striking debut, including several superb albums that paired him with pianist Ellis Larkins. But even though he was showered with praise by many critics, the course of Braff's career was not destined to be smooth. For one thing, his chosen style was not fashionably hip, and Braff, quite rightly, had no desire to change the way he played. On the other hand, Braff was praised in some quarters *because* of his apparent lack of modernity, which had the unfortunate side effect of typing him as an artist that only tradition-minded listeners were likely to enjoy. Combine that with Braff's somewhat bristly manner, which probably stems from the fierce artistic demands he places on himself, and one has the makings of a man who was born to wear the label "underrated."

"All I know," says Braff, "is that wherever I've played, people have liked what they heard. The problem was, nobody was getting to hear me enough." And with that, Braff sets off one of his typical strings of verbal fireworks—a half-serious, half-joking series of remarks that he delivers in an obsessive rush and at such a high volume level that one hardly needs a telephone to hear him. Add an exclamation point to every phrase, and you'll get some of the flavor.

"I'm a drama freak," Braff begins. "I like to dramatize a tune and I'm always trying to communicate, which is the difference between being a performer and a musician. There are many musicians, but they aren't performers, they're just instrumentalists who belong in an orchestra reading charts—which is all right, ain't nothing wrong with that. But the trouble with this world is that most of these people are on the stand today, playing seven hundred choruses!

"Loudness and softness and longness and shortness—if you're a performing animal, you know about those things. I was brought up on the two-and-a-half-minute record, where you heard a marvelous composition and little solos, returns to a theme and highs and lows, which is what I think about when I'm playing, even though sometimes I play much longer than that. I'm thinking 'stretch in,' not 'stretch out'—'in, in, in!' You see, I treat me as though I were a customer. When I'm playing I'm thinking, 'What are you doing now? Okay, that's enough of that,' so the audience always knows what I'm talking about. I mean, a truck driver can listen to Johnny Hodges and know this is something that makes him feel good—an idiot can hear those magical tones and they'll tug at his heartstrings!

"Show business—I love show business. If I had my way, I'd be up there with dancers and magicians and lights and everything. Oh, why can't I have magic, so that when I lift my horn up and want it to disappear, it vanishes out of my hand? That can be done with lights, I know it can! Oh, why can't I be tremendous? If I were a star, I'd have such fun! Sinatra—why don't I get the exposure he gets? Maybe I should call him up and threaten him. No, no, I'd better not do that—that is not the way to go. But why did they ruin everything? I mean, this is the worst world I've ever lived in. All I want to do is go over the rainbow, to someplace better than where I was. And why can't I have my own talk show?"

Sorting through this barrage of vintage Braff-isms, with its built-in wryness and its wild swings in mood, one simultaneously feels that almost none of it, and all of it, should be taken at face value. Braff really does want to be "tremendous" and all the rest. But even as he bursts at the seams with the need to impose his ego upon the whole world, he is self-aware enough to know that his gifts are best suited to the relatively intimate medium of the cornet. In fact, when Braff pours his turbulent soul through that horn, it seems that the sheer pressure of his drive to communicate to one and all is what makes his music so powerful in a nightclub setting—as though one were bearing witness to a beauty that could, at any moment, explode.

"Ruby is a traditionalist," says Braff's longtime friend Tony Bennett, "in the sense that he knows the roots and the treasures—Louis Armstrong, Judy Garland, Bix Beiderbecke, and all the rest. But then, having learned from them, he takes that knowledge and flies with it in a very modern way. Like all great jazz musicians, Ruby is right in the 'now,' and when people get a chance to hear him, they're always moved. I remember last year, I went to one of those really hardnosed ASCAP [American Society of Composers and Performers] meetings that the Songwriters Hall of Fame puts on. Every big composer was in the audience, and a whole bunch of artists performed, but it was more of a social occasion until Ruby came out to back a singer. He played a few solos and obbligatos, and suddenly it was like everyone was swooning. They didn't know who Ruby was, and then when they heard this magnificent horn, they just went 'Wow!' But that's what Ruby can do to you if he gets a chance."

Ruby Braff died in 2003.

PART IV

Moderns and After

DIZZY GILLESPIE
[1977]

"*Roots!*" Someone had mentioned Alex Haley's book, and Dizzy Gillespie wasn't about to let it pass. "Listen," said the great trumpeter, "I've been following roots longer than *Roots*. Why, my great-grandmother was the daughter of an African chief. How do I know? Twenty years ago they gave me a day in my hometown—Cheraw, South Carolina. And on my way to the reception I stopped at the house of this guy named James Poe. Poe was my mother's maiden name, and she used to work for these people, nursing their twin boys.

"I walked right up to the front door, which was unheard of then. But I'd be damned if I was going to the back after being all over Europe, an international star. I rang, and Mrs. Poe came to the door. She didn't know who I was, but she saw this black face, turned I don't know what color, and started to say, 'We aren't buying nothing,' or whatever. So I started talking—fast. I told her I was Mrs. Gillespie's son and this was my day in Cheraw and I thought I'd come by and pay my respects. 'Mr. Poe is not seeing anybody,' she said. 'Mr. Poe is sick.' But he must have heard my voice inside. 'Is that you, John Birks?' he said. 'Yeah.' 'Come on in here, boy.' So I went in and there he was, about eighty years old in a wheelchair. 'Boy,' he said, 'we're proud of you. Been all over the world, ain't you? Saving your money? Guess you've got a nice little bundle.' 'Mr. Poe,' I said, 'let's not talk about money. You probably got Confederate money under the bed.' And we laughed with that. Then he said, 'You know, your great-grandmother would be proud of you, too. You didn't know her, did you? She was a remarkable woman. My grandfather went all the way to Charleston to buy her because she was the daughter of a chief.' 'Well,' I said, 'call me your *majesty* then!' And he cracked up.

It's typical of Gillespie to find humor where most of us could see only pain, but the ironic note of triumph he sounded that day was also a very real one. Two generations removed from slavery (his grandfather was born before the Emancipation Proclamation), John Birks Gillespie is artistic royalty, a genius who played a key role in shaping jazz, our major native art form.

For Gillespie, music began at home. His father, a brickmaker by trade, led an amateur band and played a large variety of instruments. As a boy, Gillespie experimented with the string bass and the trombone, and then at twelve borrowed a trumpet from the boy next door. That was it. Formal musical studies weren't in the picture, though. And Gillespie emphasizes that being self-taught furthered the growth of his own style.

"A style develops when you hear something that you want and then go about getting it in your own way," he explains. "That's why my jaws and neck stick out when I play. I heard something and that was the only way I could get it—because I didn't have a teacher. And that's how style arrives—the way you play, not the actual notes."

By the time the Gillespie family moved to Philadelphia in 1935, Dizzy was skilled enough to get a job in a local band led by Frank Fairfax. The young Gillespie modeled his playing after Roy Eldridge, listening to that virtuoso's Saturday night broadcasts with the Teddy Hill band from the Savoy Ballroom. Not only did this imitation process challenge Gillespie's ear and technique, but it also helped to win him his first job. Eldridge left Hill to go with Fletcher Henderson, and when the leader sought an Eldridge-style trumpeter to take his place, there was Gillespie, who had come to New York looking for work with another band. Engagements followed with Cab Calloway, Lucky Millinder, and other Swing Era orchestras, but Gillespie was soon hearing new ways to play and trying them out at after-hours clubs like Monroe's and Minton's. The name for the new music—bebop—was yet to come, but Gillespie, pianist Thelonious Monk, drummer Kenny Clarke, and others were hammering out its fundamentals. "I don't think of it as a revolution," Gillespie reflects, "I think of it as a progressive revelation. We used to sit down and look at a regular chord and say, 'Man, we should make the flatted fifth here.' We changed the chords around and made two or three chords out of one."

Recordings from that period show that Gillespie was venturing beyond his stage of Eldridge worship. But as much as the music speaks of things to come, it took another element to bring Dizzy and bebop to ripeness—alto saxophonist Charlie Parker. "I met him briefly in Kansas City when I was with Cab," Gillespie remembers, "and about a year and a half later [in 1943] we played together with Earl Hines. That's how our association began. Both of our musics demonstrated what happened after we met. It's the direct cause—I know it. I didn't play that way before I found him, and he didn't play that way before he found me."

Unfortunately, the Hines band in which Parker and Gillespie were partners made no recordings because of a musicians union dispute with the record industry. But after the recording ban was lifted, Bird and Diz—who had been working in a combo on 52nd Street—finally came together in a studio. The first recording session, in February 1945, wasn't a complete success due to the drummer's rather metronomic timekeeping. But a May 1945 date gave us "Salt Peanuts," "Shaw 'Nuff," "Hot House," and "Lover Man"—recordings whose impact on fellow musicians and fans it would be difficult to exaggerate. "Thad Jones told me once," Gillespie says, "that he was in the Navy in Hawaii, resting in his bunk, when a record of mine came on. He fell right out onto the floor. Because, he said, that was exactly the music he'd been looking for."

For bebop's creators it may have been, as Gillespie says, a case of "just going about our business." But to his audience, the man from Cheraw became a cultural demigod. Thousands of young men turned themselves into replicas of Gillespie—sporting bop berets, bop glasses, and bop ties, and trying their best to grow mustaches and goatees. And behind it all, carrying bebop beyond mere faddishness, were those magnificent sounds that truly said something new. No trumpeter had played the instrument with greater speed, range, and harmonic daring. Undoubtedly sophisticated, bebop was reaching out to the boundaries of musical experience, but underneath, as Gillespie explains, "there's a fundamental quality to it. It's drum music translated to melody instruments. And that's why it's lasting."

Sophistication plus fundamentals. The farthest out and the nearest in. Many of Gillespie's solos from the forties begin with what sounds like a shout or a scream that reaches straight back to the origins of black music, to field hollers and spirituals. More than thirty years after they were recorded, improvisations like "Night in Tunisia" and "52nd St. Theme" are still breathtaking. One suspects they always will be.

Bebop's growing popularity led Gillespie to form a big band, which folded after an ill-advised southern tour. But the second Gillespie orchestra, organized in 1946, made it over the hump. At its best this was a truly fearsome ensemble, featuring avant-garde arrangements and the dramatic conga playing of Cuban-born percussionist Chano Pozo. By 1950, the big-band era was drawing to an end, and Gillespie disbanded his orchestra and went back to leading a small combo. The early fifties were lean years for jazz, but Gillespie's natural flair as an entertainer helped him to survive, even though he was criticized by some for the amount of comedy he mixed in. "That's all part of show business," he says. "Fats Waller and Louis Armstrong proved that. They were master musicians and yet they were great comedians."

Gradually the rebel became an elder statesman—Gillespie will be sixty this October. But in no way does he rest on his laurels. "I have to play hard. You've got to gorilla that trumpet; you must attack it. If you show any reticence towards this instrument, it will kick your ass. I don't play as much now, in terms of long solos, but I try to make what I play what should be there. Without anything superfluous."

Among the younger trumpeters, Gillespie favors Oscar Brashear, Jimmy Owens, Woody Shaw, and Jon Faddis—all of whom show traces of Gillespie influence. "Certainly trumpet players now phrase a little differently than I do," he says, "but until about ten years ago whatever somebody played was within the framework I'd laid out. Miles Davis? I asked him recently, 'What are you doing?' and he said, 'You know, you taught me.' 'Wait a minute,' I said, 'what you learned from me about harmony and things like that ain't got nothing to do with what you're playing now.' Then he tried to explain what they were doing with chords, scales, and electronics, but it didn't make sense, it didn't instruct me. So I still don't know what he's doing."

As for jazz's future in a world of rock and so-called fusion music, Gillespie is hopeful. "Rock's got a lot of rhythm, I'll tell you that. And rhythm will carry you through, I think, because rhythm is basic. The rock guys who are really sophisticated have got it. You see, our jazz rhythm—'chuck-a-ding, chuck-a-ding, chuck-a-ding'—we've gone past that now. The bass player does one thing, the drums and the guitars do something else, and they all stay out of one another's way."

Sooner or later when you're talking with Gillespie you have to notice his vitality and optimism, his sheer appetite for life. It's a quality he largely attributes to his religion, the Bahai faith. "I'd always believed," he explains, "but I never had anything to program my belief in the right direction. But the Bahai faith is the personification of everything I've believed from the beginning. To wit: We all come from the same sources—now is the time for all mankind to be unified in every aspect of human endeavor, including a world government.

"They teach you that each individual, spiritually, is at his own level. So you take that into account in all your dealings with mankind. If you see a guy acting off-the-wall, his spiritual level is at a low ebb. So you treat him like that. But the ones who are at the level where you are, you treat them that way. You hardly ever get into any arguments. Because hate—boy, hate takes up a whole lot of energy. And when you're using that up, you could be doing something to better your own condition." Hardly the thoughts of a man you'd call Dizzy. But, in the words of Teddy Hill, the bandleader who hired him to replace Roy Eldridge forty years ago, "He is Dizzy like a fox."

Dizzy Gillespie died in 1993.

THELONIOUS MONK
[1982]

THELONIOUS Sphere Monk, jazz innovator, pianist, and composer, died early today, after suffering a stroke on February 5, according to an official at the Englewood Hospital, Englewood, New Jersey. That was the gist of the story that came over the wires last Wednesday, and it was accurate as far as it went. But much more needs to be said about Thelonious Monk, because his immense contribution to the music of this century is so easily misunderstood.

His very name suggests eccentricity, and there was behavior to back up that image—the sly, elflike dance steps that Monk (a physically imposing figure) sometimes would indulge in after a piano solo; the unusual titles of many of his compositions ("Misterioso," "Epistrophy," "Off Minor," "Nutty," "Ba-lue Bolivar Ba-lues-are," and "Rhythm-a-ning"); and his reclusive role in recent years (he last performed in public in 1975). Yet if the notion of eccentricity is extended to Monk's music, nothing could be further from the truth, for he may have been the most logical composer-performer jazz has yet produced. Listen, for example, to Monk's composition "Little Rootie Tootie," which, like his "Locomotive," Luckey Roberts's "Railroad Blues," and Duke Ellington's "Daybreak Express" and "Happy Go-Lucky Local," belongs to the long jazz tradition of pieces that imitate the sound of railroad trains. An impressive portrait, with its chugging chords perfectly capturing the sound of a steam engine leaving the station, "Little Rootie Tootie" becomes an astonishing musical discourse after the theme has been stated and the piano solo begins. Like Alexander Pope's spider, who "feels at each thread and lives along the line," Monk spins out a steadily evolving pattern of musical thought in which the most practical and the most abstract virtues become one thing. Simultaneously delicate and strong, as joyful as a nursery rhyme and as grave as a hymn, "Little Rootie Tootie," like so many of Monk's creations, has an unshakeable aura of finality to it, as though his way were the only way to proceed. And it is this quality of utter completeness, as rare in jazz as it is in any other music (or any other art for that matter), that made Monk a master.

Born in Rocky Mount, North Carolina, on October 10, 1917, Monk grew up in New York City, where he began studying piano at age six. He played the organ in church and toured with an evangelist (returning to those roots when he recorded the hymn "Abide With Me" in 1957). But his principal influences were the great Harlem stride pianists, particularly James P. Johnson and Fats Waller. Full of elaborate keyboard decoration, their music was essentially composed, not improvised—or at least not improvised from the inside out, as the music of jazz's major horn soloists would increasingly come to be. And so it was Monk's role to recapture for jazz the virtues of compositional form, to make every note part of a total statement while also making sure that the shaping impulse was in no sense a diminishing one.

That last point is crucial, for Monk emerged in the early 1940s, when such artists as Dizzy Gillespie, Charlie Parker, and

Bud Powell were proposing harmonic and rhythmic ideas so radical that an equally daring formal response to their music seemed unlikely. And yet the idea that Monk's music was a response to bebop should not be taken too literally, for Monk was always himself, following the skein of his own logic and impervious to fashion. His complex yet concise structures baffled some of the new musicians, yet Monk managed to find key interpreters—in particular, vibraphonist Milt Jackson and drummers Art Blakey and Max Roach. It is no coincidence that these men were percussionists, for the central impulse of Monk's music is rhythmic. Listen to any of his compositions and one hears time being divided in new ways—more discontinuously (or so it seems at first). But then one realizes that the angular gaps between each phrase are charged with an almost ferocious rhythmic power, that the mind of the composer is leaping from crag to crag like a mountain goat, ignoring the easy and familiar and, in the process, redefining the essential.

There are those who disparaged Monk's skills as a pianist, apparently feeling that lickety-split finger exercises are what jazz piano technique is all about. But as critic Paul Bacon once wrote, "[Monk] relies so much on absolute musical reflex that Horowitz's skills might be unequal to the job." Only a few of Monk's compositions have entered the standard repertoire, though two that have, " 'Round Midnight" and "Ruby My Dear," remain imperishable almost no matter who plays them. But the apartness of most of his music is another sign of its nature and value, for such pieces as "Criss Cross," "Four in One," "Evidence," "Hornin' In," "Skippy," "Trinkle Tinkle," "I Mean You," and "Bye-Ya" defeat surface interpretation. If they are to be performed by anyone other than their creator, they must be met on their own ground; and the number of jazz musicians who can do that has been limited and probably always will be. In fact, while Monk embodied the essence of jazz as much as any man, if only because his music was suffused with profound blues feeling, when one looks at the iron-clad strength and solidity of his art, it is clear that he had few, if any, genuine counterparts within jazz. His stern sense of order, his ability to yoke together the most disparate materials and make them yield a series of primal, profoundly satisfying sums—these are not virtues one finds in many twentieth-century artists of any kind.

MONK IN MOTION
[1982]

L ONG before his death last February 17 at age sixty-four, it was obvious that Thelonious Monk was one of jazz's premier composers, along with Jelly Roll Morton and Duke Ellington. From the deservedly popular " 'Round Midnight" to such less-familiar gems as "Who Knows," "Skippy," and "Gallop's Gallop," Monk created more than seventy compositions, and, in addition to his own recordings, they are now his legacy. But as new recordings of Monk's music begin to arrive—tributes from other artists and previously unissued material from the master himself—one wonders about the nature of that compositional legacy.

If Monk had been a composer in the Western classical tradition, his scores would be relatively straightforward blueprints for future performance, structures that any sympathetic interpretive artist could bring to life. But Monk, like Morton and Ellington, was a quintessential *jazz* composer, a man whose music cannot easily be separated from the way he and his chosen cohorts performed it, night by night. That is, Monk's works were not composed and then interpreted, even by Monk himself. Instead, they were composed and then recomposed, coming fully to life only when the "interpreter" brings to the music all that the music itself already possesses.

That daunting yet potentially vital task was one that Monk must have faced throughout his adult life. And judging by the recordings that have emerged since his death, it is a task that should remain daunting and vital for some time to come. Chick Corea's *Trio Music* (ECM) and *Sphere* (Elektra/Musician), from the group of the same name that includes two former Monk sidemen, are the first in what will likely be a wave of tributes to Monk—though, as it happens, neither album was conceived as a posthumous salute. Half of *Trio Music*, a two-record set, is devoted to Monk compositions, and Corea says that "these tracks were recorded many months before Monk's passing and aren't intended as a memorial but as renditions of what I consider some of the classic music of the twentieth century." A similar desire to honor a still-living artist was the impulse behind *Sphere*, which, by coincidence, was recorded the day of Monk's death.

Accompanied by bassist Miroslav Vitous and drummer Roy Haynes, Corea deserves credit for choosing such seldom-performed compositions as "Think of One" and "Reflections," in addition to the often-heard " 'Round Midnight" and "Rhythm-a-ning." Also honorable is the pianist's attempt to alter his normal style—a mélange of Ravel, Bartòk, and Bill Evans—so that it fits Monk's musical world, where everything must be clearly stated and there is no room for harmonic sweetmeats or wispy impressionism. After a while, though, one begins to wonder whether Corea is really at home in this music. Once the themes have been stated, his improvisations often seem fidgety, as though he wished to abandon Monk's stern restraints and frolic a bit in some less demanding realm. But the ironclad logic of Monk's music cannot be tampered with, which is why Corea's version of the austerely graceful "Eronel" (attributed to Monk but actually written by Idrees Sulieman and Sadik Hakim) virtually destroys that piece by coyly delaying one of its key phrases. Recomposition, yes, but first one must grasp what is essential.

Such knowledge comes more naturally to the members of Sphere (pianist Kenny Barron, bassist Buster Williams, and the group's two Monk graduates, tenor saxophonist Charlie Rouse and drummer Ben Riley), and their version of "Eronel" is near-perfect, a relaxed restatement of the piece that simultaneously floats and swings. As Rouse explains in the album's liner notes, "[Monk's] compositions, if you really know them, are not the regular slow or medium or fast tempos. He usually set tempos in between. Ben [Riley] and I know the concept Thelonious wanted, having been with him for so long. We have a sense of the rhythmic pattern."

That would seem to gibe with a remark Monk himself once made, when asked why many musicians find his music hard to play. "It's not hard to play," he said, "but I know it, that's all . . . maybe." There is, however, not only a pause between Monk's "that's all" and his "maybe" but also a gap in sense, perhaps an ambiguity—one that "Sphere" inadvertently highlights. Barron, Rouse, and the rest are excellent interpretive artists, but they avoid the challenge of recomposition, as though Monk's "that's all" meant "this far and no further." So *Sphere* presents us with a warmly affectionate and attractive portrait of Monk, but one in which there is little sign of the galvanic creator who can be heard on three new-old albums from the master himself: *Live at the It Club* and *Live at the Jazz Workshop* (both on Columbia) and *Thelonious Monk/Gerry Mulligan: 'Round Midnight* (Milestone).

The *It Club* and *Jazz Workshop* sets, four records in all, were recorded on October 31 and November 4, 1964, by Monk's working group of the time (Rouse, Riley, and bassist Larry Gales). The repertoire on the two albums overlaps, with seven compositions being played on both nights; yet Monk's need to recompose his music makes these dual versions of "Well You Needn't," "Bemsha Swing," and the rest into quite different experiences. In almost every case the *It Club* performances are more intense, for this must have been one of the best nights this band ever enjoyed. Rouse, who could be a lackadaisical soloist, is pushed to the point of near-delirium, and Monk himself is in equally ferocious form. There is his massive, staggered-chord passage on "Ba-lue Bolivar Ba-lues-are," the way he works a fragment of "Blues in the Night" into his solo on the same piece, the sheer aggressiveness of his playing on "Well You Needn't," and a great deal more. Turning to the *Jazz Workshop* album, one hears less electricity, less heat. But how much and how intriguingly Monk's approach to "Well You Needn't" has changed in just four nights, as he finds a jumping, Savoy Sultans–style groove that makes you want to at once laugh and dance.

A tune-by-tune comparison of the *It Club* and *Jazz Workshop* albums yields many such riches. But even more fascinating, as fascinating as any Monk performance that comes to mind, is his twenty-two-minute solo piano exploration of " 'Round Midnight" on *Thelonious Monk/Gerry Mulligan: 'Round Midnight.* Three-quarters of the two-record set is devoted to original and alternate takes from the August 13, 1957, session that paired Monk and baritone saxophonist Mulligan—a meeting that failed to strike sparks, though Monk and bassist Wilbur Ware are in good form and Mulligan solos handsomely on "Sweet and Lovely" and " 'Round Midnight." Then there's the other " 'Round Midnight"—the solo piano version, which comes from the April 5, 1957, session that produced the album *Thelonious Himself.*

The originally issued take of this " 'Round Midnight" was one of Monk's masterpieces, an intense, nearly seven-minute rumination on his most famous theme. But now we have that take plus the music that immediately preceded it, Monk's extended attempt to decide just how he wanted to handle " 'Round Midnight" on that particular day. He starts and stops no less than seven times before beginning the final performance, which may suggest that this newly issued material is a collection of scraps that would have been better left unreleased. But the incompleteness of these trial runs is a small price to pay for what we get in return, an almost literal opportunity to read Monk's mind.

Probably aware that he was not going to attempt a complete take for some time, Monk takes hold of " 'Round Midnight" as though he has never encountered it before—poking at its rhythms, stretching its harmonies and melodic shapes this way and that until the " 'Round Midnight" we already know seems about to disintegrate. But what appears to be disintegration is really a microscopic musical analysis, as Monk breaks his composition into its smallest component parts in order to discover anew what it is actually made of. Once Monk has sifted through the fragments a few times, we too know what " 'Round Midnight" is made of—a series of irreducible, crystalline motifs, each one as potentially beautiful as the familiar whole and each one, so it seems, capable of generating a very different " 'Round Midnight," depending on which facets Monk wants to highlight.

So even though the final version of " 'Round Midnight" is one of Monk's masterpieces, the takes that precede it aren't really incomplete at all. Instead they suggest that the seemingly unshakable logic of Monk's music was built upon a ceaseless questioning of the forces that held together his own music, or anyone else's music for that matter. From that point of view, there could be more than one way to take Monk's "It's not hard to play, but I know it, that's all . . . maybe" response to the question "Why do musicians find your music hard to play?" In one sense, Monk's answer obviously means, "Maybe it's hard for them because I know how it should go, and they don't." But that floating, semi-isolated ". . . maybe" also seems to look back at "I know it" and "that's all" and, in a very Monk-like way, set them syntactically adrift—as though he were saying something like, "But what all is this 'it' that I know? And to what extent, and in what ways, do I actually know it?" "I know its" chasing after "maybes," radical risks undertaken in the face of radical doubt— perhaps one source of Thelonious Monk's profound musical logic was his sense of how hard won the order he made actually was.

HERBIE NICHOLS
[1987]

*T*HE *Complete Blue Note Recordings of Herbie Nichols* (Mosaic) leaves no doubt that the late composer-pianist stands along-

side Monk, Bud Powell, and Charles Mingus as one of the key
language makers of modern jazz. Born in New York in 1919,
Nichols died of leukemia in 1963, having been unable throughout most of his career to work in contexts that were attuned to
his unique musical message. But in 1955 and 1956, the owner
of the Blue Note label, Alfred Lion, brought Nichols into the
studio on five different occasions, first with bassist Al McKibbon
and drummer Art Blakey and then with bassist Teddy Kotick
and drummer Max Roach. The resulting body of work, expanded
now by many unissued takes and several previously unheard
compositions, is the gist of Nichols's "difficult yet alluring" legacy—to borrow the terms used by the set's passionate annotator,
trombonist Roswell Rudd, who has devoted much of his own
career to proclaiming the virtues of Nichols's music.

Startlingly oblique but with firm roots in the Harlem stride-
piano tradition of James P. Johnson and Fats Waller, Nichols's
ideas at first seem closely allied with those of Thelonious Monk,
which were nurtured by similar sources. But the Monk comparison has worked to Nichols's disadvantage, leading some otherwise careful critics to think of Nichols not only as one of
Monk's minor offshoots but also (by comparison with Monk) as
a man who didn't really improvise, in the sense of inventing new
melodies, but instead merely restated his pieces over and over,
encrusting them in layers of structurally arbitrary decoration.
The truth lies elsewhere, though. Like Art Tatum, who also has
mistakenly been dismissed as an essentially decorative player,
Nichols was one of the few genuine harmonic thinkers in jazz—
not only in terms of the weight he placed on harmony but also
because he was so innovative in that realm.

His music is based on what might be called "a counterpoint
of harmonic signposts." For Nichols, every chord, every note, is
brimful of directional force, is suffused by intense but often ambiguous impulses to move toward specific harmonic resting
places. And those resting places may be fairly close at hand or
rather far away, with "close" and "far" having both spatial and
temporal meanings—depending upon one's sense of the distance
in pitch between the initial and the resolving event, the amount

of time it will take to travel from one of them to the other within the evolving musical discourse, and the amount of resistance the harmonic medium will mount to the move that Nichols has just proposed. But these impulses are, again, often ambiguous (or perhaps that should be "richly ambivalent"). While, at a given moment, Nichols suggests that he is about to move *this* far and in *that* direction, in the next moment he will play something that suggests he is moving toward a different goal—which is nearer or farther away, both in space and in time, than the previous one.

A bit bewildering at first, and an approach that calls for careful listening, this counterpoint of harmonic vectors yields enormous dramatic dividends, enabling Nichols to establish and comment upon a kaleidoscopic range of moods with remarkable flexibility and wit. (In this sense, Nichols should be compared to Ellington and, in some moods, to Billy Strayhorn.) Rudd, for example, describes Nichols's "Sunday Stroll" as "pure psycho-drama" and identifies the piece's component parts as (1) "walking along"; (2) "everything's OK; it's peaceful today"; (3) "a wave of solemnity creeps over the scene"; (4) "a ray of hope"; and (5) "reconciliation, doxology, a true release."

No less important are the structural aspects of Nichols's approach. As one directional signpost or vector follows another, the play between their oblique, qualifying, even contradictory messages eventually stands revealed as the language principle of his music. Consider, for instance, the two takes of Nichols's "Shuffle Montgomery"—a wryly amiable, self-mocking piece that Rudd rightly claims is "one of the greatest riff tunes ever dreamed up by anybody." On the originally released version, the harmonic tensions of "Shuffle" are resolved almost immediately, with a charming, almost coy, autumnal sweetness—as though the music were saying, "Oh, yes, oh, yes, oh, yes." But on the alternate take, at least one of those moments of potential resolution is left unresolved; and now the music says, "Oh, yes, oh, yes, oh . . . but maybe not."

When Nichols is at his most magisterial—as he is on such masterworks as "The Gig," "Hangover Triangle," and "The Spinning Song"—composition and improvisation become one, and our perception of where we are, how fast and in what direction we are moving, and what "objects" are passing in front of our eyes seems to alter with a surrealistic fluidity and wit. This is also a music of humane warmth and humor and a vivid sense of swing, which is animated in intriguingly different ways by master percussionists Blakey and Roach. And it's all there to be heard on *The Complete Blue Note Recordings of Herbie Nichols*.

The Mosaic Nichols set is now out of print. Its contents are available on Blue Note but without Roswell Rudd's marvelous essay.

OSCAR PETERSON
[1982]

"**H**ELP, Martha, I've been run over by a piano! What? Well, judging by the treadmarks, it must have been a Superfunk Riffmaster. Yeah, I know—that kind of evidence won't hold up in court. But just before it hit me, I got a good look at the guy behind the keyboard. That's right, Oscar Peterson."

It all started innocently enough, as I waited for Peterson to begin his first set. Drummer Martin Drew stepped onstage and set the tempo—a brisk one, as you might expect. Next, bassist Nils-Henning Ørsted Pederson joined in. And then came, as the woman who announced the act put it, "the Oscar Peterson." I don't know whether she meant to say "*the* Oscar Peterson" or forgot to throw in the last word in "the Oscar Peterson Trio." But somehow "the Oscar Peterson" sounded just right, a generic phrase with an undertone of threat to it, like "winter weather" or "the cops."

The first tune was a standard whose title escapes me, even

though Peterson finally turned it into a variation on "Milestones." In any case, things started off with such a carefree sense of swing that I forgot to brace myself for the assault. But after some attractive ideas were stated in a relaxed manner, the temperature of the performance suddenly shot through the roof. Finger-busting runs, twangy blues clichés, crashing block chords, silent-movie tremolos—the whole thing was a technical extravaganza that drew wows from the crowd. But as I picked myself up from under the table, I wondered what, in musical terms, had actually occurred.

When Peterson shifts into high gear, which is where he likes to be, I hear little more than a series of hammered-out riffs—the kind of brief, streamlined phrases that were so rhythmically intoxicating in the hands of the 1930s Basie band or guitarist Charlie Christian. But riffs are seldom interesting in themselves. Instead they are the musical equivalent of iron filings, meaningful only when they are shaped into larger designs by the magnetic force of swing. Yet you won't find much design in Peterson's music. Gobbling up the tune, the keyboard, and the listener's ear and nerves, his riffs come at you like a pool of piranhas—an assault so compulsive that your only choices are escape or surrender.

Of course, there is a lot of drive to Peterson's music, but as Miles Davis once said of him: "Nearly everything he plays, he plays with the same degree of force. Oscar is jazzy; he jazzes up the tune." Given that jazziness—the way Peterson attacks almost every piece from the outside and reduces it to piano fodder—you might think he'd be better off if he calmed down a little. But more often than not, the opposite is true, for one step away from Peterson's mechanical frenzy there is a genuine frenzy that can be quite exciting.

On "Caravan," taken at an exhaustingly swift tempo, Peterson was pushed to the point where all of his pianistic resources were vital if anything coherent was going to occur. Sparked by the challenge he had given them, Peterson's fingers and mind at last began to work in tandem; and the ideas he came up with as he scurried around the keyboard had an urgency and rightness that could not be denied. So even though the rest of Peterson's set was a musical hit-and-run job, I guess I'm willing to nurse my bruises. Overdrive is Oscar Peterson's most effective gear, and his music begins to make sense only when he wheels his screeching keyboard right to the edge of a cliff.

STAN GETZ
[1984]

F ROM the time he made his first recordings as a precocious eighteen year old, tenor saxophonist Stan Getz has been writing an autobiography in sound. Or perhaps that should be an autobiography in sounds, if by "sound" one means the personal tone-quality a man obtains from his instrument. Over the years, Getz's always lovely tone has passed through a number of phases—from a downy-soft purr to a knife-edged iciness, from a pleading moan to today's full-bodied warmth. And the path traced by this sonic quest may be the best evidence we have of who Stan Getz was and is.

Born in Philadelphia in 1927 and reared in the Bronx, Getz went on the road with trombonist Jack Teagarden's big band at age fifteen, in part because he already was an accomplished instrumentalist but also because World War II was heating up and many musicians in their twenties were in the service. In the next few years, Getz played with Stan Kenton, Randy Brooks, Buddy Morrow, Jimmy Dorsey, and Benny Goodman, and by the time he joined Woody Herman in 1947 and recorded the two performances that made him famous, "Summer Sequence IV" and "Early Autumn," his life was a volatile mix of artistic sophistication and emotional callowness. A star soon after "Early Autumn" was released, Getz was then just twenty-one, and perhaps that is why his sound in those days had a boyish tenderness to it that seemed to come directly from the sound of Lester Young, the great tenor saxophonist who had made emotional sensitivity his trademark. But even though Getz says that he "surely is a Lester Young disciple," he insists that other players helped to shape his style, particularly two of his early bosses, Teagarden and Goodman. "I was at a very impressionable age when I worked with them," Getz explains, "and even though their instruments were different from mine, they were both such beautiful players that they had to affect me. So if I'm to be called a direct disciple of Lester Young, I would say that the difference between me and the other players who loved him had something to do with Goodman and Teagarden."

By the late 1940s quite a few jazz tenor saxophonists sounded quite a bit like Young. But Getz was separated from the rest of the Lestorians by his caressing lyricism ("I'm a romanticist from the word 'go' ") and the sheer ease with which he could handle his horn—his ability, as one critic said, "to translate into action any idea that came to mind." Given such resources, Getz seemed to have few problems in his musical life after he left Herman to make such best-selling records as "Long Island Sound" and "Lady in Red." A shrewd judge of talent, he assembled one fine group after another during the early 1950s, including a remarkable quintet that included guitarist Jimmy Raney and pianist Al Haig, a quartet in which pianist Horace Silver received his first recognition, and another quintet that featured valve-trombonist Bob Brookmeyer. Emotionally, however, this was a period in which, as Getz says, he "was involved in the twilight zone of jazz." Addicted to narcotics for several years, in 1954 he tried to hold up a drugstore, and after his arrest he wrote a poignant open letter to the editor of *Down Beat* magazine, portraying himself as an immature, "too much, too soon" victim of youthful success.

"Yes, I've had some bad things happen to me," Getz says, reflecting on those days, "particularly my involvement with drugs and alcohol, both of which I've conquered. But I did hang in there on the road, and in the long run I think I got something out of it. At the very least, contact with other players and working every night for years and years does hone your music. Also, I believe that I was always very spiritual in my playing, which seems to be what people have responded to over the years. It seemed like they knew there was a spiritual person inside me, trying to get out from under the depths of degradation."

Locked in that struggle, Getz spent the latter part of the 1950s in Denmark, returning to this country in the early 1960s with body and soul intact and with his greatest triumphs ahead of him. First came *Focus*, the 1961 album that Getz regards as his favorite, which found him soaring over a string-orchestra backdrop scored by Eddie Sauter. In 1962 Getz kicked off the bossa nova craze with his version of Antonio Carlos Jobim's "Desafinado," which was followed by a similarly successful collaboration with João and Astrud Gilberto, "The Girl From Ipanema."

Getz's working group at this time was another gem that included vibraphonist Gary Burton and drummer Roy Haynes, and though there was another dark period for Getz at the end of the decade when he spent two years in Spain, he returned to action in 1971 with another remarkable combo (pianist Chick Corea, bassist Stanley Clarke, drummer Tony Williams, and percussionist Airto Moreira), recording an album with them (*Captain Marvel*) that perhaps marked the dawn of Getz's true musical maturity. By now his sound is as warm and rich as that of any of the great players, and his sense of swing, which used to have a tense, compulsive edge to it, flows with a relaxed grace. And always there is his cascade of fresh musical ideas, which seems all the more remarkable when one considers that Getz has been playing for almost forty years, often in settings where he is the major solo voice.

So how does Getz keep things fresh night after night? And how does he account for the newfound power of his playing, which enables him to push the mike aside and still fill the room with sound? "The last time I came to Chicago," Getz says, "I had a new drummer, and after the first week or so, he said to me, 'I don't believe how big your sound is. I've worked with some powerful tenor players, and you have a bigger sound than any of them.' I think that's because I try to vibrate the brass, not the reed, which is hard to do because the saxophone is a reed instrument. But when you get that brass vibrating, you've really got something. A while ago we did a concert in San Francisco in a hall where we didn't use any mikes, and afterwards this kid came up to me and asked what kind of sound system we were using. He said he'd never heard that kind of sound before. 'Yeah, you're right,' I said. 'It's called *acoustic* sound.' As for keeping things fresh—if I didn't keep my music fresh, I think I'd be terribly unhappy. After all, what else do I have?"

Getz's current quartet consists of one holdover, pianist Jim McNeely, and two newcomers, bassist David Williams and drummer Ralph Penland, a group, Getz says, "that's really clicking together. Ralph is not just a basher—he has done a lot of work with singers—and David is a natural talent who has a special 'ping' to his attack. The chemistry is out of sight, and we're having a wonderful time."

Elsewhere things look rosy, too. There's a soon-to-be-released album on the Elektra/Musician label that pairs Getz with pianist Albert Dailey, and this summer he'll be performing the *Getz Variations*, a new work for tenor saxophone and computer-generated sound that was written for him by composer Dexter Morrill. "I teach at Stanford in the summers," Getz says, "so we'll do it there first. Then we'll take it to the Pierre Boulez Center in Paris and from there to Berlin and Cologne, because the Germans are interested in that computer stuff. My part of it is completely improvised, though. I'll be alone onstage, surrounded by a bunch of speakers."

Alone onstage. Despite all the fruitful musical partnerships that Getz has engaged in over the years, that's the way one tends to think of him—as a solitary, pensive, and ultimately courageous figure, lost in the music as he tries to make his cold metallic saxophone vibrate with the warmth of life.

Stan Getz died in 1991. Donald Maggin's biography of him, *Stan Getz: A Life in Jazz*, published in 1996, makes clear in alarming detail (though no one who knew the man could have been surprised by this), that on the personal level Getz's life was consistently chaotic and that he often was as hurtful to others as he was to himself. While talking to Getz, I had showed him a passage from Robert Pinsky's poem "History of My Heart" in which Pinsky, an amateur jazz saxophonist in his teens, compared the "Listen to me" aspects of playing a jazz solo to the cries of "Look at me, Ma!" that young children aim at their bored or indifferent mothers as they venture deeper into the water at the beach. Getz's response to this passage—at once rueful, amused, and probably calibrated to take account of his interlocutor's identity as well as his own—was, "Very Jewish . . . very Jewish." Another passage came to mind then, though I didn't mention it—the second sentence of Isaac Rosenfeld's autobiographical novel *Passage From Home*: "I was fourteen, a precocious child, sensitive as a burn." I next spoke to Getz several years later—in the meantime having done an interview with Gary Burton (it appears below) in which Burton, when asked how he acquired his taking-care-of-business skills as a bandleader, said: "I've often said to Stan Getz that I learned all the things *not* to do from my three years with him, as far as how to be in the business, how to deal with promoters, and all that sort of thing. Stan has been out on the road since he was fifteen and never got a chance to grow up." The Burton interview had been published at least two years before, and in a newspaper, the *Chicago Tribune*, that Getz wasn't likely to see in the normal course of things. But when we crossed paths again, Getz began by repeating what Burton had said and made it clear how much those words had injured him. Sensitive as a burn, indeed.

One final Getz memory. The first time I had a chance to review Getz in live performance came in the early 1980s. He was in exceptional form that night, and the review was enthusiastic. The next day I got a telephone call at work from Getz. He'd read the review and asked, with disarming flattery, "Are you a musician?" He went on to say that he liked the review so much that he wanted the club in Boston where he would be playing the following week to have a copy so it could be blown up and placed on a placard outside the club. Could you, Getz asked, make a copy of the review and send it along to the club in Boston? "Sure, no problem." "Would you be able to do that today?" "I guess." And then the kicker: "Could you blow it up yourself?"

WOODY HERMAN AND STAN GETZ
[1985]

Today both men are leaders, in every sense of the term. But when Woody Herman and Stan Getz first crossed paths, in August 1947, the thirty-four-year-old Herman already was something of an elder statesman, having led his own band for a decade, while the twenty-year-old Getz, soon to become the star tenor-saxophone soloist in Herman's great Second Herd, was even more callow than he appeared to be—a budding jazz master who was still a troubled boy at heart. It took just two Herman recordings to make Getz a star—the last movement of Ralph Burns's extended tone-poem *Summer Sequence,* and Burns's later transformation of that movement into a separate piece titled "Early Autumn." And there can be little doubt that the sheer youthfulness of Getz's playing on those recordings is what gave them their broad appeal—as he evoked in sound that near-pleading need for romance that resides in the souls of so many adolescents. Indeed, when Getz and other former members of the Second Herd reminisce about their days with the band, the image of a bizarre jazz summer camp comes to mind—with Herman as the sympathetic but earnest counselor who had to ride herd, so to speak, over a very enthusiastic but sometimes dangerously wild, even self-destructive, group of young men.

"Music," Getz says. "Music, music, music—that's what life in that band was like. And sports, too. We had a softball team—

[trombonist] Earl Swope was a tremendous athlete who had a tryout as a third baseman with the Washington Senators, and a lot of the other guys were very good. I'll never forget the time we beat Harry James's band in a doubleheader. We came out there in our undershirts, and they had these uniforms on; I think at that point Harry [a rabid fan] hired his guys for how good they played baseball, not music. But as scraggly as we looked and as hungover as some of us were, we still won, and I got about nine hits in fourteen at-bats. Harry was so mad afterwards that I think he fired his whole band."

At the heart of the Second Herd was the band's famous sax section—tenor saxophonists Getz, Herbie Steward, and Zoot Sims, and baritone saxophonist Serge Chaloff. Dubbed the "Four Brothers," after the Jimmy Giuffre composition that featured their inventive solos and smooth ensemble sound, the unit was hired en masse in Los Angeles in the summer of 1947, a year after Herman had disbanded his electrifying First Herd. "I was searching for a specific kind of saxophone player," Herman recalls, "and the ones who were suggested to me were all more or less hanging out on the beach at Santa Monica. There was Zoot, Stan, and Herbie—a beautiful musician whom few people remember anymore. The only guy we imported was Serge; we brought him in from Boston."

"We were working at this Mexican ballroom in east Los Angeles," Getz adds, "three tenors, a trumpet, and a rhythm section—the voicing was [arranger] Gene Roland's idea—and [drummer] Don Lamond suggested to Woody that he come hear us."

"Unfortunately the Second Herd was before its time," Herman continues, "and I lost money on it. But I loved it anyway. Leading bands is my hobby, you might say, and it's a hobby I happen to believe in." The Second Herd was before its time because it was, from top to bottom, a bebop band—full of players who had absorbed the new musical lessons of Charlie Parker and Dizzy Gillespie. While the Second Herd's tenor saxophonists were inspired by the gliding swing of Lester Young, their solos were also marked by a boppish rhythmic tension. And the band's arrangements were full of orchestral restatements of bop's angular solo ideas. On Ralph Burns's arrangement of "I've Got News for You," for instance, the sax section plays Parker's "Dark Shadows" solo note-for-note, doing so with a skill and zeal that still seem remarkable. And the massed trumpets of the Second Herd often shrieked to the sky à la Gillespie at his most flamboyant—an effect that thrilled the hip portion of the audience but tended not to soothe dancers.

Unfortunately, nonmusical aspects of bebop were part of the Second Herd, too. "I really didn't have much trouble with the guys," Herman recalls, "as long I could keep them awake. I wasn't familiar with the behavior of people who were using junk [i.e., heroin]"—to which Getz adds, "I could tell some stories, but I'd better not." (In Ira Gitler's oral history of jazz in the 1940s, *Swing to Bop*, ex-Herman vibraphonist Terry Gibbs states that "out of the eighteen guys in the band, about eleven were really strung out.") Close to chaos at times ("Once we started a show," says Gibbs, "and six guys were there"), the Second Herd managed to leave behind an imposing legacy of music—even though it made far fewer recordings than it should have, thanks to an American Federation of Musicians recording ban that kept the Second Herd out of the studios from December 1947 to December 1948.

"From the very beginning," says Getz, "that band was something special. I remember our first rehearsal, at a place on Santa Monica Boulevard. Ralph Burns came in with a brand-new, pretty difficult chart on 'Lover Come Back to Me'—about five pages' worth, it overlapped the music stands—and that band read it down and swung it without a moment's hesitation. Putting guys together, Woody was great at that. And once he puts them together, he knows how to develop each guy's musical personality." "Yes," Herman says, "I've tried to do that throughout my career as leader. We all deserve some special attention, and I try to find out how and when to give it. I think every individual is worth the bother."

Getz left the Second Herd early in 1949—not, as one might expect, because he wanted to become a leader himself (even though that is what lay in store for him) but, so he says, because of an incident that seems to speak of the same emotional vulnerability one can hear throughout his famous "Early Autumn" solo. "We were going to play at the University of Illinois in Urbana," Getz recalls. "It was the first night of a tour with Nat Cole, and we were driving down there on a cold, cold day with lots of ice on the road. Everybody else went on the bus, but Ralph Burns had a new yellow Ford convertible, and he and Serge Chaloff and I decided to drive down together. The traction on the Ford wasn't good enough, though, so we had to stop in this little town and phone Walt Yoder, the manager of the band. After we told him what happened, he called back and said that he was going to have the express train to St. Louis flagged down at the local station so we could get to the job. We went to the station, the train came by, they threw the flare out, and it took the train about half a mile to stop. Then as we were walking down the track we heard sirens. We didn't find out what was going on until we learned that when the express was flagged down, a brakeman on a local got off to see what was happening, and he slipped on the ice and was decapitated by the express. Well, when I heard about that, something happened inside me. I felt so bad that I just lost heart and decided I was going to leave. They had a big band; they could have done with three saxes that night instead of five. And Ralph wasn't even playing piano then. I don't know; it just did something to me."

Despite that sad conclusion to his Herman days, Getz has fond memories of the Second Herd and the man who led it. "Woody was a great guy to us," Getz says, "probably the fairest man I ever worked for. He was so egoless and democratic. He'd call a tune and if one of us would say, 'Ah, let's play this one instead,' he'd say, 'OK, we'll do it.'"

After his Third Herd of the mid-1950s, Herman stopped counting; and while at times he has been forced to cut down to a medium-sized combo, his band (now called the Thundering Herd) is still going strong—a breeding ground, Herman says,

"for people who will be known as giants in the future." Be that
as it may, it is the music of the First and Second Herds that will
make Herman last—for in their various ways the scorchingly hot
First Herd and the cooler and more cerebral Second Herd produced some of the most exciting music ever to come from a
large jazz ensemble. Getz, on the other hand, has made his mark
as a ceaselessly virtuosic soloist and as the leader of a series of
excellent small groups. (The list of musicians who got their first
big break with Getz includes Gary Burton, Chick Corea, Stanley
Clarke, and Bob Brookmeyer.) Always among the most popular
jazz performers, Getz became something of a pop star in the
early 1960s, when his best-selling recordings of "Desafinado"
and "The Girl From Ipanema" made him the king of the bossa-
nova craze.

"I suppose I could have become the Guy Lombardo of the
bossa nova," Getz says. "But I didn't want to do that, which is
why I never played more than a few of those tunes each night.
You have to stay fresh and creative, and I think Woody feels the
same way. When I was with him, I could tell that he adored
standing up there, listening to good musicians play. And that's
still his secret. He just enjoys listening to good players."

Woody Herman died in 1987.

AL COHN

The first of these four pieces, which appear here minus some re-
dundancies but in the order in which they were written, records a
change of heart toward, and I hope an increase in understanding
of, the music of tenor saxophonist Al Cohn (1925–1988). The three
pieces that follow touch upon different aspects of Cohn and place

him in the context of several of his musical partners and peers (Lee Konitz, Zoot Sims, and Allen Eager).

[1979]

EVERY jazz fan likes to think he can tell who the truly valuable players are the first time he hears them. But Al Cohn, one of the finest tenormen jazz has to offer, was for years my personal stumbling block, an artist whose message I pretty much misunderstood. Encountering him initially in the mid-1950s, I thought of Cohn as a Lester Young disciple gone awry. He seemed to lack both the lithe swing of his eventual frequent partner Zoot Sims and the harmonic agility of Stan Getz, while his big tone was (so I thought) rather sour and unwieldy.

What I failed to grasp then was the individuality and quality of Cohn's thought. First, his harmonic imagination is one of the most profound in jazz, although he uses it quite subtly, never dazzling the listener with effects that disturb the developing line. The feeling one gets from his solos might be described as "constant pressure," as he outlines the harmonic pattern of each piece and then establishes its strength by pushing steadily at its boundaries. Melodically, Cohn is a structural player, too, seamlessly bonding one thought to the next. And he is drenched in the blues—or rather he must have realized long ago that the blues and the keening, minor-mode chants of Jewish cantorial music have a great deal in common. But most of all, rhythm is the area where Cohn has become a master.

Listening to his older recordings, I realize that occasionally he did have problems with swing because his heavy tone needed an agitated base to keep it aloft. Now, however, his lines rumble forth with irresistible rhythmic power, and one hears an artist who truly thinks in sound—reminiscent, if the comparison isn't too farfetched, of Johannes Brahms, another musician who achieved mastery after a lengthy, sober apprenticeship.

[1980]

IT's the first set at the Jazz Showcase, and alto saxophonist Lee Konitz, as he has done so often throughout his career, is coaxing sounds out of silence. Or perhaps silence is coaxing sounds out of him, for Konitz's gravely sincere art seems always to have been based on the assumption that music of requisite purity can emerge only when the corresponding purity of silence is given its due. The song he plays is the charmingly cobwebby standard "Weaver of Dreams," and Konitz, accompanied by bassist Jim Atlas and drummer Wilbur Campbell, approaches it as though he were rediscovering that improvisation is possible. His solo begins with abrupt tongued phrases that then are smoothed out into longer, flowing lines so firmly rooted in the theme that the point at which Victor Young's melody has become Konitz's personal creation is difficult to define.

Then tenorman Al Cohn joins Konitz on "Yardbird Suite" and is simply ferocious, a man who seems to have been born again as a musician since he cut back on his labors as an arranger. Initially inspired by Lester Young, Cohn has built his sound into a huge, elementally dark force. And the rhythmic undercarriage that supports all this tonal and melodic weight is so imposing in itself that one feels that Cohn, in his rebirth, has revived the aesthetically rather dormant soul of Sonny Rollins as well.

Cohn is alone with the rhythm section now, and he plays "Do Nothing Till You Hear From Me" at a very down tempo, as though he were out to prove that his recent gains in rhythmic power enable him to set into useful motion what seems likely to be inanimate. And he does just that, roaring like a lion of Judea. (Cohn and Konitz may be the two quintessentially Jewish jazz musicians—Cohn a fierce Maccabean rabbi of the tenor saxophone, Konitz the alto's Talmudic scholar.)

[1982]

D ENTED here and there and almost devoid of their original bright finish, the tenor saxophones of Al Cohn and Zoot Sims look like they've been through the Thirty Years War, which in one sense is true. It was more than three decades ago—in January 1948—that Cohn met Sims, his new sectionmate in Woody Herman's Second Herd, and began a musical partnership that has grown steadily in meaning. Both were first-generation Lester Young disciples, and each had found a personal style within Young's fruitful universe—Sims favoring a light, gliding, almost breezy approach while Cohn's manner is deep-toned and rhythmically aggressive, with a moaning lyricism at its core.

Several years ago a friend half-seriously suggested that each of the first wave of Lester Young disciples built his style on a specific Young solo. Al Cohn was "Tickle Toe," Zoot Sims was "Blow Top," Brew Moore was "Pound Cake," and so forth. Listening to Cohn and Sims at the Jazz Showcase Wednesday night, that notion seemed to make a good deal of sense, especially when Cohn quoted "Tickle Toe" toward the end of a fast bossa nova. And it made even more sense the next day, when I played the original "Tickle Toe" and "Blow Top." There, on "Tickle Toe," were the hallmarks of Cohn's style—the dense, burrowing harmonic sense and the urgent, driving swing—while the sun-drenched ease of Young's "Blow Top" solo was equally in tune with Sims's lighter, more lyrical approach. This type of influence redounds to the credit of all parties concerned—reminding us, on the one hand, how multifaceted Young's art was and, on the other, how subtly and honestly Sims, Cohn, and all the other "brothers" were able to respond to their master's voice, or perhaps that should be "their master's voices."

Today, of course, Sims and Cohn are full-fledged masters themselves. The latter, especially, grows in stature with each passing year, to the point where it's hard to think of another tenor saxophonist who plays with such consistent seriousness and weight. Not that Cohn is an unduly sober improviser, for his sense of humor is as sly as S. J. Perelman's. The "Tickle Toe" quote, for instance, was sandwiched into a very unlikely harmonic cul de sac, as though Cohn wished to prove that he could state any idea at any time and get away with it—in the same way that Perelman would place a foppish, Anglophile locution alongside a phrase that spoke of the world of lox, bagels, and pastrami on rye.

Sims is more variable these days, perhaps because his music depends so much on the freshness of his lyrical impulse. Swinging comes so effortlessly to him that Sims can give pleasure even when he falls back on familiar patterns. Yet when he really "sings," as he did Wednesday night on his own familiar piece "The Red Door"—linking each phrase to the next so gracefully that the entire solo seemed a single thought—one realizes that beneath Sims's familiar rhythmic ease there is another, richer level of invention. Circumstances dictate how often that side of Sims rises to the surface, and playing alongside Cohn is one of the circumstances that does the trick, for both men were at or near the peak of their form. Cohn and Sims must have played "The Red Door" many thousands of times, but every time it swings open on something new.

Zoot Sims died in 1985.

[1986]

As magnificently as Al Cohn played Tuesday night at the Jazz Showcase, I'm sure that even Cohn would admit that attention must be focused on his tenor saxophone partner for the week, Allen Eager. While Eager did venture into town in 1982, it would seem that this engagement marks his real return to action—one that, in jazz terms, might be compared to the news that Arthur Rimbaud had stumbled out of Africa to present us with a book of new poems. Eager, you see, is among jazz's mystery men—a precociously brilliant disciple of Lester Young who made his first recordings in 1946, when he was only nineteen, and then played alongside Fats Navarro in Tadd Dameron's band on 52nd Street before he wandered off into different realms. Among other things, Eager became engaged, as he once put it, "to a girl from one of the wealthier families in the United States," hung out in Paris with the international jet set, turned himself into an expert race-car driver, and, in the 1960s, encouraged Dr. Timothy Leary to use LSD wholesale and for "kicks" rather than in a controlled, experimental fashion.

It was, one assumes, quite an odyssey. But playing the tenor saxophone had less and less to do with it—until, in the late 1970s, Eager ended up as a night clerk in a Miami Beach hotel and once more decided to pick up his horn. The road back was not easy, and in 1982, Eager's musical reflexes seemed a bit out of sync. But now the battle seems to have been won, because on Tuesday night Eager sounded quite lovely from the very first: oblique, unique, and intensely swinging.

The first tune of the night, based on the changes of "Exactly Like You," found Cohn in the lead—and his leonine, almost oratorical rhythmic power left his partner grinning with pleasure. Then Eager took over, and one was transported to another, more intimate realm—one that is governed by the Young-derived dream of a melody that need never end. What that means in purely musical terms is that Eager often plays through the changes—anticipating the next harmonic shift by finding an ambiguous area that enables him to be where he's going to be harmonically before he really gets there. And so the line sweeps on without a break, while Eager seems at once bemused and delighted by the whole affair—as though he were regarding his handiwork from a coolly distant point of view.

Cohn, on the other hand, is passionately present at all times—an urgent dramatist who highlights his noble ideas until each solo has the weight and shape of a full-fledged composition. As much as any improviser who comes to mind, Cohn perfectly balances rhythm, melody, and harmony so that at every moment he is moving forward on all three fronts. And as for his tone, on "O Grande Amor" Cohn's descents into the lower register had a bassoonlike richness that brought Serge Chaloff to mind. Obviously inspired by Cohn's example, Eager grew stronger and more inventive throughout the night. One hopes that his return is permanent.

Allen Eager died in 2003.

ART PEPPER

The first of these two pieces about Art Pepper was written two years after the second; they appear here in reverse chronological order because, in effect, the obituary attempts to sum up Pepper's life and artistic achievement, while the second piece, a response to Pepper's autobiography, *Straight Life*, tries to explore the reasons why an artist who lived in such a turbulent, frequently self-destructive manner could produce music whose key trait was an often exquisite orderliness and grace.

[1982]

THERE will be no more of Art Pepper's passionate, exquisitely structured music. One of jazz's great alto saxophonists, Pepper died Tuesday morning of heart failure in a Los Angeles-area hospital, never having regained consciousness after he suffered a stroke six days before. He was fifty-six.

"A pioneer of progressive jazz" was the way one wire-service obituary spoke of him, and to the degree that there ever was such a music as "progressive jazz," Pepper did bear some relation to it—but only because, having worked successfully within

"progressive" contexts, he defined their limitations by effortlessly transcending them. An artist whose sense of musical order
was seemingly innate, he was often stimulated by complex external structures, but in their absence his own form-giving qualities were rich. The "pioneer" tag is also dubious, for Pepper—
unlike, say, Lester Young, John Coltrane, and Charlie Parker—
did not inaugurate a broadly influential style (though there were
a few Pepper disciples). Nor was his attitude toward the jazz
artists who preceded him in any sense iconoclastic. A trio of
Swing Era players—alto saxophonists Benny Carter and Willie
Smith and tenor saxophonist Joe Thomas—were his initial in-
spirations, and the symmetry and warmth that characterized
their music were qualities Pepper never relinquished. But his
own symmetries, for all their grace and apparent ease, bore the
marks of intense internal pressure, while his warmth and humanity were those of a man who had to define and test himself
anew each time he picked up his horn.

From the first, self-expression was Pepper's goal, and in that
sense, aided by his natural ear and burgeoning instrumental fa-
cility, he was a jazz musician long before he became familiar
with the music. The vital familiarizing process took place while
Pepper was still in his teens, at jam sessions in Los Angeles's
Central Avenue district. Joining Stan Kenton's orchestra after
brief stints with the bands of Gus Arnheim and Carter, Pepper
recorded his first solo, "Harlem Folk Dance," in 1943 and, after
Army service and work as a Los Angeles-based freelancer, he
returned to Kenton in 1947. This was the period when Pepper
became a star of sorts, and on "Art Pepper," the piece that Kenton trumpeter Shorty Rogers wrote for him in 1950, and on the
1951 "Over the Rainbow," recorded with Rogers's octet, Pepper's
suave lyricism and knife-like rhythmic zeal already marked him
as a special artist.

It was in this period that Pepper became a heroin addict,
which led over the next two decades to long absences from the
scene and several jail terms. But in the midst of this external
chaos, Pepper was perfecting and deepening his music. From
1956 to 1960, his first stage of true maturity, he produced one

masterly recorded performance after another: "Besame Mucho," "I Surrender Dear," "Pepper Pot," "Old Croix," "What Is This Thing Called Love?" "All the Things You Are," "Rhythm-a-ning," "Winter Moon"—the list is a long one. But eventually the authorities and Pepper's personal demons had their way, and he was not to make another significant recording until 1975.

Pepper returned to jazz with all his skills intact and with his expressive range having increased under the weight of his long ordeal. On any given night until the very end—his last Chicago performance, which took place only two weeks before his stroke, was typical—Pepper challenged himself to the utmost. In his life, Art Pepper seemed to be skating at the edge of an abyss. And yet his music managed to encompass that sense of danger, seeking and finding a wholeness that was, so it seems, denied to its maker.

[1980]

LIKE most autobiographies that purport to tell all, *Straight Life: The Story of Art Pepper* is a tissue of genuine revelations and willful posing, in which the desire to speak the truth is at war with the author's need to paint himself as a romantic victim. But because *Straight Life* was written by a major jazz musician, the book does tell us a great deal—about the so-called "jazz life" and also about the tensions that affect almost every artist who functions in the modern world.

There are any number of nineteenth- and twentieth-century artists whose lives and whose work expressed an inner emotional turmoil that bordered on self-destruction—Poe, Rimbaud, Van Gogh, Scriabin, Hart Crane, the list could go on and on. But the hallmarks of Art Pepper's music are lucidity, grace, and a meticulous sense of order. How, one wonders, can those qualities be reconciled with a life so internally chaotic that much of *Straight Life* reads like a suicide note?

The title of the book, borrowed from that of Pepper's swift little melody on the changes of "After You've Gone," is deliberately ironic, because "straight" is the one thing the alto saxo-phonist's life has never been. Born on September 1, 1925, in Gardena, California, he was the byproduct of a brief, stormy romance. His teenaged mother wanted an abortion, his father married her only because he wanted the child to live, and much of Pepper's youth was spent away from both parents, in the care of his stern paternal grandmother.

The account in *Straight Life* of those early years is grim, but it would have meaning only to Pepper's friends if it were not for his great musical gifts. From the first he seems to have been a "natural," with a drive toward self-expression that logically led him toward jazz, although the account of his youthful initiation into that world strikes a note of naiveté that echoes throughout the book. Told by a guitarist that "these are the chords to the blues . . . this is black music, from Africa, from the slave ships that came to America," Pepper recalls that "I asked him if he thought I might have the right to play jazz." Musically, the an-swer to Pepper's question obviously was "yes," as it was for Bix Beiderbecke, Pee Wee Russell, and many other white jazzmen. But the fact that Pepper felt compelled to ask (or says that he did—the anecdote sounds a little too pat to be literally true) suggests that emotionally he would forever feel uncertain that his unquestioned ability to play jazz made him part of the jazz community.

While still in his teens Pepper worked in predominantly black bands led by Lee Young and Benny Carter and hung out in Los Angeles's Central Avenue district, where a free and easy racial comradeship prevailed. "There," Pepper recalls, "every-body just loved everybody else, or if they didn't, I didn't know about it." Young, remembering that same era, says, "It wasn't about 'whitey' this and 'whitey' that. It was about good musi-cianship and people respecting one another for the talents that they had."

Pepper's talents, which evolved further during a stint with Stan Kenton's orchestra, required him to forge his own style, one that owed a debt to black jazzmen but was significantly different in that his music seemed increasingly to have uncertainty and isolation as its subject. Then, after a tour of Army duty that led to the disintegration of his first marriage, Pepper returned to Kenton and found, in 1950, what was for him to be the "answer"—heroin. At this point in *Straight Life*, Pepper makes no excuses. Having found "no peace at all except when I was playing," he felt, under the influence of the drug, that "I loved myself . . . I loved my talent. I said, 'This is it. This is the only answer for me . . . whatever dues I have to pay.' I realized that from that moment on I would be, if you want to use the word, a junkie. And that's what I still am."

If *Straight Life* were an exemplary tale, Pepper's career from then until now would be an unbroken account of personal and artistic disintegration. But while he would spend more than a third of the following three decades in jail on various narcotics charges and would involve himself in a mutually self-destructive second marriage, these are also the years of Pepper's greatest musical triumphs. One answer to this seeming paradox might be that *Straight Life* is a con job, an attempt by the author to paint himself as a larger-than-life rogue. But even if the grimmer anecdotes in the book are discounted, Pepper's physical presence today is enough to confirm their essential truth. A strikingly handsome man at one time—reminiscent of Tyrone Power, according to a friend—Pepper is now someone whose haunted, ravaged face clearly proclaims that he has never needed to conjure up imaginary demons.

Straight Life finally does give us the information we need to resolve the split between Pepper's willfully disordered life and his carefully ordered music. Indeed, the answer may be found in an aspect of the book that at first seems quite frustrating—in the author's reluctance to talk about his music and in his corresponding eagerness to relate the lurid details of his sex life, drug addiction, and prison experiences.

That music is important to Pepper is believable only if we already know his music; otherwise *Straight Life* might be the story of any junkie. But soon we realize that, for Pepper, music, drugs, sex, and prison life are, in one sense, all of a piece—or rather, they all seem to be jumbled together in one area of his mind, a realm in which instinctual intelligence exists alongside childlike cunning, in which self-determined forms of order and expression blend into the trials of shame and pride that a law-breaker's life tends to bring. For example, Pepper states with special pride that he has never been an informer, never turned in a drug connection. From his point of view, that is an honor-able, certain, and essentially private act, a matter between peers in a closed society. And in their various ways, drug use and sex share similar qualities. One gets high or one does not, in the privacy of one's own nervous system. One satisfies oneself and one's partner or one does not, also in relatively private circum-stances. And so Pepper feels free to boast about all these things.

But music is an exception for him because, like all forms of art, its ultimate meaning cannot be private, cannot be controlled by the artist; other people will take what the artist creates and make of it what they will. Of course, in the jazz world, partic-ularly the world of the black jazz musician, communal agree-ments have often prevailed between the musicians and the au-dience, and almost always among the musicians themselves. But Pepper no longer seems to trust either of those communities, if he ever did. From his point of view, the comradeship of Central Avenue is gone forever. Instead, the isolated modern artist par excellence, he tries to create his own private world—striving for perfect, spontaneous order because only then will what he cre-ates remain within his control. And, of course, every time he performs, he fails, for his music becomes more lucid and mov-ing to us, and less private to him, the closer he comes to formal perfection.

So, for Art Pepper, the tensions remain; and as *Straight Life* demonstrates, they periodically become too great to be borne. But for us, one step removed from Pepper, the tensions are re-solved. And that is the final paradox, that his music may do more for us than it can ever do for him.

SONNY STITT
[1981]

GOING to hear saxophonist Sonny Stitt, the question that inevitably arises is, how serious will he be about his music tonight? Will he coast along, relying on his fluid technique and bottomless anthology of bebop licks, or will he decide (to borrow a phrase from one of his mentors, Charlie Parker) that now's the time and fully commit himself to the act of improvisation?

With those thoughts in my head, I ran into drummer Wilbur Campbell at the door of the Jazz Showcase at the Blackstone Hotel (where Campbell, pianist Willie Pickens, bassist Milton Suggs, and Stitt are appearing) and asked him some version of that inevitable question. "Well," said Campbell, "last night he was serious as cancer." A glance at Stitt, determinedly adjusting the mouthpiece of his tenor saxophone, suggested that Campbell's assessment was true. And when Stitt began the first set with an up-tempo blues, his initial, fresh-toned phrase clearly proclaimed that he was eager to play.

Having made his mark as an alto saxophonist before he turned to the tenor in 1949, Stitt approaches both instruments as though he were splitting the difference between them. Within his Lester Young–derived tenor sound there is a keening, altoish cry, and he shades the edges of his hardcore Parkerish alto tone with a tenorlike breathiness. Getting back to that blues, one noticed right away that Stitt was in unusually fine form. The lilting swing of his lines was a delight; and when he fastened upon a comfortable riff (which, on a typical night, he might have chewed over for half a chorus), he dropped it long before its savor was gone and leaped on to something new.

Sheer joyfulness is a quality I've seldom associated with Stitt, who at age fifty-seven has behind him an endless string of potentially mind-numbing gigs. (If all the blues choruses he has played were laid end to end, the resulting monster solo might last a solid month.) But on this night Stitt seemed to have re-vitalized himself, found a way to fall in love with his music all over again. And as the set continued, each tune was kicked to a higher level of exuberance.

On "The Shadow of Your Smile," which began with a dancing cadenza, one noticed anew Stitt's perfect sense of pitch, which in his hands is transformed into a rhythmic device, a way of giving each note a special bell-like "ping." And "Star Eyes," with Stitt switching to alto, proved that the fluidity he achieves on the instrument can be quite personal, not merely a carbon copy of Parker. Best of all was Denzil Best's line on "I Got Rhythm" changes, initially titled "Denzil's Best" and then "Allen's Alley" until it became known as "Wee." Beginning on alto and returning on tenor, Stitt used his mind, his technique, and his heart to shape two marvelous solos—fresh chapters in a musical book that both he and the audience seemed reluctant to put down. And then he went out with the blues again—at the same tempo as the first tune, but somehow not the same groove. The accumulated choruses of Sonny Stitt's life may be close to endless, but nights like this make a permanent mark.

Sonny Stitt died in 1982.

JACKIE MCLEAN
[1977]

WHEN I first heard Jackie McLean play the alto saxophone, more than two decades ago, he immediately became, to my way of thinking, an essential musician—one of those artists whose work speaks so directly to the emotions that his listeners feel they know the man behind the horn. In fact, the recordings that document McLean's career amount to a vivid personal and musical autobiography—a tale whose secondary characters include almost every important name in modern jazz.

For instance, on his initial record date in 1951, the nineteen-year-old McLean was surrounded by a cast that included Miles Davis, leader of the band and a close friend; childhood pal Sonny Rollins; and Art Blakey, who eventually would become McLean's boss. And visiting in the control booth was no less a figure than Charlie Parker, McLean's idol and mentor. The young altoist acquitted himself well on that session, which can be heard on Davis's album *Dig*. But today McLean considers it "one of my worst experiences. Bird's presence made me very nervous. And I was sick, too—addicted to drugs."

By 1951, McLean had been a heroin addict for two years, and he would remain one until 1965, when he kicked the habit under the guidance of Dr. Marie Nyswander, who pioneered the methadone treatment for drug users. To some, those are unpalatable facts that would be better off ignored. Yet the story of McLean's survival and growth as a musician cannot easily be separated from his struggle to survive and grow as a man, a struggle in which narcotics addiction played a major role.

Born in Harlem, McLean grew up in a neighborhood that was saturated with music. Among the jazz giants who lived within walking distance were Duke Ellington, Nat Cole, Don Redman, Andy Kirk, and Coleman Hawkins. Hawkins's recording of "The Man I Love" was an early influence on McLean ("I was fascinated by Oscar Pettiford's bass solo where you could hear him breathing"), and then he was totally captured by tenorman Lester Young. "Pres made me want to play the saxophone," he recalls, "but my mother bought me an alto instead of a tenor. I didn't know the difference yet, and when I found out, I told her it was the wrong horn. 'Well,' she said, 'you're going to have to make it sound like the right horn.' " And that is essentially what McLean has done. His potent sound—always heated, sometimes fiercely acrid, and with his phrases often descending into the alto's lower register—is living proof of Ornette Coleman's claim "that you can play flat in tune and sharp in tune, that some intervals carry that human quality if you play them in the right pitch."

As a teenager, McLean already was moving in fast company. Among the young players in the neighborhood were Rollins, pianist Kenny Drew, drummer Art Taylor, and a host of similarly gifted musicians who soon fell by the wayside. Heroin suddenly was quite prevalent in Harlem, and McLean and most of his friends became addicts. Parker, every young musician's idol at the time, was known to be a drug user, and it is often assumed that the teenage addicts were following Bird's example, linking heroin with hipness. But McLean, who was there, has a different assessment of the situation.

"What you have to ask," he says, "is why this happened in the 1940s and not in the twenties or thirties. Starting in 1946 and continuing until quite recently, they just opened the door and let drugs into the inner-city communities. Who are 'they'? I don't know if I want to say that the crime syndicate was behind it or if it was the United States government. But you must remember that the government owed a great debt to men like Lucky Luciano and Vito Genovese, who had kept the docks free of labor trouble during the war. Then, when the war was over, the government turned its back and let them bring drugs in. A lot of politicians knew about it, looked the other way, and made a lot of money in the process. So the whole question of hipness was secondary. When I was seventeen, a capsule full of heroin cost a dollar. I could walk out of my house—and I lived in a good neighborhood—and see all of my friends who weren't musicians vomiting in the gutters or nodding on the corner. In fact, I was the last one in my group to become addicted. I remember the day I went over to [trumpeter] Lowell Lewis's house to practice, and he opened the door and said, 'Well, Jackie, you're by yourself now.'"

McLean admits that his years of drug use were filled with "ugliness and horror." But he is not one of those converts to the straight life who view their escape from addiction as a modern-day version of *The Pilgrim's Progress*. A realist, he emphasizes the uncomfortable fact that heroin helped him to feel "relaxed and confident. I don't mean the stuff makes you play better, but it does eliminate stage fright. I was able to play things in public that I would never have attempted otherwise."

McLean rose to well-deserved prominence during the 1950s as a member of important bands led by Charles Mingus and Art Blakey. But he really blossomed in the following decade when he was one of the few established musicians who responded positively to the innovations of the avant-garde. He quickly realized that young turks like Ornette Coleman and Eric Dolphy were in the vanguard of a continuing revolutionary tradition, perhaps because the altoist had close personal and musical ties to the revolutionaries of the bop era—Parker, Davis, Blakey, Mingus, Bud Powell, and Thelonious Monk. Without altering the basic premises of his music, McLean soon was an avant-gardist himself, producing such vital albums as *Let Freedom Ring* and *One Step Beyond*. And he also became quite a talent scout, discovering and showcasing drummer Tony Williams, vibraphonist Bobby Hutcherson, and trumpeter Charles Tolliver. In recent years, he has been combining musical journeys into the future with forays into the past. Since 1970 he has taught jazz history at the University of Hartford, where he is now chairman of the Department of Afro-American Music.

"I've become quite interested," McLean says, "in some of the almost-forgotten figures from the early 1900s—men like Ford Dabney, Will Vodery, and James Reese Europe, who were the precursors of Fletcher Henderson and Don Redman in the development of the big band. And since I've learned what field hollers are, I can listen to Charlie Parker and literally hear them in his solos. Not that Bird was making intentional references to the past—it just happened that way because field hollers were among the early roots of the music.

"I focus on the innovators in my courses, and as it happens, most of them are black musicians. Often my students question that emphasis, and I tell them, 'Well, you know about Tommy Dorsey and Benny Goodman.' But there are a number of white musicians who have had an innovative impact on jazz—Bix Beiderbecke and Frankie Trumbauer, for example. What they were playing in the 1920s was beautiful and quite different from what other people were doing."

Because academic duties don't permit McLean to play in public as often as he would like, the altoist is looking forward to his Jazz Showcase engagement. His frontline partner will be trumpeter Ira Sullivan, and the rhythm section will include Chicago stalwart Wilbur Campbell, the man McLean calls "my favorite drummer in the world." With compatriots of that stature, this McLean visit to the Showcase should be an event to remember.

SONNY ROLLINS

This response to the music of Sonny Rollins served as the liner notes for a reissue of Rollins's 1955 album *Worktime.*

[1972]

MOST jazz fans, myself included, tend to view the process of jazz creation in a dramatic, even romantic light. If the artistic product is turbulent, passionate, noble, etc., we feel that the circumstances surrounding its creation must have been similar in tone. As one has more contact with musicians, though, one discovers that it is rarely that simple—musical events that to the listener seem immensely dramatic may have been created in a casual, "let's get the job done" manner. I mention this as a mild corrective, for if ever there was a recording that deserved the term "dramatic," *Worktime* is it.

The situation was this: Sonny Rollins, who by 1954 had established himself as the best young tenorman in jazz, moved to

Chicago for most of 1955 and "woodshedded" (that apt jazz term for artistic self-examination). He emerged to join the Clifford Brown/Max Roach Quintet, and when he recorded *Worktime* on December 2, 1955, it was his first appearance on record since October 1954, when he recorded as a sideman with Thelonious Monk.

Worktime was a dramatic and startling event, then and now, because it revealed that during his sabbatical Rollins had made a quantum jump in every area of musical procedure. He was no longer "the best young tenorman" but a major innovator whose achievements would have implications for the future course of jazz that have not yet been exhausted, either by himself or by all those he has influenced. Most obviously, there was an increase in rhythmic assurance and sonoric variety on Rollins's part. But these and other seemingly technical gains were all in the service of a shift in sensibility, a unique attitude toward his material that had only been hinted at in his previous work.

I imagine that everyone who admires Rollins's music has commented on its humorous quality, though there seems to be agreement that "humorous," by itself, is not an adequate description. David Himmelstein has added the information that it is "the humor of inwit, of self-consciousness or, as Sonny once aptly put it, the consciousness of a generation nourished on '*Lux*—you know, the *Radio Theatre,*'" and Max Harrison has given us the terms "sardonic" and "civilized irony." But the best guide I have found to the sensibility that emerges on *Worktime* is a remarkable article by Terry Martin titled "Coleman Hawkins and Jazz Romanticism" that appeared in the October 1963 issue of *Jazz Monthly*. In commenting on Hawkins's version of "Until the Real Thing Comes Along" (which can be heard on the album *Soul*) Martin says that "the whole is a finely shaped drama. Dramatic structure may in fact point to the core of Hawkins's art. He handles his materials with the ease and cunning of a great dramatist, and as with great drama the meaning may not correspond exactly with what the characters are made to say. It is the personae and the relations generated between them that contain the essence of the achievement."

Much of this also applies to Rollins, though his kind of drama differs in form and content from Hawkins's. A comparison between "Until the Real Thing Comes Along" and "There Are Such Things" from *Worktime* may show what the differences are. As Martin points out, one of Hawkins's methods is to make an initial statement that is romantic in character and then juxtapose it with "highly emotive rhythmic figures" that eventually lead back to the original mood. It is as though he were saying, "Yes, romance does exist, but I want to show you the tough reality that lies underneath." Structurally, Hawkins's drama is double in effect but single in method—i.e., allowing for foreshadowing devices, he presents one persona at a time—while with Rollins the method as well as the final effect is double (at the least). No statement is allowed to rest unqualified by him for more than a few measures, and often the very tone quality and accentuation with which a phrase is presented is felt as an ironic commentary upon it.

The implications of such an approach are numerous. For one, even though Rollins can retain and heighten the pattern of linear motivic evolution that was hailed enthusiastically by Gunther Schuller as "thematic improvising," the effect of constant renewal produced by his simultaneous or near-simultaneous expression of multiple points of view is, I believe, the more radical and lasting development, for it enables the soloist to achieve an emotional complexity that before was largely the province of such orchestral masters as Duke Ellington, whose every band member is potentially a musical/dramatic character. Also, it opens the door to a new view of the jazz past, for the improviser can now range beyond the apparent boundaries of style and make use of any musical material that his taste for drama can assimilate.

Rollins's frequent use of such unlikely vehicles as "There's No Business Like Show Business," "Sonny Boy," "In a Chapel in the Moonlight," "Wagon Wheels," and "If You Were the Only Girl in the World" can be seen in this light—for while one wouldn't swear that none of these pieces (and there are many more like them) appeals to Rollins on essentially musical grounds, it's a safe bet that he is drawn to them because he likes to evoke, toy with, and comment upon their inherent strains of corniness, prettiness, and sentimentality. And by bringing orchestral/dramatic resources into the range of the individual soloist, Rollins may have given to jazz just the tool it needs to survive the apparent exhaustion of the emotional resources open to the improviser whose relationship to his material is one to one, which is what I think can be heard in the later work of John Coltrane.

The finest tracks on *Worktime,* for me, are "There's No Business Like Show Business," "Raincheck," and "There Are Such Things." Notice, in particular, the utterly unexpected insertion of the verse of "Show Business" (where Rollins is accompanied only by Morrow's strong bass line) right after the theme statement. What results is quintessentially Rollins-esque, a compulsively swinging, seriocomic tour de force that at once embraces and bemusedly holds at arm's length the flag-waving fact of Ethel Merman's existence.

HANK MOBLEY

The first of these two pieces was the liner notes for a reissue of Hank Mobley's 1957 album *Poppin'*. (The reference there to Nietzsche supposedly commenting on Mobley's style was a would-be serious joke. Nietzsche did write those words, in his essay "Contra-Wagner," but he was referring to the music of Georges Bizet.) The second piece was a posthumous appreciation.

[1982]

IN the mid-1950s the Blue Note label yielded momentarily to supersalesmanship, releasing such albums as *The Amazing Bud Powell, The Magnificent Thad Jones,* and *The Incredible*

Jimmy Smith. That trend was dormant by the time Hank Mobley became a Blue Note regular and unfortunately so—a record titled *The Enigmatic Hank Mobley* would have been a natural. "To speak darkly, hence in riddles" is the root meaning of the Greek word from which "enigma" derives; and no player, with the possible exception of pianist Elmo Hope, has created a more melancholically quizzical musical universe than Mobley, one in which tab A is calmly inserted in slot D.

Though he was influenced by Charlie Parker, Sonny Stitt, and, perhaps, Lucky Thompson, Mobley has proceeded down his own path with a rare singlemindedness, relatively untouched by the stylistic upheavals that marked the work of his major contemporaries, Sonny Rollins and John Coltrane. In the words of Friedrich Nietzsche, not previously known for his interest in jazz, Mobley's music is "without grimaces, without counterfeit, without the lie of the great style. It treats the listener as intelligent, as if he himself were a musician. I actually bury my ears under this music to hear its causes." And that is the enigma of Mobley's art: In order to hear its causes, the listener must bury his ears under it. In a typical Mobley solo there is no drama external to the developing line and very little sense of "profile"— the quality that enables one to read a musical discourse as it unfolds. Not that high-profile players—Rollins and Dexter Gordon, for example—are necessarily unsubtle ones. But to understand Mobley the listener does have to come to terms with complexities that seem designed to resist resolution.

First there is his tone. Always a bit lighter than that of most tenormen who worked in hard bop contexts, it was, when this album was made, a sound of feline obliqueness—as soft, at times, as Stan Getz's but blue-gray, like a perpetually impending rain cloud. Or to put it another way, Mobley, in his choice of timbres, resembles a visual artist who makes use of chalk or watercolor to create designs that cry out for an etching tool. Harmonically and rhythmically, he could also seem at odds with himself. For proof that Mobley has a superb ear, one need listen only to his solo here on "Tune Up." Mobley glides through the changes with ease, creating a line that breathes when he wants it to, one that that is full of graceful yet asymmetrical shapes. And yet no matter how novel his harmonic choices were—at this time he surely was as adventurous as Coltrane—Mobley's music lacks the experimental fervor that would lead Coltrane into modality and beyond. Mobley's decisions were always ad hoc, and from solo to solo, or even within a chorus, he could shift from the daring to the sober. What will serve at the moment is the hallmark of his style; and thus, though he is always himself, he has in the normal sense hardly any style at all.

Even more paradoxical is Mobley's sense of rhythm. His melodies float across bar lines with a freedom that recalls Lester Young and Charlie Parker, and he accents on weak beats so often (creating the effect known in verse as the "feminine ending") that his solos seem at first to have been devised so as to baffle even their maker. That's not the case, of course, but even though he has all the skills of a great improviser, Mobley simply refuses to perform the final act of integration; he will not sum up his harmonic, rhythmic, and timbral virtues and allow any one element to dominate for long. In that sense he is literally a pioneer, a man whose innate restlessness never permits him to plant a flag and say, "Here I stand." Thus, to speak of a mature or immature Hank Mobley would be inappropriate. Once certain technical problems were worked out—say, by 1955—he was capable of producing striking music on any given day. New depths were discovered in the 1960s and the triumphs came more frequently; but in late 1957, when *Poppin'* was recorded, he was as likely as ever to be on form.

Much depended on his surroundings, and the band he works with here has some special virtues. The rhythm section is one of the great hard bop trios, possessing secrets of swing that now seem beyond recall. Philly Joe Jones and Paul Chambers, partners, of course, in the Miles Davis Quintet, shared a unique conception of where "one" is—just a hair behind the beat but rigidly so, with the result that the time has a stiff-legged, compulsive quality. The beat doesn't flow but jerks forward in a series of spasmodic leaps, creating a climate of nervous intensity that was peculiar to the era. Either the soloist jumps or he is fried to a crisp on the spot. As a leavening element there was Sonny Clark—equally intense but more generous and forgiving in his patterns of accompaniment. Clark leads the soloists with a grace that recalls Count Basie, and his own lines, with their heartbreakingly pure lyricism, make him the hard bop equivalent of Duke Jordan.

The ensemble sound of the band, a relatively uncommon collection of timbres heard elsewhere on Coltrane's and Johnny Griffin's first dates under their own names, gives the album a distinctive, ominous flavor; but this is essentially a blowing date. Art Farmer, for my taste, never played as well as he did during this period, perhaps because the hard bop style was at war with his pervasive sense of neatness. Possessing a musical mind of dandiacal suavity, Farmer at times sounded too nice to be true. But this rhythm section puts an edge on his style (as it did a few months later on Clark's *Cool Struttin'*), and I know of no more satisfying Farmer solo than the one preserved here on "Getting Into Something," where he teases motifs with a wit that almost turns nasty.

Adams's problem has always been how to give his lines some sense of overall design, and too often the weight of his huge tone hurtles him forward faster than he can think. But when the changes and the tempo lie right for him, Adams can put it all together; and here he does so twice, finding a stomping groove on "Getting Into Something" and bringing off an exhilarating doubletime passage on "East of Brooklyn."

As for the leader, rather than describing each of his solos, it might be useful to focus first on a small unit and then on a larger one. On the title track, Mobley's second eight-bar exchange with Jones is one of the tenorman's perfect microcosms, an example of how prodigal his inventiveness could be. A remarkable series of ideas, mostly rhythmic ones, are produced (one might almost say squandered) in approximately nine seconds. Both the relation of his accented notes to the beat and the overall pattern they form are dazzlingly oblique, and the final, whiplike descent is typically paradoxical, the tone becoming softer and more dusty as the rhythmic content increases in urgency. In effect we are hearing a soloist and a rhythm player exchange roles, as Mobley turns his tenor saxophone into a drum.

On "East of Brooklyn" Mobley gives us one of his macrocosms, a masterpiece of lyrical construction that stands alongside the solo he played on "Nica's Dream" with the Jazz Messengers in 1956. "East of Brooklyn" is a Latin-tinged variant on "Softly as in a Morning Sunrise," supported by Clark's "Night in Tunisia" vamp. Mobley's solo is a single, sweeping gesture, with each chorus linked surely to the next as though, with his final goal in view, he can proceed toward it in large, steady strides. And yet even here, as Mobley moves into a realm of freedom any musician would envy, one can feel the pressure of fate at his heels, the pathos of solved problems, and the force that compels him to abandon this newly cleared ground.

In other words, to "appreciate" Hank Mobley, to look at him from a fixed position, may be an impossible task. He makes sense only when one is prepared to move with him, when one learns to share his restlessness and feel its necessity. Or, as composer Stefan Wolpe once said, "Don't get backed too much into a reality that has fashioned your senses with too many realistic claims. When art promises you this sort of reliability, drop it. It is good to know how not to know how much one is knowing."

[1987]

"AH, yes, The Hankenstein. He was s-o-o-o-o hip." That was the response of Dexter Gordon when the late Hank Mobley's name came up in conversation a while ago—"Hankenstein" identifying Mobley as a genuine "monster," in the best sense of the term, while the slow-motion relish of "he was s-o-o-o-o hip" seemed to have both musical and extramusical connotations. But then, like so many who came to know Mobley's music, Gordon decided to qualify his praise, echoing critic Leonard Feather's assessment that Mobley was "the middleweight champion of the tenor saxophone," whose approach to the instrument (according to Feather) lacked the "magniloquence" that Gordon, Sonny Rollins, and others had brought to it.

But that is not the only way to estimate Mobley's achievement. The middleweight champ, yes, if magniloquence and size of tone are what is involved, but never merely a middleweight—for Mobley, who died last May at age fifty-five, blazed his own trail and left behind a body of work that never ceases to fascinate. Indeed, when one examines the core of Mobley's music (the twenty-four albums he recorded under his own name for Blue Note from 1955 to 1970), it seems clear that his poignantly intense lyricism could have flourished only if magniloquence was thrust aside.

Mobley's career as a recording artist falls into three rather distinct stages. The first ran from 1955 to 1958, when he made eight of his Blue Note albums, while working with the Jazz Messengers and groups led by Horace Silver and Max Roach. The second produced the magnificent *Soul Station, Roll Call, Workout,* and *Another Workout* albums in 1960 and 1961, when he was a member of the Miles Davis Quintet. And the third ran from *No Room for Squares* (1963) to *Thinking of Home* (1970). Influenced initially by Sonny Stitt, but incorporating far more of Charlie Parker's asymmetrical rhythmic thinking than Stitt chose to do, Mobley also was attuned to the lyrical sensitivities that Tadd Dameron brought to bop—an unlikely, even perilous, blend that gives Mobley's stage-one solos their special flavor. Perhaps the first critic to pay close attention to him was an Englishman, Michael James, in the December 1962 issue of *Jazz Monthly,* and James's account of the tenor saxophonist's solo on "News"—from the 1957 album *Hank Mobley* (Blue Note)—is particularly apt. "His phrases grow more and more complex in shape," James writes, "until . . . it seems that he is about to lose all sense of structural compactness. But he rescues the situation . . . and his last 12 bars, less prolix and tied more closely to the beat, imbue the whole improvisation with a unity of purpose that is paradoxically the more striking for its having tottered for a while, as it were, on the brink of incoherence."

Solos of that kind and quality can be found as early as 1955, when Mobley recorded his first album, *Hank Mobley Quartet* (Blue Note). And, as James suggests, his best work of the period is so spontaneously ordered and so bristling with oblique rhythmic and harmonic details that its sheer adventurousness seems inseparable from the listener's—and perhaps the soloist's—burgeoning sense of doubt. That is, to make sense of Mobley's lines, one must experience every note—for there are so many potential paths of development, each of which can inspire in Mobley an immediate response, that the ambiguities of choice become an integral part of the musical/emotional discourse.

And that leads to the genius of stage two, for as Mobley gained in rhythmic and timbral control, his music became at once more forceful and uncannily transparent—as though each move he made had its counterpart in a wider world that might not exist if Mobley weren't compelled to explore it. Two fine examples of that urgently questing approach are "I Should Care" and "Gettin' and Jettin'," both from *Another Workout* (Blue Note). Rather than being a direct romantic statement, "I Should Care" becomes a song about the possible contexts of romance— not so much a tale of love but a search for a place where that emotion could be expressed. (Mobley does this by building his solo around "balladized" bop phrases whose angular tensions, here made more languid, serve to test the romantic dreaminess, which in turn tries to subdue those "realistic" intrusions.)

Mobley's sensitivity to context is present in a different way on "Gettin' and Jettin'," as he pares down his lines toward the end of his brilliant solo in order to invite the active participation of drummer Philly Joe Jones. (Mobley's interaction with drummers is a story in itself—his exceptional taste for contrapuntal rhythmic comment bringing out the best that he and such masters as Jones, Art Blakey, and Billy Higgins had to offer.)

Stage three of Mobley's career has its virtues, too, and if such recordings as *A Caddy for Daddy* (Blue Note), *Dippin'* (Blue Note), and the first side of the recently issued *Straight No Filter* (Blue Note) were all we had, Mobley still would be a major figure. But as John Litweiler has pointed out, Mobley "consciously abandoned some degree of high detail in favor of concentrating his rhythmic energies," which gave his music a bolder profile but left less room for the jaw-dropping ambiguities of his stage one and stage two work. Above all, though—and to a degree that is matched by few jazz soloists—Mobley invites the listener to think and feel along with him. Indeed, his commitment is such that a commitment of the same sort is what Hank Mobley's music demands.

TINA BROOKS

This piece about tenor saxophonist Tina Brooks (1932–1974) was the liner notes for Brooks's album *Minor Move.*

[1983]

IT is an eerie, uncomfortable fact that only one of the men who appears on this recording is still alive. But among the many musicians whose careers have been cut short by one aspect or another of the so-called "jazz life," there are some special cases—artists whose acutely sensitive, often melancholic music seems to have predicted that their time with us would be brief. Tenor saxophonist Harold Floyd "Tina" Brooks was such a man. And fortunately we have recordings to prove that his skills have not been exaggerated by retrospective romanticism.

Most of those recordings were made for the Blue Note label—Brooks's own album *True Blue,* Freddie Hubbard's *Open Sesame,* a Jimmy Smith and Kenny Burrell jam session date, half of Jackie McLean's *Jackie's Bag,* Freddie Redd's *Shades of Redd,* and a second version of Redd's score for *The Connection,* issued on the Felsted label under Howard McGhee's name. Collectors have been aware that at least one other Brooks-led album exists—*Back to the Tracks*, with Blue Mitchell, Kenny Drew, Paul Chambers, and Art Taylor. But for some reason *Back to the Tracks* was never released, even though the cover of the album appeared on some Blue Note inner sleeves. Now, however, thanks to Michael Cuscuna's exploration of the Blue Note archives, we have the album titled *Minor Move*. And Cuscuna reports that yet another Brooks album was recorded—with Johnny Coles, Drew, Wilbur Ware, and Philly Joe Jones.

The pre-1960 details of Brooks's career were outlined by Ira Gitler in his liner notes for *True Blue*. Born in Fayetteville, North Carolina, on June 7, 1932, Brooks moved to New York with his family at age twelve. He played C-melody saxophone in high school, and then switched to alto and tenor under the tutelage of his older brother, David "Bubba" Brooks, an Arnett Cobb–Don Byas disciple who can often be heard now with Bill Doggett's combo. But as Tina Brooks told Gitler: "Pres was the first one to really get my attention."

Professionally, Brooks's early days were spent in R&B bands (Charles Brown, Amos Milburn, Joe Morris, etc.), and he toured briefly with Lionel Hampton in the mid-1950s. He studied theory and harmony with Herbert Bourne and received less formal but apparently quite valuable guidance from trumpeter Benny Harris, with whom Brooks worked at a club in the Bronx called the Blue Morocco. It was Harris who recommended him to Blue Note's Alfred Lion, and on February 25, 1958, Brooks entered Rudy Van Gelder's studio for the first time, participating on the Jimmy Smith date that would be spread over *House Party, The Sermon*, and the recently issued *Confirmation*. Obviously impressed by what he had heard, Lion brought Brooks back as a leader on March 16, 1958, to record the session now issued as *Minor Move*. Further recording dates followed, most notably *True Blue* and *Shades of Redd*, but gradually Brooks faded from the scene. According to trumpeter Oliver Beener, a friend and a close musical associate of Brooks, his playing days had pretty much come to an end by the early 1970s. On August 13, 1974, Brooks died—a victim, Beener says, "of general dissipation."

That Brooks was a man of unusual sensitivity is obvious from his music. He was, says Beener, "a sentimentalist—his favorite tune was 'My Devotion'—and especially on blues Tina's tone sounded like a prayer." (Brooks's first name, incidentally, is pronounced "*Tee*-na," not "*Ty*-na"—a variation, Gitler explains, on Brooks's childhood moniker "Teeny.") Lester Young clearly was his primary inspiration, and in that light it is interesting that Brooks began on the C-melody sax, the obsolete horn played by Young's idol, Frankie Trumbauer. One can also detect traces of Hank Mobley, Sonny Stitt, and Sonny Rollins in Brooks's music; and there are signs that, for a time, he and his contemporary Wayne Shorter were developing along parallel lines. But as effective as he was in orthodox hard bop contexts, Brooks was essentially an individualist.

His sound, first of all, set him apart—the prayerlike tone that Beener speaks of. It was an airy, keening, often speechlike approach to the horn that instantly identified Brooks as one of those musicians for whom feeling and sound were one. Equally important were the ways in which he created an aura of resolution within restlessness. Phrase by phrase, his lines are formed so naturally that the melodic shapes seem almost tangible—three-dimensional objects that one can walk around and contemplate at will. But these purely lyrical resolutions are placed within a harmonic context that virtually denies the possibility of rest. The sonatalike patterns explored by Sonny Rollins—in which melodic and harmonic elements suddenly coalesce, releasing their accumulated tensions in cadential outbursts—are alien to Brooks's music. Instead, he hears both melody and harmony as linear forces that exist in a perpetual equilibrium, a universe in which the forming process never ceases and tensions are not resolved but transformed into the new terms of an endless lyricism. This is the world that Lester Young built, and allowing for Brooks's more hard-edged approach to rhythm, there are times when his music recalls Young's clarinet solos with the Kansas City Six. A similar comparison—more far-fetched but genuine—can be made between Brooks's music and that of Gabriel Fauré, in which the lyrical line, buoyed by wavelike shifts in harmony and rhythm, flows calmly and gracefully toward an ever-receding horizon.

While Brooks's solo on the title track of *True Blue* is the one example of his work I would preserve at all costs, *Minor Move* may be his most satisfying album—although the as-yet-unheard music on *Back to the Tracks* and the date with Coles, Ware, and Jones may alter that estimate. *Minor Move* does have some rough edges, but except for Duke Jordan and perhaps Paul Chambers, the sidemen on *True Blue* (Freddie Hubbard and Art Taylor) are outclassed by Brooks's partners on this earlier date. Lee Morgan, in 1958, was in his "bull ring" period, a time when everything he played seemed about to burst into a fanfare. He is in top form here, creating technically remarkable lines that fully express the exuberance of a man who was, at age nineteen, already a young master. Doug Watkins, according to his onetime boss Red Garland, "was a very true bass player. The note was right on, never a quarter tone sharp or flat. And his walking rhythm, his feeling, was perfect." Indeed, the sheer lilt of Watkins's lines, the way everything he played seemed to "sing," reminds me of Oscar Pettiford. As for Art Blakey, it goes without saying that he is modern jazz's premier ensemble drummer. And Sonny Clark's stature as an accompanist and a soloist steadily increases with the passage of time.

"Nutville" is a groovy, medium-tempo blues that finds everyone in good form—Clark displaying his superb sense of swing, Morgan heating up from the first chorus on and eventually leaping into implied doubletime, and Brooks soaring ahead with remarkable confidence for a man who is making his debut as a leader in very fast company. Toward the end of his solo, though, a convoluted Mobley-like passage leaves everyone unsure as to where "one" is. Presumably, that is the reason Lion and Van Gelder removed Watkins's second walking chorus, which accounts for the abrupt jump into the final statement of the theme.

Next comes "The Way You Look Tonight," a piece that Beener says was one of Brooks's favorite vehicles. It's easy to hear why, as the tenorman glides through the graceful changes of Jerome Kern's standard in a kind of lyrical overdrive. The emotional climate of his solo is almost jolly, and at one point he quotes another very romantic tune, Rodgers and Hart's "Blue Moon."

"Star Eyes" is an equally gratifying performance, one of Charlie Parker's chosen standards and a piece that Brooks was born to play. Clark has a lovely solo, with Watkins (quite Pettiford-like here) and Blakey working as one behind him. The leader is exceptionally lyrical; several new tunes could be built on the melodies he creates on this track. And don't miss his sly reference to "The Breeze and I."

The title tune is a dark, harmonically intriguing twenty-four-bar piece with a Tadd Dameron-flavored bridge built on two contrasting four-bar melodies. Here Brooks is at his most intense, as the omnipresent lyricism is drawn earthwards more firmly than usual by the harmonic pattern's gravitational pull.

Finally, there is "Everything Happens to Me." Brooks states the theme and then returns for a warm, ruminative chorus, demonstrating that the lessons of his Don Byas-inspired brother were not forgotten. Then he takes the tune out, adding a cadenza that almost pleads for the music not to end. It does, though. And so, eventually, does Brooks's life. But the grace of his artistry remains as a benediction—upon him and upon us, as well.

CLIFFORD BROWN AND MAX ROACH
[1979]

*L*IVE *at the Beehive* is one of jazz's delayed explosions. Recorded at a South Side Chicago club on November 7, 1955, the group heard here was co-led by Clifford Brown, the young trumpet master who would die in an auto accident the following

year, and Max Roach, the dominant percussionist of the bebop
era. Also present were bassist George Morrow, tenorman Sonny
Rollins (who would soon leave town as a member of the band),
and three Chicagoans—tenorman Nicky Hill, guitarist Leo Blevins, and pianist Billy Wallace. The wide-open jam session that
took place that night was captured by Roach on a home tape
machine, and until now, the music has been heard only by the
people who were at the Beehive and by a few of the drummer's
friends. Deeply wounded by Brown's death, Roach long found
himself unable to contemplate the music that reminded him of
his loss, and the mediocre sound quality of the tape seemed to
preclude commercial release. But Roach finally gave in to those
who told him that the Beehive session had to be heard. And it
turns out that the refurbished tape is more than listenable; anyone familiar with these musicians will be able to fill in the miss-
ing elements in the aural landscape.

Compared with *Live at the Beehive*, even the best of the
Brown-Roach combo's studio work sounds restrained. Immediately striking is the change one hears in Brown's playing. In a
tragically brief career that ended when he was only twenty-five,
Brown became known for his mellow, butter-smooth tone and
his ability to construct seemingly endless lyrical lines. And yet,
as lovely as it was, his music at times seemed limited by its
loveliness, which could become sweet and cute. But the Clifford
Brown heard on *Live at the Beehive* is virtually another man, a
savagely adventurous virtuoso who repeatedly rises into the
trumpet's topmost register to create patterns that seem to have
been etched in space by a needle-sharp flame. Brown excels on
every one of the album's five tracks, but he surpasses himself on
a twenty-minute version of "Cherokee." The tune, traditionally
used to separate the men from the boys, is taken at a lightning
tempo, which forces Brown's lyricism to the point of no return.
Eventually, he finds himself stabbing out phrases whose content
would be purely rhythmic if it were not for the way his sense of
tone and attack makes each note of the design vibrate with melodic meaning.

It is Roach who spurs Brown to these dangerous heights, and in the process, the drummer surpasses himself, too. Neither before nor since has he played with such abandon, and often it sounds as though two or three drummers must be at work. This multiple-player effect comes, in part, from the way Roach has tuned his drum kit. Several years before the Beehive session, he began to adjust his instruments to precise pitches. As a result Roach's playing became filled with tympanilike effects, as though he were trying to make the drums into a melodic voice. During that same period, though, a certain sobriety crept into his work, perhaps because Roach had to exert conscious control over his new resources. But at the Beehive session, all the wraps were off. Roach's explosive solo on "Cherokee" is the most startling display on the album, but in no way does he slight his role as an accompanist. Brown's solos are inseparable from Roach's support, and the drummer creates inventive patterns behind every player at every tempo from the mercurial "Cherokee" on down to the medium groove of "Walkin'."

Although the album includes skillful playing from Blevins and Wallace, the other major point of interest is the contrast between Sonny Rollins and Nicky Hill. Rollins, who was just about to establish himself as the dominant tenorman in jazz, is in generally fine form. But Hill, who precedes Rollins on "I'll Remember April" and follows him on "Walkin'," more than holds his own. An eccentrically individualistic player who died in 1965, Hill was a master of oblique construction, and his solos are surprisingly prophetic of developments to come. Particularly on "Walkin'," he ends phrases by extending a note until its harmonic meaning becomes more and more ambiguous, an insistence on the purely linear that foreshadows early Ornette Coleman.

PHILLY JOE JONES
[1980]

THERE are drummers who have had a greater influence on the course of modern jazz—Max Roach, Elvin Jones, and Tony Williams come to mind. And there are others who have more successfully parlayed their skills into commercial gain. But, from the first moment I heard him, back in 1955 with Miles Davis, no drummer has given me greater pleasure than Philly Joe Jones.

For one thing, Jones has the rare distinction of having invented a new concept of swing—one that may seem to have been superseded by later developments but one that is, in fact, as timelessly beautiful as the concept of time laid down by jazz's first great percussionist, Baby Dodds. Until Jones came along, jazz rhythm had become increasingly fluid, achieving in the cymbal-oriented work of Roach and Kenny Clarke a remarkable gliding ease. But Jones disrupted that evolution by switching the emphasis back to his snare drum, which chattered away like a machine gun, creating a stiff-legged, irresistibly compulsive drive that, as Miles Davis once said, "could make a dead man walk."

A fairly high volume level usually went along with that style, which obscured one of Jones's key virtues—the remarkable delicacy and precision of his playing. Listening to him is like watching someone weave lace out of barbed wire, as every accent, no matter how angular or explosive, becomes part of an exquisitely balanced design. In that sense Jones resembles a great dancer more than he does other drummers, and the ways in which he introduces the maximum amount of rhythmic obliqueness while still retaining his cool make him one of the most intriguingly graceful jazz percussionists. His left hand—the one controlling the stick that attacks the snare drum—is a study in itself, as it opens and closes, loosens and tightens with the rapidity of a snake's tongue. And often that always functional litheness will ripple through his entire body, leaving him frozen for an instant in a pose Fred Astaire would have admired.

But of course it is the sounds Jones produces that matter most, and here he is unique, too. The tonal range he gets out of his kit is unusually compact when compared, for example, to Roach's tympanilike spectrum of timbres, and he seems to be constantly striving for a "back-to-basics" effect. It's a dry, all-rhythm approach to drumming that could support a jazz soloist of any era, and it certainly suits the band (tenorman Charles Bowen, pianist Sid Simmons, and bassist Andy McGee) that Jones is leading now. And even though neither Bowen nor Simmons is in the same class as the men Jones once played behind (John Coltrane, Sonny Rollins, and Bud Powell, to name a few), their relative ordinariness is not disturbing because it allows one to concentrate that much more on the masterly patterns of a masterly drummer.

Philly Joe Jones died in 1985.

HORACE SILVER
[1982]

A MID all of today's talk about neoclassicism and/or revivalism in jazz, it's a treat to hear pianist Horace Silver once more, because Silver's intense, natural ties to the jazz past make it clear that most of the "neo" stuff is a nostalgic charade. Silver emerged toward the end of the bebop era, and he certainly admired the music of Bud Powell and Charlie Parker. But because he was at least as fond of various pre-bop styles—including the big-band sounds of Basie and Lunceford, boogie-woogie blues, and the rich, shouting joy of gospel music—Silver began to reshape and formalize this legacy into his own unique, old-time modern blend.

"Formalize" is the key word, because the typical Silver group combines the spontaneous fire of a jam session with the compact orderliness of a big-band chart. Solos seldom run too long, ensemble passages have a cumulative impact, and coursing through it all is Silver's superb piano work, which transforms accompaniment from a background effect into a foreground virtue, with Silver driving the horn soloists along as though they were being pursued by a locomotive. By now the styles of Silver's soloists have become formalized, too, as tenor saxophonist Ralph Moore and trumpeter Brian Lynch follow the patterns laid down by their mid-1960s predecessors, Junior Cook and Blue Mitchell. But the language feel of Silver's music is so rich that Moore and Lynch can't help but sound genuine, if only because the sheer nowness of Silver's art leaves no room for posing.

LEE MORGAN, DONALD BYRD, BLUE MITCHELL

This piece about trumpeters Lee Morgan (1938–1972), Donald Byrd (born 1932), and Blue Mitchell (1930–1979) was a response to Morgan's album *Caramba*, Byrd's *Slow Drag*, and Mitchell's *Heads Up*.

[1969]

WHEN Lee Morgan's first records appeared, he was hailed as a logical successor to Clifford Brown. There were points of similarity—a full, brass-proud tone, and a great rhythmic ease—but Morgan soon demonstrated that his musical personality was quite different from Brown's glowing good spirits. Few musicians project a personality through their instruments as directly as Morgan does (Roy Eldridge is one, and perhaps that's a clue to Morgan's virtues). I have never met Lee Morgan, but I would be surprised if he were not a witty, sarcastic, playful man. To describe the way Morgan projects this personality, I thought of mentioning separately his tonal flexibility, unpredictable choice of notes, and slyly relaxed time feeling, but, listening again, I realized that Morgan makes an inseparable emotional unity out of these devices.

Since Morgan's "The Sidewinder" became a hit, it seems as if every one of his albums, and many other Blue Note sessions as well, have a track which attempts to duplicate its mood—a repeated rhythmic pattern with a triplet feel, over which the horns play at length in an attempt to find a good, downhome groove. Lord knows the results can be depressing if the groove isn't found, but the title track of *Caramba* is certainly a success. Although the rhythmic stew has some Latin American spice this time, Morgan and Maupin make it all blues eventually.

Morgan's playing can be rather episodic, but I wouldn't trade any number of well-constructed solos for one of the dancing figures he plays here as Maupin riffs behind him. Maupin, who seems to be exploring Coltrane's material with Rollins's methods, also solos strongly on this track, and there are several passages where a Rollins-like cadence is brought off in grand style. Maupin has a hard but rich tone, and I think he would increase the emotional range of his music if he could let it become as flexible and expressive as Morgan's. Cedar Walton's solo is at first austere in its adherence to the Latin pattern. As the horns join him he moves into some delightfully relaxed and genuinely soulful blues piano.

The other excellent track, "Suicide City," reminds me that Morgan and Wayne Shorter were once close associates. The tune has that Shorter aura in which harmony tends to become sonic color rather than musical rhetoric. The rhythmic pattern is complex (at one point Billy Higgins sounds like he's playing *back-*

wards), and Morgan takes full advantage of it. Very few trumpeters (Dizzy Gillespie, perhaps) could flow through this tingling rhythmic maze with as much ease. (Listen to the way Morgan uses split tones to expand the possibilities of note placement.)

Maupin is not as rhythmically secure as Morgan here, and he occasionally displays an annoying quality that seems characteristic of younger, New York–based musicians—an alternation between so-called "inside" and "outside" playing (Joe Henderson is a prime example of this). In the "outside" passages, pieces of late Coltrane, Ayler, etc., are used merely as noise elements, and their relation to the rest of the solo seems more social than musical. The musical cynicism implied by such an attitude alarms me, but perhaps it's a symptom of what New Yorkers call the "rat race." Although the other tracks do not have the overall impact of "Caramba" and "City," each has something worth hearing.

Lee Morgan discovered his musical voice early, and he has learned to bend every means to its expression. Donald Byrd, on the other hand, seems to have been searching for an appropriate musical voice throughout his career, and his music suffers from his apparent inability to find one. The first Donald Byrd was a clear-toned trumpeter with a gift for light and graceful playing on the chords. In succeeding years Byrd used fewer notes, a brassier tone, and attempted to assimilate more blues feeling, but these were changes of costume rather than changes of heart. The Yves St. Laurent of this search for a style was Miles Davis, for Byrd has listened closely to him right up to the present. On this album you can hear Byrd play bits of Davis from *Sketches of Spain* through *E.S.P.*, few of which are well integrated.

To me, the most unfortunate of Byrd's stylistic experiments is his attempt to be a "soulful," blues-based musician. He bends notes right and left and ends many phrases on gospel-ish "ah-uhm" cadences, but it all sounds unconvincing. "My Ideal" finds him more at ease, although he invests this ballad with a hymn-like solemnity that does not always suit the melodic material. His associates perform capably, the rhythm section is quite vigorous, and Billy Higgins steps out for an indescribably hilarious vocal on "Slow Drag" that is worth the price of the record. Higgins is so naturally and soulfully himself in word and deed that one feels he could give the secret to Byrd by the laying on of hands.

When Blue Mitchell came to prominence, he was a fully formed musician, and during his years with Horace Silver, the only change was a general tightening of technical control. I don't know how a musician who was consistently inventive within the limits of Silver's style could make such a dull record as "Heads Up." Perhaps it was just a bad day in the studio, but I think the album's conception, for which pianist/arranger/producer Duke Pearson seems responsible, was the real stumbling block. The gritty sound of a medium-sized bop band (distorted by echo) is heard over a leaden "soul" rhythm on material that, for the most part, the musicians cannot approach head-on. This is a group of highly professional players, and while there are few musical mistakes here, there are few musical decisions to be made.

BILL EVANS

This piece about pianist Bill Evans and the four that follow—about pianist Keith Jarrett, vibraphonist Gary Burton, guitarist Pat Metheny, and rock guitarist/composer Frank Zappa—all touch upon what might be called the pastoral reaction or, if one were in an unkind mood, the pastoral evasion in jazz. What was being reacted to were several interrelated late 1950s phenomena: the state of the Broadway show tune tradition, which had provided jazz with so much of its basic material but which had come to be threatened from within and without; the rise of rock 'n' roll, a music that not only was at odds with Broadway-style romance and sophistication but also made it unlikely that jazz ever again would be the broadly popular "youth" music it once had been; and the advent of a full-fledged jazz avant-garde, a music that implicitly disrupted jazz's norms of craft professionalism and seemed likely to alienate a significant portion of the jazz audience. Matters of the marketplace are involved here, of course, but matters of the spirit underlie and perhaps override them. For instance, Evans's desire to defend "song form," referred to below, was based not only on his longstanding genuine affection for the forms and moods of the Broadway show tune but also on his sense that this musical-emotional world, with all its attractive, familiar, and useful habits, was now on the wane or even under attack. Thus the possibility of the pastoral almost inevitably arose, as part of the actual or imagined artistic past came to be regarded as a place of potential refuge, a realm from which a defense of the threatened "beautiful" could perhaps be mounted.

[1983]

TODAY, three years after his death at age fifty-one, pianist Bill Evans arguably remains the most influential jazz musician of our time. A list of pianists who have been shaped by Evans would run for many pages, and his influence was not confined to that instrument. Much of the technical and emotional vocabulary of contemporary jazz stems from Evans—so much so that today's dominant styles seem inconceivable without him. For one thing, he and his onetime bassist the late Scott LaFaro virtually invented the elastic, floating sense of swing that is the norm for so many contemporary rhythm sections, and his oblique, subtle harmonic patterns also are in common use. Indeed, both the breadth and likely length of Evans's influence on jazz can be compared only to the shadows cast by Louis Armstrong, Coleman Hawkins, Lester Young, Charlie Parker, Miles Davis, and John Coltrane: a veritable jazz pantheon.

But Armstrong, Parker, et al. were major creative figures, while Evans was an essentially minor artist—a charming player, at best, but one whose music was confined to a rather narrow emotional realm whose possibilities he had largely exhausted by the early 1960s. Of course, many musicians and fans would dispute that estimate. But if Evans was the minor artistic figure I believe him to be, the question of how and why he became so influential still remains. And if a limited and, in Evans's later years, quite formulaic music has shaped the approach of so many other artists, what does that tell us about the state of contemporary jazz?

To answer those questions, one has to look at the shape of Evans's career. In 1956, when he made his first recording under his own name, *New Jazz Conceptions*, Evans had yet to find a personal style, although his blend of Lennie Tristano, Bud Powell, and Horace Silver was quite promising. And much of that promise was fulfilled, particularly on the albums Evans made under the leadership of composer George Russell: *Jazz Workshop* (some of which was recorded before *New Jazz Conceptions*) and *Jazz in the Space Age*. Faced with the challenge of Russell's harmonically dense, rhythmically adventurous, complexly structured compositions, Evans produced solos that so thoroughly realized the implications of such pieces as "Jack's Blues," "Dimensions," and "All About Rosie" that he and Russell seemed to be cocomposers. Yet the bristling linear logic of those and other performances from what one might call Evans's first period proved to be something of a false trail, for his music was about to undergo a profound change.

Joining Miles Davis's sextet in April 1958, Evans went on to play a major role in Davis's *Kind of Blue* album, bringing to the music a wealth of pastel-like harmonic coloration. Perhaps it was Evans who affected Davis at this point; perhaps it was mutual. But there can be little doubt that the album's most wistfully ethereal piece, "Blue in Green," was essentially Evans's creation. And when the pianist formed his own trio in December 1959 (Evans had left Davis in October 1958; *Kind of Blue*, recorded in March and April 1959, was a one-shot return to the fold), he left behind the urgent linear drive of his earlier work and continued to work in the *Kind of Blue* manner, favoring "sprung" rhythms, delicately shaded textures, and a melodic approach in which, so it seemed, as much as possible was implied and little was directly stated. Here he found an ideal partner in LaFaro, whose remarkable technical facility and great lyrical gifts led to the creation of a new kind of piano trio—one in which the orthodox piano-soloist-with-rhythm concept was virtually abandoned, and any member of the trio could take the lead at any time.

"I'm hoping the trio will grow in the direction of spontaneous improvisation rather than just one guy blowing followed by another guy blowing," was the way Evans described his goal. But a somewhat different story is told by the four albums that Evans, LaFaro, and drummer Paul Motian made for the Riverside label between 1959 and 1961—*Portrait in Jazz, Explorations, Waltz for Debby,* and *Sunday at the Village Vanguard* (the latter two both recorded at that club during a June 1961 engagement). Listening to those recordings in chronological order, one hears an exquisitely tender romanticism subduing all other moods—so much so that the more aggressive 1959 performances ("What Is This Thing Called Love?" and "Autumn Leaves" from *Portrait in Jazz*) would have sounded unthinkably bold by Evans's 1961 standards. If "spontaneous improvisation" was the stated goal, with each new recording Evans also moved several steps further into LaFaro and Motian's lush, fluid textures—diminishing the volume level of his playing and softening its rhythmic profile until the pianist had become an almost ghostly presence, hovering near the pulse to add subtle touches of harmonic and melodic color.

The core of Evans's legacy, his 1959–61 performances were, and still are, intoxicating. But in the midst of the delicate, whirling patterns of the Evans-LaFaro-Motian trio, one could detect some potential weak points. From his first recordings, it was clear that Evans had a taste for sentimental pop tunes. (Indeed, the sugar quotient of his own most famous composition, "Waltz for Debby," is quite high.) Now, Evans's fondness for such ditties as "Someday My Prince Will Come," "Alice in Wonderland," and (in later days) "People," "Make Someone Happy," and "The Love Theme from *Spartacus*" is not a sign of weakness in itself. After

all, Thelonious Monk and especially Sonny Rollins have chosen
to deal with material that was no less sweet and sentimental.
But in emotional terms, Evans often seemed to be as much at
the mercy of those songs' hyper-romantic moods as any follower
of the Hit Parade—either that or perhaps he believed that he
could purify and exalt such music through sufficient applica-
tions of subtlety and good taste.

Rollins, on the other hand, could take a campfire ballad like
"In a Chapel in the Moonlight" or a mock cowboy song like
"Wagon Wheels" and transform its corniness into strength by
building into the performance an ironically humorous view of
the song's sentimentality, not to mention his own (and the entire
culture's) taste for such sentiment. In jazz it's not just the material but the artist's attitude toward it that counts. When Rollins
got his hands on extremely sentimental tunes, he not only knew
just what they were but also was able to express and play with
that awareness—thus providing his listeners with a seriocomic
venture into emotional realism (for all of us have a residue of
sappiness in our souls that must be dealt with from time to
time). But when Evans handled "Make Someone Happy" or
"What Kind of Fool Am I?" as though they were not sugary
kitsch but songs that deserved all the tastefulness he could lavish
upon them, he was as close to being emotionally fraudulent as
the most cynical, manipulative cocktail lounge virtuoso.

Now, Bill Evans was not in fact such a cynic, if one can
judge a man's state of mind from his music. Instead, he seemed
to believe that the genuine prettiness of, say, "When I Fall in
Love" was just one step away from the beautiful. And it is this
wistful faith, implicit in so much of Evans's music, that the difference between the "pretty" and the "beautiful" is only a matter
of degree that probably accounts for Evans's vast influence—
above and beyond the attractiveness and usefulness of his specific musical techniques.

The period of the initial Evans Trio (1959–61) also saw the
advent of Ornette Coleman, whose music, with its spontaneously
varied harmonic patterns and its near-total rejection of anything
that might be thought of as pretty, seemed to threaten the very

existence of what Evans once referred to as "the song form." One could argue that Coleman's music (and that of Coltrane, Cecil Taylor, Albert Ayler, et al.) was not intended to threaten anything but was merely the music these men wanted and needed to make. But the threat was present nonetheless, especially to those younger artists who had grasped some of the implications of the so-called new music while still feeling unable or unwilling to sever their ties with the song form's reassuring pleasures.

That is not to suggest that a strict progressivism should apply in jazz or in any art. But radical developments arise only when there are preexisting tensions—the sense, for instance, that the usefulness of previously prevailing techniques is at or near an end. And while that may not turn out to be the case, once a Coleman or a Coltrane comes along, the decision to continue working within a preexisting musical mode almost unavoidably becomes a conservative act—a decision to do something and a decision *not* to do something. So, through no fault of his own, Bill Evans's music has become one of the means by which almost two generations of jazz musicians have skirted the artistic problems that Coleman and others uncovered, not to mention the solutions they proposed. Reassured by Evans's music that the song form can live and flourish, his disciples occupy themselves with finding ever more subtle harmonic byways and increasingly more oblique means to float above the pulse. More power to them, one might think, except that the romanticism of Evans's style cannot be separated from his purely musical techniques. And as his disciples have massaged that romanticism several times over, its inherent weaknesses have become more evident.

Consider the album *Bill Evans: A Tribute,* on which fourteen prominent pianists—including George Shearing, Teddy Wilson, John Lewis, McCoy Tyner, Chick Corea, Herbie Hancock, Richie Bierach, and Joanne Brackeen—are heard in solo performance. The members of the pre-Evans generations fare best, with Lewis's chaste, tender version of "I'll Remember April" a particular gem. And there is some strong playing from the first generation of post-Evans figures, particularly Hancock and Corea. But when one gets to the second- and third-generation pianists, especially Brackeen and Andy LaVerne, an odd, curdled hysteria enters the music. Seemingly aware that Evans's techniques demand a romantic statement of some sort, but unable to find such an impulse within themselves, in its place Brackeen and LaVerne supply a thick, inflated rhetoric—the musical equivalent of a bad pastoral poem in which nymphs and satyrs frolic about, even though both the poet and the culture have ceased to believe in the dream that those mythical beings represent.

Judging by his recordings, it would seem that Evans himself occasionally found that dream equally difficult to inhabit. Consider the performance of Jule Styne's "People" that appears on his 1975 solo album *Alone (Again)*. A virtually static, mechanically sentimental song, which was found wanting on those counts by no less a judge of popular music than Frank Sinatra, "People" still might have been the basis for an interesting performance if Evans had done something to reshape its structure or to question its abject pathos. But instead he just plays the tune over and over again for more than thirteen minutes—always keeping the nagging melody in the foreground. Now there can be little doubt that Evans was fully in control of this performance; throughout *Alone (Again)* he is alert and technically secure. So why, then, does he keep hammering away at "People" until the listener wants to scream?

Perhaps Evans was aware for once that he could not purify the mechanical kitsch of such songs, no matter how subtly he embroidered them, and he therefore decided to let "People" stand on its own and even to emphasize its essential banality. So Evans's "People" is an awful thing to listen to, a grinding musical torment. But in terms of his entire career it can be read as a momentary, and oddly moving, union of self-awareness and self-disgust—Bill Evans's pained farewell to a world of sweetness and light that part of him always must have sensed was false.

Second thoughts are called for here, for several reasons. First, Peter Pettinger's biography of Evans, *Bill Evans: How My Heart Sings*, published in 1998, has brought to light a great deal of information about Evans's life. Second, some of that information has to do with Evans's varying patterns of drug use and their possible effects on the music he was making during any given period of his career. Finally, it was not until 1984 that the first two albums by Evans's final trio (with bassist Marc Johnson and drummer Joe LaBarbera) were released—a freshet that would be followed by a veritable geyser. Beginning in 1989 with the release in Japan of the eight-CD set *Consecration*, and followed in 1996 by the six-CD set *Turn Out the Stars* and in 2000 by the eight-CD set *The Last Waltz*, some twenty-two hours of music recorded in live performance by Evans in the final year of his life have been made available. And it is the feeling of many of Evans's admirers that these recordings, particularly the *Turn Out the Stars* set, constitute a major—perhaps a climactic—development for him.

I don't agree by and large, but there is no question that the music of Evans's final trio was an advance over, say, the music Evans was making in the early 1970s, a period during which even the sympathetic Pettinger acknowledges that "Evans . . . settled for long stretches of meager invention, stringing together stock phrases and motives." And Pettinger adds that "the methadone which he was taking, with its sedative effect, may have been a contributing factor." (Methadone is an opium-based substitute for heroin, the drug to which Evans had been addicted since the late 1950s.) It seems fair then to speculate that the driven, harried, feverish quality that crops up on the recordings from Evans's final year, and that to my mind disturbingly marks the *Turn Out the Stars* set in particular, was linked to Evans's late-1970s turn to the stimulant cocaine as his drug of choice.

There are any number of great jazz performances that could be described as driven, harried, and feverish—Bud Powell's "Un Poco Loco" is one obvious example. But if Powell's "Un Poco Loco" is driven, harried, etc., it is expressively so—the anguish, if you will, pervades every strand of the musical fabric and is mastered there, or at least exhilaratingly confronted, in the terms of Powell's art. But the latter-day Evans often sounds like a man on the run (and not only because of his longstanding tendency to rush), strewing forth pianistic "gems" in an attempt to distract or evade pursuers.

This is, again to my mind, especially true of the four lengthy and much-vaunted performances of Miles Davis's "Nardis" on *Turn Out the Stars*. While the harmonic virtuosity of Evans's playing on the five-minute-or-so solo passages that begin each of those perform-ances is undeniable in one sense, it finally seems more fidgety than reflective (a series of paths that either lead nowhere in particular or back to the place where Evans started). Questions also arise—as I think they do in most of Evans's music after the death of Scott LaFaro in 1961—about how genuinely lyrical this supposedly quint-essential jazz lyricist actually was.

"One extremely striking aspect of the Evans approach . . . is his strong melodic sense," wrote Orrin Keepnews in the liner notes to Evans's 1958 album *Everybody Digs Bill Evans*. "Bill is funda-mentally a lyrical pianist, a 'pretty' player in the best meaning of that word. . . . This strong melodic sense is also very much in evi-dence on 'up' numbers." The performances on *Everybody Digs* sup-port that view, especially "Tenderly," which seems to have been conceived as a single melodic strand and which concludes with a thrilling passage in which the pianist rushes upwards toward what we sense must be his ultimate melodic goal and is thrown back no less than five times, only to ascend triumphantly on his sixth and final attempt. One suspects that this performance involved a good deal of pre-planning, but even if it did not, the adventure of Evans's melodic impulse literally enacts a confrontation between ecstasy and restraint, as he gives us a line that "desires" a release, is repeatedly blocked, and then magically overleaps the barrier.

Increasingly, however, Evans was constructing what Pettinger rightly describes as an "essentially harmonic world." On "I Wish I Knew," from the 1961 album *Explorations,* Pettinger notes "the large-scale substitution . . . of new harmonies for the songbook changes. The . . . songsheet made do with half a dozen or so basic chords. Evans's reconstruction . . . employed nearly three times as many, changing mostly by the half bar. In this way a simple song could be enriched, strengthened, and transformed."

Transformed, yes—enriched and strengthened, perhaps not. A more or less simple popular song that also is a good one has a certain organic unity—a working balance between its harmonic, melodic, and rhythmic components. Alter that balance by a "large-scale substitution of new harmonies," and do the components of the song remain in balance? And if not, what can be done about this? As it happens, on "I Wish I Knew," Evans has a good answer: he adds to the mix, as Pettinger says, "the infinite shades of his tone production," thus nudging the song's melodic and rhythmic components into the same realm of luxuriant ambiguity that his substitute harmonies already occupied. And it is this balance (as I wrote in 1983) that worked so well for him up through the death of LaFaro, as Evans "moved several steps further into LaFaro and [Paul] Motian's lush, fluid textures—diminishing the volume level of his playing and softening its rhythmic profile."

What was increasingly at stake in Evans's music of this period was the pianist's acute sensitivity—musical and otherwise. One thinks of the emotional buffeting he reportedly received from some audiences and fellow band members because he was the only non–African-American member of the Miles Davis Sextet and of his resulting "determination," says Pettinger, "not to isolate himself from the [band's] drug-grounded fellowship. In fact, not content with being a mere addict, he was determined to be the worst junkie in the band." Evans's companion of the time, Peri Cousins, adds: "I have a theory about his addiction. When . . . he kicked it, which he did on numerous occasions, the world was . . . too beautiful [for him]. It's almost as if he had to blur the world for himself by being strung out."

Quite articulate about his music, in a 1964 interview Evans said this: "The only way I can work is to have some kind of restraint involved, the challenge of a certain craft or form and then to find the freedom in that. . . . I think a lot of guys . . . want to circumvent that kind of labor." Then there is this Evans statement: "I believe that all music is romantic, but if it gets schmaltzy, romanticism is disturbing. On the other hand, romanticism handled with discipline is the most beautiful kind of beauty."

Plausible words, perhaps, but the value that Evans seemingly places on restraint in itself leads one to ask, what is being restrained and why? Evans's "challenge of [working within] a certain craft or form" is not merely an account of his own necessary practice; it lends to that practice an aura of moral virtue ("I think a lot of guys . . . want to circumvent that kind of labor"). In other words, for Evans certain sorts of musical labor are not only valid but they also validate. And should an aesthetically valid outcome be reached in a seemingly nonlaborious manner, that can be disturbing. Thus in 1964, after acknowledging that the brilliant, lucid, and "completely unpremeditated" two-piano improvisation that he and Paul Bley played on George Russell's 1960 album *Jazz in the Space Age* "was fun to do," Evans says: "[But to] do something that hadn't been rehearsed successfully, just like that, almost shows the lack of challenge involved in that kind of freedom."

Drawing a comparison between Bach and César Franck in his *Man and His Music: Romanticism and the Twentieth Century*, Wilfrid Mellers refers to the "tension [in Bach's music] between linear independence and the dramatic logic of harmony." In early Evans, as in Bach, that tension was alive, rich, and fruitful; in much later Evans, as in much Franck, logical and increasingly elaborate harmonic labor seemingly exists to curtail, if not defeat, linear melodic independence. (Pettinger says of Evans's 1966 composition "Unless It's You"—and the same could be said of many latter-day Evans improvisations—"The interest was mostly harmonic . . . , the significance of almost every note [of the top line] dependent on its attached harmony.")

One thinks again of Evans's recording of "Tenderly," with its dramatized joust between restraint and the desire to break away from it, of Evans's acute sensitivities, and of his apparent attempt to damp them down after the death of his uncannily empathetic musical partner Scott LaFaro. In 1983 I began by referring to Bill Evans as a minor artist. What I would say now is that Evans was an artist whose conflicts threatened to overwhelm his gifts, and that it was his fate to spend much of the latter part of his career making a music in which those conflicts were in effect disguised, even denied.

KEITH JARRETT
[1982]

IF the "human potential" movement (est, Scientology, and all the rest) develops a need for liturgical music, Keith Jarrett should be its Bach. Seated at the piano Saturday night at Orchestra Hall, Jarrett celebrated the self (not his own self as much as *the* self) with a neo-religious ecstasy that was both impressive and . . . I was about to say appalling, but let's leave it at "impressive" for the moment, and I'll fill in the blank later on.

Jarrett's concerts typically consist of two completely improvised solo-piano ruminations, which on Saturday amounted to about seventy minutes of music, separated by an intermission. He began with (and often returned to) a rumbling bass pattern that sounded as though it had been abstracted from a spiritual. Transformed into a soft, graceful stomp, this motif traveled in the direction of gospel music (a short trip, to be sure) before branching off in two different directions—first a hint of bluegrass twang and then a solemn, deeply chorded hymn that resolved with a nutlike sweetness.

At this point, the ten-minute mark or thereabouts, Jarrett stopped, bothered by some coughs from the audience. Still lingering in the air, that sweet cadence may have been the goal of Jarrett's journey, as a friend later remarked; but now the pianist had to take a long detour in order to find it again. And this side trip was, for me, the most fascinating part of the concert.

Picking up the hymn-tune feel again, Jarrett swiftly expanded it into a piano version of a Bach organ chorale. Increasingly chromatic and increasingly intense, this passage began to acquire some of the choked eroticism of César Franck, with the erotic aura highlighted by Jarrett's passionate groans and moans, not to mention his standing pelvic thrusts at the keyboard. One already knew that extreme chromaticism and the physical side of romance have been closely associated since the days of Wagner's *Tristan*. But as Jarrett pushed his musical odyssey toward early Schoenberg, it seemed he was out to give the audience a kind of *Tubby the Tuba* tour of late-nineteenth- and early-twentieth-century classical music.

What made this both impressive and (I'll fill in the blank now) weird, was that the sounds Jarrett produced apparently were directed at himself as much as at the audience. A pianist of great technical expertise, Jarrett is also, in some massively naïve way, his own audience—a man determined to forget all that he knows of the musical past each time he sits down at the keyboard, yet a man who, in the act of improvisation, tries to remember as much of that past as he can. Of course this leaves the rest of the audience at the mercy of Jarrett's wayward memory, with our kicks depending on whether the things he "discovers" are, on any given night, discoveries for us, too. So if his music is to have its proper effect, it calls for an audience as naive as he is—either that or an audience that can will itself into naïveté, as Jarrett seems to do. In either case, a kind of romantic tampering with the self is the goal—an attempt to wipe the mind clean and then discover, with an innocent, newborn bliss, a "you" that's better than the one you forgot.

GARY BURTON
[1984]

"To know what the instrument can do," wrote Cecil Forsyth in his classic book, *Orchestration*, "one must have heard a good player. Arpeggios, scale-passages, repeated notes, successions of thirds and sixths and brilliant glissandos are all executed with accuracy and a lightning-like rapidity." The instrument Forsyth had in mind was the xylophone, but he just as well could have been speaking of the vibraphone, the xylophone's first cousin in the world of mallet percussion. And no one better fits Forsyth's description of what a good player can do on such an instrument than Gary Burton.

There were important vibes players in jazz before Burton—notably Red Norvo (originally a xylophonist), Lionel Hampton, and Milt Jackson. But even though Burton would be the first to salute his predecessors, from the moment he appeared on the scene in 1960 it was obvious that new standards of vibraphone virtuosity were being set. For one thing, Burton habitually plays with four mallets instead of the normal two, which enables him to produce a cascade of notes and chords in a short span of time. And more often than not, Burton makes good musical use of his startling facility, bringing to the vibes a pianolike textural richness.

Equally significant is the shape of Burton's career. Starting out as a sideman with George Shearing and Stan Getz, he became a leader at the relatively tender age of twenty-four and has remained in control of his own musical destiny ever since—nurturing a number of future stars in his band (including guitarists Pat Metheny and Larry Coryell) and pioneering such trends as "jazz-rock," "jazz fusion," and the lyrical, pastoral style that has come to be associated with the label for which Burton records, ECM.

Burton's current quartet includes young Japanese pianist Makoto Ozone, and Ozone's sudden rise to prominence ("He seems to have the entire piano world at his fingertips," said a critic for the *New York Times*) is giving his musical mentor a not-unpleasant sense of déjà vu. "Makoto is just twenty-two," Burton says, "and he reminds me so much of myself when I was that age, working with Stan Getz. I see him going through a lot of the same experiences I went through, confronting his talents and learning how to channel them, deciding what to do next and how you want to handle your career. In the last year or so I've begun to realize my age. It's an eerie thing to suddenly see myself as an older, established player."

Thinking of Burton in those terms also is a little eerie from the listener's point of view, for in physical appearance and mu-

sical manner there always has been an air of boyish innocence
about him. Born and reared in southern Indiana, Burton still
seems to be a white-bread-and-mayonnaise kind of guy who just
doesn't fit the normal image of a jazz musician. Of course,
there's a lot of fiction built into that supposedly "normal" image,
which depicts the jazz artist as someone who has, at the least,
"paid a lot of dues," if indeed he isn't a romantic rebel with a
penchant for self-destructive behavior. But there does seem to
be something unjazzlike about the stability and calm good sense
with which Burton has taken care of business all of these years.

"My generation of musicians—Chick [Corea], Herbie [Han-
cock], Keith [Jarrett], and so forth—arrived at a very fortunate
time," Burton says. "We were at the turning point, when jazz
came out of the saloons and the seamy side of life and became
respectable. In a way, we owe it to our predecessors, some of
whom went through years of drug addiction and alcoholism and
making very little money and being taken advantage of by promoters and record companies and all the rest. By the time we
came along, it seemed that the industry finally had begun to
grow up.

"One of the things that helped us tremendously was the advent of rock, because all of a sudden rock became the bad boy.
We were welcome in colleges, where we hadn't been welcome
before, because they would much rather have a jazz concert
than a rock concert. Also, the trend among the musicians themselves when I was growing up was to be a good businessman,
to be well-educated, to not be foolish and waste your talents, to
be in control of yourself so you could take advantage of the
opportunities that came along. I've often said to Stan Getz that
I learned all the things not to do from my three years with him
as far as how to be in the business, how to deal with promoters
and all that sort of thing. Stan has been out on the road since
he was fifteen and never got a chance to grow up.

"No, I've never 'scuffled,' as they say. Since I started, I
haven't been without work for more than two or three weeks at
a time, which was the period between my gigs with Shearing

and Getz. And my career has gone steadily upward, so by all outward appearances I've had everything go my way. If I got really personal, though, I could tell you about all the things that have happened to me in my life that I consider my tragedies and disasters. I think that even the most outwardly lucky-appearing people have their personal tragedies, which instill in them a feeling of what frustration and sadness and grief are all about. Now, you don't expect a nineteen-year-old to have an understanding of those deeper feelings, and I certainly didn't when I was that age. I remember I used to get the criticism that my music didn't have any emotional depth, that I was just too happy all the time. But what do you expect from a kid who was just out of high school and making his first record? What else would I feel?"

That first record featured Burton with some players who lived on the borderline between country-and-western and jazz, and this blend is something that often has appeared in Burton's music. Apparently taking the place of the blues feeling that usually is at the core of jazz, it has evolved into the Midwestern-lyrical strain that he and Pat Metheny have done so much to popularize.

"Growing up in southern Indiana," Burton says, "I heard a lot of country music, and I wasn't exposed that much to jazz, except on records. Even then, the records I got weren't the hip East Coast albums, so my early projects were more reminiscent of the kind of phrasing you would hear from a bluegrass band. Certainly a lot of guitar players from the Midwest came under the same kinds of influences. Also, there's a lot of similarity between bluegrass and jazz. Rhythmically, you have a definite beat going on, and you're improvising over chord changes, and the big attraction is instrumental prowess. It's a feeling that has blended into the jazz scene in recent years."

Indeed it has, especially after Burton emphasized its open-air, pastoral quality, which has a great deal in common with the wistfully muted lyricism of Bill Evans. But this style seldom is hospitable to the bold displays of instrumental personality that once were so common in jazz; and in the midst of these musical purple mountains and amber waves of grain, one sometimes wonders whether jazz has lost much of its realistic, big-city emotional grit.

"There has been a tendency for elements in the music to be leveled out," Burton says, "and now you get less and less of that distinct individual-player sound. But it's an old emphasis, this thing of having an individual sound and style. It dates back to the days when jazz was dominated by horn players, which isn't the case any more. All the leading players used to be saxophonists or trumpeters, but now we're living in the age of the rhythm section. Today's leading players are pianists or guitarists or bassists or drummers, and all the major groups tend to be rhythm-section oriented, with maybe one horn player out front. The emphasis has shifted, and the last thing I'd want to be now is a horn player. There's much less work available to you, and the choices are much narrower."

But if Burton wouldn't want to be a horn player, is he glad to be a vibraphonist? After all, despite Norvo, Hampton, Jackson, and Burton (not to mention such stalwarts as Bobby Hutcherson and Walt Dickerson), no vibes player has made the kind of major artistic breakthrough that affects the way other jazz artists play their instruments.

"Probably no vibraphonist will ever do that," Burton says, "and that's a source of frustration to me. Playing this instrument is both a blessing and a curse. It's a blessing in that I've never had much competition on the instrument, in my opinion, and I did get early recognition because I played an instrument that few people played. If I had been just one of the many piano players around, my career might not have gotten off the ground as quickly as it did. But at the same time, the vibes is an instrument that's primarily used in jazz, so I don't have opportunities in classical music or rock. And it's not an instrument that's in every band, like the drums or the bass or the piano, so vibes players almost always end up being leaders in order to give themselves a format in which to perform. So I suppose I'll never wield as much influence as I might have been able to if I had played a more conventional instrument.

"Being a jazz vibes player is not as a rare as being a jazz accordionist or kazoo player; it's about on par with being a jazz flute player. They do exist and there have been some good ones over the years, but when you think of your favorite musician, it's not likely that a flute player or a vibes player will come to mind. I remember a few years ago I got a review in London where the guy's opening line was, 'I've never liked the vibes, but from all the players to choose from, I suppose Gary Burton is . . . ' 'Boy,' I thought, 'what a weird bias that is.' I mean, critics aren't the only ones who categorize and use labels; musicians do that all the time. We have everybody classified in various little niches, and we'll say, 'He's a mixture of this and that,' or 'Now he's doing this kind of thing, instead of the other kind of thing he used to do.' But what kind of prejudice is it that doesn't like a whole *instrument?*"

PAT METHENY
[1982]

JAZZ may be the word that best describes the kind of music guitarist Pat Metheny's group plays. But ever since he joined vibraphonist Gary Burton as a precocious twenty-year-old back in 1974, Metheny has been a category unto himself. Swinging hard at times, the first of his eight albums on the ECM label, *Bright Size Life,* showed traces of bluegrass and country music, which is natural because Metheny, born and reared in Lee's Summit, Missouri, a suburb of Kansas City, remains a down-home product of the American Middle West. Later recordings, which led to the formation of his own very successful group, made it clear Metheny also has a lingering affection for rock 'n' roll. Then there is the twenty-minute title track of his widely praised album *As Falls Wichita, So Falls Wichita Falls*. Created by Metheny and composer-keyboardist Lyle Mays, it is a virtual galaxy of abstract computer-synthesized electronic tones that sounds like a blend of Steve Reich, Sibelius, Aaron Copland, and Vangelis's sound track for *Chariots of Fire*.

That desire to explore the outer limits of computerized electronic-musical technology, coupled with a lyrical dreaminess, also surfaces on Metheny's most recent album, *Offramp*, where it is hard at times to tell who is producing what sounds on what instruments or whether in the conventional "human minds guiding human hands" sense there are *any* instruments being used. Yet *80/81*, the album that preceded *As Falls Wichita* and *Offramp*, is as humane, earthy, and, yes, as jazzlike as can be, with Metheny finding much common ground with former Ornette Coleman sidemen Dewey Redman and Charlie Haden. And the two albums before that were very rock-oriented (*American Garage*) and as countrified as a bluegrass banjo festival (*New Chatauqua*). The unifying element in Metheny's music would seem to be Metheny himself, who always communicates a distinct, recognizable personality, whether he is playing acoustic or electric guitar or twisting the dials of synthesizers. So we began by discussing the question of how musical personality can be communicated in an increasingly electronic age.

> KART: When I started listening to jazz back in the 1950s, the electric guitar had already been "conquered," so to speak. You could immediately identify every good player. But I have trouble (and I don't think I'm alone in this) in detecting differences among players of the newer types of electronic instruments. Is this a listener's problem or is it one that the players have, too?
> METHENY: At this point I think it's a problem with the instruments more than anything else. As soon as you introduce elements other than the actual human person touching the wood, metal, or what have you of a real instrument, there's one more step between the point where the person and the music interact. Hundreds of years ago when the piano first hit, that same problem was there, and for a while some people must

have felt that the piano was overly mechanical. But gradually players evolved who could deal with the piano's limitations and take advantage of its possibilities, coming up with different kinds of music that fit the instrument. When you start talking about the guitar, though, something that all guitar players have to accept (at least I've accepted it for a long time) is that the guitar in jazz is not one of the major instruments. The key breakthroughs that have happened over the years—Louis Armstrong's, Charlie Parker's, John Coltrane's—have not been made on the guitar. To me the closest thing to a breakthrough on the guitar was Jimi Hendrix. He was the first guy to make it an *electric* guitar, to get a really wild, human sort of sound.

As far as synthesizers go, there's even more distance between the person and the instrument than on the guitar or the piano. Not only do you have to press down a key, when you press down that key, you're not even triggering a mechanical action—you're triggering an electronic oscillator that responds to whatever numbers you've happened to program into the machine. So that's a lot of the problem. The tone quality of these instruments is something that is more or less bought in a store, which means that the only real distinction you can get from player to player is their choice of notes and the kind of phrasing they use.

Now I'm coming on a little negative, which might seem strange since I'm obviously very involved with these instruments. And I do think that a case can be made that there are certain virtues that acoustic instruments have that electronic instruments will never have. But I also feel that electronic instruments have possibilities that are unique to those instruments. That's what I'm interested in, because I like the idea of dealing with instruments that haven't been dealt with before. It's just a little bit harder, but it's a lot of fun, too.

It's interesting for me to see the way musicians who are a generation or so older than I am react to electronics. I've got this really hip instrument called the Synclavier, a very sophisticated digital computer. Jack DeJohnette is my next-door neighbor, and when he comes by he seems so overwhelmed by the electronics of it, so bemused. While for me, the electric guitar was the first instrument I ever played, so I've been dealing with all those knobs and everything from day one. To me, electronics are only a tool—a way to get to something, not an end in itself.

KART: There seems to be an affinity between your music and Ornette Coleman's. Your first album had a Coleman tune on it, you've played with Dewey Redman and Charlie Haden, and some of your own pieces sound very Coleman-like.

METHENY: I've never played with Ornette, but I have spent some time with him and really enjoyed it. The title track on *Offramp* is inspired by him. What I like about Ornette's music— the thing that Dewey and Charlie are so great at and the thing I try to emulate—is implying the harmony in the melody. All Ornette did is take things one step further, so instead of having to resolve in such and such a key and at such and such a point you can really go anywhere. That's what Ornette means to me, more than sort of going bananas.

KART: How important was the accident of your provincial upbringing? I've always felt that Coleman [who was born and reared in Fort Worth, Texas] was able to respond so freely to the blues and country music because they were more accessible to him in Fort Worth than they would have been to a young jazz musician who was growing up in, say, New York. Was that the case for you in Lee's Summit?

METHENY: Well, I've never felt a real allegiance to any one style of playing. I'm a firm believer in having a bebop foundation, but at the same time that I was playing bebop in Kansas City I was into the Beatles and all the country music around there that you couldn't get away from even if you wanted to. And I always liked all of it. I feel sorry for people who don't like a lot of different kinds of music. I can get off hearing Dolly Parton sing, and I can get off hearing Miles Davis. If I had to say which is more valuable, I would say Miles. But I can still get a blast from "Stairway to Heaven."

KART: Another accident that might not be accidental is the way your music is used so often as a segue between stories on [National Public Radio's news show] "All Things Considered." Obviously you have a fan at NPR. But that also suggests that your music has a kind of readily recognizable timeliness built into it, because there's nothing more "right now" than the news.

METHENY: It isn't only NPR. At the beginning of the Indianapolis 500 [broadcasts], you always hear "Cross the Heartland," and after the Lakers won the NBA title, they put together a six-minute slow-motion piece of their entire season that had "Are You Going With Me?" [from *Offramp*] in the background. And you can hear "Phase Dance" on everything from TV magazine shows to Roto Rooter commercials. I always like it when our music is used that way, even though they chop it up, because it means that we're conveying some sense of our generation and our time. I don't know if what we play is going to be a "classic" music. There might be a couple of tunes that will last. But I do think that in ten or twenty years you'll be able to listen to a tune like "San Lorenzo" and feel something about the time it came from. That's a lot of what jazz is, being a reporter on the times.

KART: Speaking of "Are You Going With Me?"—on that tune and on most of the first side of *Offramp* (not to mention a good part of *As Falls Wichita*) I'm not sure what instruments are involved or who's playing what.

METHENY: I know. It's getting pretty weird in that department. On the first tune ["Barcarole"], the high part that almost sounds like a trumpet is me on guitar synthesizer, and the low part (the "bump, bump" sound) is me on digital guitar. Everything in the middle is Lyle. What's really weird on "Are You Going With Me" is that there are no overdubs. A lot of the parts are being played by a machine, this computerized sequencer thing, and then we play on top of it. I've wondered about the ethics of doing that, because the computer is really generating most of the sounds you hear. I just tell myself that over the long run the method you use to get some music happening is insignificant. But if you think that the electric-versus-acoustic controversy was intense, stick around. Very soon it's going to get to the point where there will be a whole generation of musicians, great musicians, who have never learned to play an instrument, people who don't play in real time. These new instruments—the computer sequencers, the drum machines, and so forth—allow you to render anything you can think of. It's going to be really wild to see what happens.

KART: You've said that the presence of an audience is so im-

portant to you that you can be playing by yourself and think
that the music sounds terrible and then think that it sounds
great the moment someone who wants to listen comes into the
room. In those situations does the way you play change, or is
it the way you feel about the music that changes?

METHENY: The music changes. After playing thousands of
gigs over the years, my feeling is that the audience brings the
music. They have almost total control over what we sound like
on a given evening, depending on how intently they're listening.
That's one of the reasons I stay out on the road so much, to get
new information about this mystery. It has nothing to do with
how loud they clap or how much they scream or anything like
that. It's this sense of "you play, they listen, and then you play
because they're listening." It just keeps spiraling. Then if you
play something and you get a sense that they haven't heard
what you've just played, you start to lose interest in connecting
up the details. It's real hard to explain, and I wish I could do it
more clearly. I do know, though, that it's something you can
never plan on. You can play New York and know that Ornette
and all these other intent listeners are out there, and it just isn't
happening. Then you can play Ames, Iowa, or someplace like
that, and the music takes off.

KART: You were teaching guitar at nineteen, an age when most
people are students. Were you ever just a kid? Or are you still
a kid in some ways?

METHENY: Well, I've had a real strange life. When I was fifteen, I was working six nights a week in Kansas City, and I feel
like I've been fifteen ever since. But that's true of a lot of jazz
musicians. [Drummer] Paul Motian—he's fifty-one, and he
could be fifteen. I toured with Sonny Rollins this spring, and
Sonny could be twelve. I don't mean that we're childish in any
way, but there's something about this music that keeps you
young. It's always new. No matter how good you get, you're still
right at the beginning.

FRANK ZAPPA
[1969]

A sage I invented once said, "The only event that might merit the term 'progress' would be an increase in the percentage of intelligent human beings." And he added, "Those who work toward this goal are known, variously, as fools, clowns, and prophets."

For purposes of economic gain and protective coloration, Frank Zappa and the Mothers of Invention have promoted themselves as a group of truly weird people. Well, the Mothers may have their eccentricities, but no more than other musicians I have met, and Zappa himself is a man of striking sobriety. Sometimes, he even made me feel frivolous.

Zappa is standing onstage in front of ten thousand or so people, most of them under twenty-one, at an open-air concert last summer. He says to the audience, "We've just had a request for 'Caravan' with a drum solo" (the fruit of a Mothers routine on "America Drinks & Goes Home"). Laughter. Shouts of "yeah!" "Now we may play 'Caravan' with a drum solo, or we might refuse to play 'Caravan' with a drum solo. Which will it be? We think we'll let you decide." (All of this is delivered in a light, mocking tone of voice.) An applause-meter-type test indicates that the crowd does not want "Caravan" with a drum solo. "All right, we'll play 'Wipeout'" (the nadir of early-sixties schlock rock). Which they proceed to do, in three tempos at once. The mindless riff of "Wipeout" melts like plastic.

Consider this scenario: A bright young boy is attending a Southern California high school. It is 1955. The Korean War has just wound down. The boy is prey to all the adolescent agonies—acne, young love, dumb teachers, the rigid status system of the American high school, etc. He doesn't particularly want to grow up and be a successful anything. There is a music called rock 'n' roll that expresses his condition. He likes the music, maybe loves it. Because he is musically talented he begins to play it.

But soon several things disturb him. First, he is musically curious, so he begins to explore other kinds of music—jazz, perhaps, certainly the twentieth-century classical avant-garde. After this, the musical limitations of rock 'n' roll seem obvious. Second, he sees that popular music, and rock in particular, serves its consumers in ways they fail to recognize. It diverts their anxious energy into rhythmic response and lulls their sorrows with romantic fantasy. It helps to render them harmless, or at least controllable. And behind all this there is a chain of promoters, DJs, record company executives, and on up who are making a living on the music. This makes the boy angry. He resents being used and manipulated. Perhaps he eventually resolves to do something about this.

On every Mothers album, aside from *Ruben and the Jets*, this statement is printed on the sleeve: "The present-day composer refuses to die! Edgar Varèse, July 1921" (on *Ruben and the Jets* it reads: "The present-day Pachuco refuses to die! Ruben Sano, June 1955"). Varèse was born in Paris in 1885 and settled in New York in 1916. His distinction as a composer lies in his acceptance of the harsh sonic environment of the modern city as his musical material. Out of this "noise," with a scientist's precision, he created a new musical order. Although Varèse's music can be violent, it is never programmatic or sentimental. He masters his environment on its own terms.

Zappa begins the second half of the concert by saying, "Ian Underwood will now play for you the Mozart Piano Sonata in B flat." Underwood begins to play the first movement of a Mozart piano sonata (K. 281). He plays it very well.

I asked Zappa about his recent run-in at the London School of Economics, and he said, "I was invited to speak at the London School of Economics. So I went over there and asked, 'What do you want me to say?' So here's a bunch of youthful British leftists who take the same youthful leftist view that is popular the world over. It's like belonging to a car club. The whole leftist mentality—'We want to burn the fucking world down and start all over and go back to nature.' Basing their principles on Marxist doctrine this and Mao Tse-tung that and all these clichés that they've read in their classes. And they think that's the basis for conducting a revolution that's going to liberate the common man. Meanwhile, they don't even know any common men. With their mod clothes, either that or their Che Guevara khakis. It's a fucking game.

"I do not think they will acquire the power to do what they want to do, because I'm positive that most of them don't really believe what they're saying. I told them that what they were into was just the equivalent of this year's flower power. A couple of years before those same schmucks were wandering around with incense and bells in the park because they heard that that was what was happening in San Francisco. The first thing they asked me was what was going on at Berkeley. I was thinking to myself, 'What, you guys want to copy that too?' It's really depressing to sit in front of a large number of people and have them all be that stupid, all at once. And they're in *college*."

Zappa introduces the first piece on the concert as "a chamber piece for electric piano and drums." The title, I believe, was "Moderato." A chamber piece is exactly what it is. The drum part takes typical rock rhythms (wham-wham-awhamma-bambam) and stretches out the space between beats to the point of abstraction. The result is a series of percussive timbres suspended over a void. The music verges on the Hollywood sinister (background for some awful, invisible monster) but the close interaction between the two players (at times each seems to be imitating the other's part) gives the piece an extravagant formal vigor.

Zappa, like most moralists, is pessimistic about people in the mass. Perhaps he even wants to punish them. The rest of the group seems considerably more optimistic, and occasionally there are good-natured clashes of will.

ZAPPA: All those mediocre groups reap a huge profit, because people really *like* what they do. The more mediocre your music is, the more accessible it is to a larger number of people in the United States. That's where the market is. You're not selling to a bunch of jazz aesthetes in Europe. You're selling to Americans, who really hate music and love entertainment, so the closer your product is to mindless entertainment material, escapist material, the better off you're going to be. People will dump a lot of money into a bunch of young pretty boys who are ready to make music of limited artistic merit so long as they can sell a lot of it.

KART: What about your gestures of contempt towards your audience?

ZAPPA: I don't think the typical rock fan is smart enough to know he's been dumped on, so it doesn't make any difference. Those kids wouldn't know music if it came up and bit 'em on the ass. Especially in terms of a live concert, where the main element is visual. Kids go to *see* their favorite acts, not to hear them. We work on the premise that nobody really hears what we do anyway, so it doesn't make any difference if we play a place that's got ugly acoustics. The best responses we get from an audience are when we do our worst material.

(Mothers keyboardist) DON PRESTON: Oh, how can you say that?

ZAPPA: It's true, man. "Louie, Louie" brings down the house every time.

PRESTON: People were *booing* the last time you played that. One guy wanted "Louie, Louie," so you said, "OK, we'll play 'Louie, Louie.' " *"Booo!"*

ZAPPA: Maybe they were booing because we didn't play "Midnight Hour" instead.

KART: Isn't it difficult to function as musicians when you feel that no one is listening?

PRESTON: *I* don't feel that way.

ZAPPA: I think most of the members of the group are very optimistic that everybody hears and adores what they do onstage. I can't take that point of view. I get really bummed out about it. Because I've talked to [the audiences], and I know how dumb they are. It's pathetic.

PRESTON: But they do scream for more when we do a good show.

ZAPPA: They scream for more and more because they paid X amount of dollars to get in, and they want the maximum amount of entertainment for their money. It's got nothing whatever to do with what you play. Stick any group on there and let them play to the end of the show.

KART: Do you have a solution to this situation?

ZAPPA: Yeah. I'm not going to tour anymore.

KART: Do you think rock will survive?

ZAPPA: Rock won't die. It will go through some changes, but it ain't going to die. They predicted it too many times in the past. Remember "The limbo is coming in, rock 'n' roll is dead"? There've even been some concerted efforts to kill it. But it will survive because there'll always be several very smart producers and record companies who are interested in giving people what they want instead of what they need.

During the concert the Mothers play several long numbers where everybody gets a chance to blow. Because several of the players have extensive jazz backgrounds, their playing in this context clarifies the differences between jazz and rock improvisation. An essential quality of the jazz solo is the sense it conveys of forward movement through time, which is among the byproducts of the jazz soloist's role in even the simplest contexts—establishing and revealing his identity. In the typical rock solo this kind of forward movement rarely occurs. Instead there is an amount of space to be decorated, with the emotional curve (excitement to ecstasy) a foregone conclusion. That's why many jazz listeners find rock solos boring, no matter how well played. They're like someone brought up on Beethoven who listens to a raga and says, "I dig the rhythm, but we're going around in circles. Where's the development?"

In many rock solos, guitar solos especially, there is an essentially theatrical relation between the player and what he's playing, and the most "exciting" parts occur when it sounds as if what he's playing has got the upper hand. The drama is that he's supposedly conjured up a screaming musical monster, and now that beast threatens to overcome him. The excitement comes from watching him master the "beast," surrender to it, or get even altogether and smash or burn the instrument. When someone like Jimi Hendrix presents this arguably sexual fantasy, the results can be Wagnerian. The Mothers undercut this setup quite neatly. The soloists go through the outward motions of getting "hot," but their precision of accent and the care they give to motivic development prevent any "loss of control" effect. The reaction of the audience to this was curious. Zappa would stomp off a number that had "Watch Out! Explosion Ahead!" written all over it, and people in the audience around me would murmur "Yeah" with a near-blank look of anticipated ecstasy settling on their faces. When, by the end of the piece, no explosion had occurred, they looked vaguely bewildered, although they applauded, of course.

The Mothers have made six albums so far, and *Absolutely Free, We're Only in It for the Money,* and *Uncle Meat* are worthy of anyone's attention. Their first album, *Freak Out,* is interesting but unformed, *Mothermania* is an anthology, and *Ruben and the Jets* is an extreme parody of fifties rock 'n' roll. Listening to all the albums in one sitting reveals an interesting facet of Zappa's musical procedure—in the pieces with lyrics, the often elaborate rhythmic and melodic patterns are tied directly to the words (one beat and one note to each syllable, with few large melodic intervals). This effect carries over into the instrumental pieces, where the tight rhythmic-melodic motifs expand and contract as if they had a life of their own. It's an airy, bracing music, and the play of intelligence in it is so prominent that one must respond in kind. Zappa thinks that *Uncle Meat* is "the best album in terms of overall quality," but his favorite music is on *Lumpy Gravy,* the album where he directs a large orchestra. It's hard for me to tell why he thinks so, for what comes through is a collage of rock and classical parodies that are disconnected by any standard. Perhaps he has in mind the album *Lumpy Gravy* might have been, because both he and drummer Bunk Gardner mentioned that the Los Angeles studio men on the date were unable to cope with some of the music and played without much spirit on what they did manage to record.

Frank Zappa might be described as a cultural guerrilla. He sees that the popular arts are propagandistic in the broad sense—even when they masquerade as rebellion they lull us into fantasy and homogenize our responses. So he infiltrates the machine and attempts to make the popular forms defeat their traditional ends—his music doesn't lull, it tries to make you think. Obviously, he's balanced on a narrow edge. On the one hand, he's faced with an audience whose need for homogeneous response is so great that they can make *his* creations fit *their* desires. On the other, he must in some way reach a mass audience or his efforts are useless. And, of course, there's money, too. He's only human. But, whatever the outcome, there is still the music, and if any of us are around in twenty years, I think we'll be listening to it.

Frank Zappa died in 1993.

MCCOY TYNER
[1981]

IN 1963 the classic John Coltrane quartet (Coltrane on tenor and soprano saxophones, McCoy Tyner on piano, Jimmy Garrison on bass, and Elvin Jones on drums) was in residence in Chicago at McKie's Disc Jockey Show Lounge. Those in the audience who had heard the group before were aware that each night there would be at least one full-scale musical assault, an attempt to climb the glass mountain of ecstasy by sheer force of will. And when Coltrane launched into "Mr. P.C.," a swift minor blues, one knew that this was it.

The leader dropped out after stating the theme, and the field of battle was left to Tyner and the rhythm section. At first, the pianist skated brilliantly ahead; but the ever-rising turbulence of Jones's drumming forced Tyner to dig deeper, summoning up fierce chordal patterns that were only a shade less percussive than the barrage that was falling all around him. The solo went on and on until, at about the fifteen-minute mark, piano, bass, and drums seemed to have fused into a single entity. And it was then that one noticed a nearby patron doing something unusual.

Methodically, and in time to the music, he was beating his head on the bar—hard enough to cause some pain to himself, or so it seemed, but obviously not hard enough that he would be forced to stop. But what was truly unusual about this event is that it was, in one sense, not unusual at all. The passion these musicians were pouring forth seemed to call for an extreme response—shouts of awe and affirmation at the very least and, if it came to that, pounding your head on the bar.

McCoy Tyner doesn't recall that particular evening at McKie's, but he recalls many just like it. "That whole band played very intensely," Tyner says. "During my time with John, the concept was to do as much as you can, to express as much as possible. And the setting was just right for a sideman; it was a glorious position to be in. Also, the atmosphere was different then, very creative and in some ways closer to the real core of the music. It wasn't like it is today, when you have these bastardized concepts and offshoots."

The "real core" versus "bastardized concepts and offshoots," that is Tyner's way of referring to the period that began just about the time he left Coltrane in 1965 and continues to this day—the era of "jazz-rock" and "jazz fusion" that has found any number of players (including some very gifted artists) diluting their music in an attempt to reach a mass audience. Tyner has never done that, and if one needed a living definition of the "real core of the music," any number of his performances would fill the bill. But his lifelong adherence to the core has not been without its moments of temptation.

"I was approached at one time or another," Tyner recalls, "and told that if I did this or that I'd get to a wider audience. But after you come up through a band like the Coltrane band, it's really hard to turn left. A lot of [the commercialization of jazz in the 1970s] had to do with economics. There were monies available, and while there have always been a few jazz people who have been able to . . . well, we've always felt a little cheated when we see a guy who can only play four chords and suddenly he's a millionaire. That bothers a lot of people. So some people said, Why not? Jazz seems to be being kicked around, and this other opportunity is over here. And a lot of them just fell head over heels into it, to the point where they lost touch with anything that resembled the true music. It was a real test of your commitment. And I guess if I hadn't come up the way I did and learned what I had learned, it would have been easy for that to happen to me."

Born in 1938 in Philadelphia, Tyner acquired his sense of commitment from many sources. The city was a hotbed of jazz creativity, and when Tyner settled on the piano at age fifteen, he was able to share ideas with such young turks as trumpeter Lee Morgan, pianist Bobby Timmons, and bassist Reggie Workman. Senior advisers were important to Tyner as well, including composer Cal Massey, pianist Hassan Ibn Ali, and Coltrane himself, whom he met for the first time in 1955. But the key influence on him was Bud Powell, the genius of the bebop piano, who lived around the corner and practiced at Tyner's house. "I feel very fortunate that I met Bud Powell when I was a teenager," Tyner says. "He opened up doors for me and showed me the possibilities. But even though I admired his music, I knew that I could never play like Bud Powell, that I could never be him. I realized then that I would have to be myself, that you can't really contribute if you're copying somebody."

Though Tyner's earliest recordings, made with trombonist Curtis Fuller and with the Art Farmer–Benny Golson Jazztet when he was only twenty-two, are a bit unformed by the standards of his later work, they are already quite personal. The rate of harmonic change is slowed down, melodic and rhythmic patterns extend sinuously through entire solos, and already there is a hypnotic, spiritual undertone to the music. Those tendencies were developed throughout Tyner's time with Coltrane, which began in 1960. And by the time he made his last album with Coltrane (*Meditations,* in 1965), the level of dissonance in his music and his ability to shape that dissonance to his own ends had increased so radically that Tyner was almost as much of an avant-gardist as Cecil Taylor.

But after Tyner formed his own quartet in 1970 and began to record prolifically for the Milestone label, it became clear that his music, for all its power and intensity, would always retain a basic songfulness. Dark and brooding at some times, joyful and exuberant at others, Tyner's playing might be thought of as one long piano solo—an attempt to discover, state, reshape, and decorate a vast primal melody. While so single-minded an approach may sound tedious, Tyner's music has, for the most part, remained fascinating and fresh, thanks to the passion he brings to it. But how, one wonders, does he maintain that level of intensity night in and night out, especially when his style of piano playing calls for the stamina of a champion athlete?

"Well," he says, "if you play for John Coltrane, you're going to build some muscles. But it's a tough life, much tougher than most people realize. Over the years I've developed, out of necessity, the attitude that music is my profession. I make a livelihood from it, so I've come to think of myself as an artist but with a businessman's approach. Of course, as an artist there are certain demands that are placed on you and certain demands you place on yourself. And my job is to make sure that those demands match up. It's a challenge to know that when you go to perform you've got to be in top-notch shape, but it's very rewarding, too.

"I had a guy come up to me once and say, 'When I was in Vietnam in a foxhole, I had a tape of your music with me and it helped me get through the war.' Those are the things that make you think your life has been worthwhile, that make you realize that during your time on this planet you really did make a contribution to humanity."

WAYNE SHORTER
[1987]

ALL by itself, it seems a rather ordinary announcement: "The quartet of tenor and soprano saxophonist Wayne Shorter will be appearing November 19–23 at the Jazz Showcase." Place some context around those words, though, and they become potentially explosive, for Wayne Shorter is the reluctant dragon of jazz—a man whose reemergence onto the scene after more than a decade under wraps is, to say the least, eagerly anticipated. A vastly influential figure since the early 1960s, when he starred with Art Blakey's Jazz Messengers and then with Miles Davis, for the last fifteen years Shorter has virtually disappeared within the atmospheric textures of Weather Report, the popular jazz fusion group he co-leads with composer-keyboardist Joe Zawinul. But now, at age fifty-two, Shorter at last seems willing to do what many feel he should have been doing all along—step forward and make the kind of sweeping musical statements that an artist of his talent, intellect, and experience surely must have been storing up inside.

The initial evidence of Shorter's return to the fray is *Atlantis,* the first album he has made under his own name in eleven years. But even though *Atlantis* marks a definite advance over recent Weather Report efforts (the gemlike details of the album's nine Shorter compositions make most of Zawinul's stuff sound simple-minded), *Atlantis* does strike an ominous note. While there are a few moments when Shorter's solo horn pokes through the album's densely multitracked sonic fabric, nowhere on *Atlantis* does he actually improvise. Considering Shorter's immense improvisational gifts, not to mention the central role improvisation has played in the career of every major jazz artist, that is a puzzling development—as though Walter Payton had announced that from now on he would only play defensive back.

Speaking from New York, in the midst of a tour that has taken him from California to Europe and that will wind up early next year in Japan, Shorter seems pleased with the way *Atlantis* turned out. But in the next breath he insists that the album's gently wistful mood-painting is not the kind of music he is performing with his new quartet. "It's a bad band," Shorter says, "a real bad band." (In the inside-out world of jazz jargon, "bad" means exceptionally good.) "The chemistry, or whatever you want to call it, is definitely working. The piano player, Tom Canning—he was Al Jarreau's musical director for a number of years, just one of those knowledgeable guys. Gary Willis on bass has been with Hubert Laws. He's from North Texas State [University], the place where the Tower of Power guys came from. The drummer, Tom Brechtlein, was with Chick Corea for seven years. And as for what we're doing in person, you're going to hear some—what do they call it?—'chainsaw murder.' Well, let me use a better analogy, a more positive one. Last night we were playing something, and it got so strong that I had an urge to get on the microphone and go, 'Kong, Kong, Kong, Kong'—you know, like this movie monster is coming toward you."

Ah, yes—to those who latched on to his music back in the 1960s, "chainsaw murder" and "Kong, Kong, Kong, Kong" are just what one hopes to hear from Wayne Shorter. During that period Shorter was one of the most *dangerous* players to ever pick up a horn—a man whose solos were described by various critics as "quietly maniacal" and "clinically precise," full of "abrupt changes of mood" and "wild satanic humor." A good example of Shorter's early, fruitfully disruptive approach to improvisation is the solo he took on "June Night" from the album *Kelly Great*, made in 1960 under the leadership of pianist Wynton Kelly. The tune is a lightweight pop ditty, and it's performed by the group with a coy, two-beat stroll. But as Shorter slides into his solo with a vast languid swoon, his listeners suddenly find themselves in a surrealistic fun house, dropping through unexpected trap doors and on the receiving end of some ghostly musical shocks. At one point, for instance, Shorter rises to a pitch of apparently genuine ecstasy, spitting out a rapid-fire figure like a man who has been plugged into a light socket. A moment later, though, Shorter repeats this phrase with the delicately miniaturized grace of a music box, as though he were letting us know that the appearance of soloistic ecstasy may be just that—not a take-it-to-the-bank emotional fact but a cool, even cold-blooded, act of the will that then can be toyed with or even mocked. In fact, the whole idea of the jazz solo—the assumption, prevalent since the days of Louis Armstrong, that the improvising musician is making a spontaneous personal statement—is something that Shorter's way of making music often has kept at arm's length.

"When they play or paint or write or do anything of that sort," Shorter explains, "a lot of people assume that what they're doing at the moment, that emotional thing, is the nth degree of creativity. Because they believe that what they're doing is a pure emotional expression, it's supposed to be sacred or magical or mystical or whatever. Well, as far as I'm concerned, it's not. The act of creation is not magical or mystical or any of those things, even though it can be thought of that way and received that way.

"You wonder sometimes why millions and millions of people go for certain things. Well, when people cleave unto things, most of the time they do so because they're in a life condition that makes it possible and necessary for them to do that. They want that magic. In music, for instance, I don't care how much you like it, you're going to see first and then you're going to hear. When people see me onstage, I can tell that some of them are looking at me with a kind of wonder. The listening, if it does come, always comes after that."

As elliptical as his musical thought, Shorter's explanations often seem to call for explanations themselves. But his need to push aside the idea of the heroically inspired soloist seems to have arisen from a belief that he himself lacks certain heroic traits, that sense of ego that drives so many artists to venture to and beyond the limit. Born under the sign of Virgo (in Newark, New Jersey, on August 25, 1933), Shorter once said that "people under Virgo tend to take consistent and insistent notice of details. Virgo people, for example, make good doctors, lawyers, and secretaries. But they also tend to fear the large responsibilities that go with greatness and accordingly, if they ever become great, it happens almost involuntarily."

In Shorter's case, though, thousands of listeners have been eager to thrust greatness upon him, despite his unwillingness to step into the spotlight. "Yes," Shorter admits, "I know there's been this hue and cry—'We want to hear more of you' and all that stuff. So in that sense, in terms of having my own band under my own name, I'm a late bloomer. But there's something that is happening now as a result of me being the way I am. When I say I'm a late bloomer, I also mean that something is manifesting itself in my life right now in terms of the environment. The environment is everything, and, just like a mirror, it is reflecting that late blooming and saying 'Well done.' Because it's happening that way in its life at the same time it is in mine. We're all blooming late, but we are blooming."

In addition to *Atlantis* and his solo tour, Shorter has been working on another intriguing project, the Bertrand Tavernier film *'Round Midnight,* which is based on the relationship between the late pianist Bud Powell and his French friend-guardian, Francis Paudras. "The film is about the music and what was going on around it at that time," Shorter says. "You know, 'the life.' I was over there [in France] working on it about six weeks, and at the end of my workload Bertrand asked me, 'What name do you want to be in this movie?'—because in all the dialogue I had there was nothing that required my character's name to be spoken or revealed. So I said I wanted to be called Lamont Cranston. And Bertrand laughed and laughed, because he knows all about *The Shadow,* about Lamont Cranston and Margo Lane.

"I met Bud Powell in 1959, when I went to Europe with Art Blakey. Bud came to my room and I played [Powell's composition] 'Dance of the Infidels' for him. Before that he had asked me for forty francs—or rather he said, 'Do you have forty francs?' And I said 'yes' and laid the money on the table, thinking he wanted it for a drink or something. Then Bud sat down and said, 'Play me something,' and after I did, he just walked out. So this summer, when I was working on the movie, I met his daughter, Celia, and asked her about what had happened.

" 'When Daddy walked into that room,' she told me, 'he really didn't have money on his mind. And when he walked out without touching it, that was because you'd already paid him. He was checking you out. And he left that way because he was satisfied, because he felt that everything was going to be in good hands.' "

Such an encounter, one suspects, would have made a good episode of *The Shadow*, assuming Lamont Cranston had been willing to delve into the world of jazz. And there can be little doubt that the darkly romantic careers of Powell, Parker, Fats Navarro, and so many other bebop stalwarts had a profound impact on Shorter's view of things—as he tried to figure out how (if, indeed, at all) this beautiful music could be separated from the self-destructive lifestyles that so often seemed to surround it. To take only one of many possible examples, none of the four men who performed with Shorter on "June Night" back in 1960 (Wynton Kelly, trumpeter Lee Morgan, bassist Paul Chambers, and drummer Philly Joe Jones) is among the living. "Well," Shorter says, "I did it. I'm still here. And Herbie Hancock is still here. Jimmy Smith is still here. Dizzy Gillespie is still here. I ran into Diz last week in Berlin, in my dressing room. He had played his set, and he and Joe Zawinul were waiting around to hear me play. Diz used to be kind of rotund, you know, but he has lost a lot of weight and looks very good."

One is grateful, of course, that Wayne Shorter has managed to survive when so many of his peers were struck down. But the fans who come to hear him this week at the Jazz Showcase will be wondering whether Shorter's music has survived and flourished as well. If Shorter's "chainsaw murder" quip means that he is once more playing all out, everyone should be happy. But if the style he adopts is that of *Atlantis*, with little or no improvisation in store, some listeners are bound to be disappointed.

"Well," Shorter says, "to me the word 'jazz' means no categories, a refusal to be locked into a style of any kind. Most people think of a style as a direction, but direction doesn't mean too much to me. Because if you get locked into playing a style in order to appease those people who need that style to point out the way for them, it becomes a way of comfort, both for them and for you. Of course, a style can be a different direction, one that has a challenge to it. But even then, it's still a comfort, because it is a direction. So instead of direction, I go more for what I call 'value creation.' No matter what it is, if value comes out of it, I say, go ahead."

ORNETTE COLEMAN

The following four pieces about Ornette Coleman are a review of
one of his earliest recordings, an interview, and reviews of his 1980s
band Prime Time and the band of the same period, Old and New
Dreams, that included former Coleman associates Don Cherry,
Dewey Redman, Charlie Haden, and Ed Blackwell.

[1974]

ORNETTE Coleman worked with this group (cornetist Don
Cherry, drummer Billy Higgins, bassist Charlie Haden, and
pianist Paul Bley—the nominal leader, who recorded the group
in live performance) for six weeks between his first and second
studio recording sessions, sometime between March 1958 and
January 1959. The logical question is, how does Coleman sound
at this early date, freed from studio pressures and united for
the first time with Haden? Well, he sounds great, much more at
ease than on his first album, *Something Else*. And even though,
compared to what was to come, there is something of the
gawky adolescent to the Coleman we hear on *Live at the Hill-
crest Club*, no other recording of his has a comparable feeling
of looseness and spontaneity until the *Town Hall Concert* album
of 1962.

And do these tracks tell us something about Coleman that
we didn't know before? I suppose not, but merely because
they're beautiful in themselves and unexpected messages from
the past, they do help to explain why the most successful innovator of the sixties (successful in the sense of producing performance after performance that really worked) should in the long
run have had such a negligible effect on his contemporaries and
successors, compared to the impact of men like John Coltrane
and Eric Dolphy. (Very few players showed Coleman's literal im-
print, and if there were others who grasped the principles of his

music without wishing to sound like him, they must have decided that these principles couldn't be applied by them.)

It comes down to this—Coleman is both a pre-tonal and a post-tonal player, and, in a sense (a very fruitful one for him), he reads the history of tonality backwards to its pre-tonal state. What enabled him to do so, in addition to innate genius, was the accident of birth that placed him in a provincial center (Fort Worth, Texas) where Charlie Parker's latest stretchings of triadic harmony could be heard alongside musics—blues, rhythm and blues, cowboy ballads, and what have you—that were either pre-tonal or so crude in their tonal functions as to be pre-tonal by implication. You can call it naïve or the ultimate sophistication, but sensing the relation between a music in which tonality was on the brink of ceasing to function and musics in which it functioned quite simply or hardly at all, Coleman was able to preserve what for him were the plums of tonality—the emotional colors of triadic harmony, especially the most basic ones (who aside from Monk has made so much of the octave jump?)—without adopting tonic-dominant cadential patterns and phrase structures.

This explains why the internal rhythm of Coleman's solos often has a bouncy, downhome lope to it, à la Swing Era alto saxophonists like Pete Brown and Tab Smith or proto-R&B figure Louis Jordan (even though Coleman will interject phrases of startling asymmetry, and even though that internal rhythm has a floating, precisely controlled relation to the stated beat of the bass and drums). Conversely, the men who were most involved in stretching triadic harmony to its furthest limits to date in jazz, Charlie Parker and Art Tatum, also were the men who carried the subdivision of the beat to its furthest point to date—because such subtleties of accentuation were necessary to throw into relief, and so make articulate, melodic lines whose harmonic implications otherwise might have been inchoate.

On "Klactoveedsedstene," Coleman and Cherry play Parker's spiky theme with tremendous élan, which should settle any lingering doubts about Coleman's rhythmic control and confirm that his sometimes radically simple rhythmic choices were real choices and not the results of any instrumental incapacity. The analogous simplifications of his melodic-harmonic universe can be heard best here on "The Blessing," where he takes a mellow, strongly organized solo highlighted by a subtle sotto voce passage of implied doubletime. Improvisations like this—"Peace" on *The Shape of Jazz to Come* is another—reveal that however free Coleman is of tonic-dominant functions (in the sense of not needing to touch home base at specific intervals), his music has plenty of cadential possibilities that he can find as emotion dictates. And it is these moments of resolution, which give back to us the most primary pleasures of triadic harmony cleaned of the grime of long use, that ultimately divided Coleman from his contemporaries. However much they might respect a pre-tonal universe and make gestures toward it, they lived in a post-tonal world and could not read the history of tonality as Coleman did. But if his route has turned out not to be one that others could take, perhaps that makes the beauty he has given us all the more treasurable.

[1986]

WHEN alto saxophonist-composer Ornette Coleman's first recordings were released in 1959 and 1960, a good many musicians and fans felt threatened by the titles of the albums alone—*Something Else!, Tomorrow Is the Question, The Shape of Jazz to Come,* and *Change of the Century.* Such banner-waving phraseology, which seemed eager to proclaim that previous styles of jazz were about to become obsolete, could be dismissed as an excess of promotional zeal. But Coleman's music proved to be even more controversial than the verbal package that was wrapped around it.

Labeled "free jazz," it was a way of playing that seemed to break a host of musical rules—doing away with the more-or-less orderly harmonic language of Western concert and popular music and dispensing as well with the theme-and-variations forms and the symmetrical phrasing that such harmonic thought implies. Then there was the actual sound of Coleman's alto saxophone. Raw and even raucous at times, it often deviated from the norms of "correct" pitch, in much the same way a country blues singer might bend his voice or his guitar strings for expressive effect. In fact that apparently primitive side of Coleman's art turned out to be its most threatening (and, for some, its most appealing) trait—a sign that if jazz were going to advance, it might not do so by continuing along a path of sophistication and complexity that paralleled the recent development of Western concert music.

While Coleman's innovations were in their own way remarkably sophisticated and complex (and carefully ordered as well), they also were firmly linked to jazz's most primal roots—a "return to the source" that entranced many open-minded listeners but inadvertently challenged almost everything that the most advanced pre-Coleman players thought they knew. So the lines of controversy were drawn, with such knowledgeable critics as Martin Williams insisting that Coleman's music "represents the first fundamental re-evaluation of basic materials and procedures for jazz since the innovations of Charlie Parker," while trumpet master Miles Davis weighed in on the other side with, "Just listen to what [Coleman] writes and how he plays it—if you're talking psychologically, the man is all screwed up inside."

That fuss was, and still is, a source of pain to Coleman—even though, aside from making his music in the ways he sees fit, he has played almost no part in it. "I was," Coleman explains, "always a victim of how they used me, which is why I haven't had as much success in the music business as I might have had. You see, in the Western world when someone unknown comes along and does something really well, what happens is that they ask another person for his opinion of what that first person has done. And if that second person says it's good or it's bad, only then do most other people start thinking 'maybe it is good' or 'maybe it is bad.' And I've had it both ways.

"I'm not mentioning names, but I remember one trumpet player who came up to me [in 1959, when Coleman first performed in New York] and said, 'I don't know what you're doing, but I want to let the people see me playing with you. Why don't you play some blues and let me come up and play.' So I said, 'OK,' and we did some song that he [obviously Coleman is referring to Miles Davis] had played with Charlie Parker. Then when they asked him what he thought of my music, he said, 'Oh, the guy's all messed up—you can tell that just by listening to him.' And it wasn't true."

Indeed it wasn't. And for proof that Davis himself must have known that, one need only listen to his mid-1960s recordings, which find Davis incorporating ideas that were proposed several years before by Coleman's early trumpet partner, Don Cherry. "Oh, for sure," Coleman says, when Cherry's influence on Davis's playing is mentioned. "But what I'm saying is that some people who are doing things in front of the public have used their positions to not be threatened, and others have used their positions to make me seem as if I didn't belong where they are."

Among the unthreatened ones, as far as Coleman's music is concerned, is guitarist Pat Metheny, who is as much in front of the public as any of today's jazz instrumentalists. Having paid verbal and musical tribute to Coleman on several occasions, Metheny has now collaborated with his idol on a new album, *Song X.* Those who think they know Metheny's music may wonder what he and Coleman have to say to each other—not only because the saxophonist has never shown the least inclination to modify his own musical vision, but also because Metheny is often thought of as a soft-core, pastoral-tinged virtuoso with an excessive taste for electronic gimmickry. But on *Song X* Metheny wholeheartedly places himself at Coleman's disposal, while the master is stimulated in turn by the guitarist's empathetic support. In fact, the album includes several startling passages in which Metheny, having used computerized technology to "sample" Coleman's sound and then incorporate it into his guitar synthesizer, is able to play alongside Coleman in such a way that one seems to hear two Colemans at the same time—with the second "Coleman" line actually being produced by Metheny's instrument.

"The equipment Pat has," says Coleman, "is so advanced it's

like an F-16. When he uses it, all of a sudden it sounds like the solo I'm playing turns right into the one he's playing. [The album] was very exciting. But I didn't want to make a record just because Pat was a fan of mine. I felt that if there was something we could do together so a record should be made, then we'll do it. So I told Pat, 'You come to New York and study with me and work on it, and if it comes out that way, then we'll go into the studio.' He did that, and I think it came out really well for him.

"What was the collaboration like? Well, I've always told the people who play with me that I would like to improvise as if we were writing compositions. And that's the hardest way to improvise, because most people have got to have some kind of map to go by—whereas I've always said that you don't need that map once you know where it is you're going, and if you've gone there before you certainly don't need to keep looking at it. So I would write something, and Pat would write something, and I would say, 'The reason that doesn't work is because it's limited to this particular key or this particular sound,' and then we'd work on it some more.

"After all, the thing that's so amazing about music is that from Mozart to Monk to Bach to Charlie Parker to Muggsy Spanier to whomever, all the music that's been played in the Western world has been played with the same twelve notes. People keep thinking about styles and categories, but the category is just the person; it's not the music. I remember once I was looking for a bass player, and [guitarist] James Ulmer told me about this kid in Brooklyn. So I called him and he came over to play with me and he was just fantastic. He couldn't read or write music, he just played pure natural. And every note he played was the exact right note. That just proved to me again that the ability to express yourself has to do with who you are and not with what someone says you can or can't do because of something you need to know before you do what you do.

"But that particular quality of expressiveness is not as abundant these days because everybody goes to the same fountain—to the television and things such as that. And therefore they forget who they are because someone tells them that they're not them. What I'm saying is that the 'civilized' system we've inherited doesn't mean that there has been any advance in creativity. This system has just enabled everyone to have some relationship to each other without our having to necessarily be related to each other."

A typical dose of Coleman's gnomic wisdom, such remarks have the same effect as his music, as an initial sense of homegrown oddity and awkwardness is replaced by an awareness that not only does almost all of what Coleman says make sense, but also that the sense he makes could be made in no other way. It has been a long road for Coleman—from his boyhood in Fort Worth, Texas, to his years of experimentation and frustration in California, his period of celebrity and controversy in New York, and the many years after that during which he has learned that his search for "players who are independently in tune with themselves" also involves a search for listeners who possess similar virtues. Yet as difficult as that road has been at times—and as much as Coleman has come to realize that the very strength and humaneness of what he has to give tends to stir opposition—he has never deviated from his course.

"It seems," Coleman says, "like there's a music you think you need in order to get away from your problems, whatever those problems might be. But some music doesn't have anything to do with that. It's just like water, you know—part of the elements, a music that has something to do with being in existence. And it just happens that some people play music that way, which is why they're cast as 'outsiders.' I never thought of myself as an outsider, though. I just thought that people would understand and get something out of what I played once they got over the fact that their memories wouldn't allow them to understand what was going on in the present. That's what's so good about the album Pat and I made. Because of his age [thirty-two] and my age [fifty-six], you can realize that when people say things aren't what they used to be, it doesn't have anything to do with that. It has to do with the truth, the truth of what you actually believe."

[1982]

WITH Ornette Coleman due in town this Saturday, Old and New Dreams' visit to the Jazz Showcase at the Blackstone Hotel becomes doubly delightful. The band is three-quarters of Coleman's best unit (trumpeter Don Cherry, bassist Charlie Haden, and drummer Ed Blackwell) plus tenor saxophonist Dewey Redman, another Coleman associate and a player directly inspired by his former leader. Coleman no longer plays the way Old and New Dreams does; and why should he, when he sees other realms to conquer? But there is every reason for Haden, Cherry, et al. to keep bringing this classic style to life, because it is less a style than a good-sized world view in which new musical treasures can always be found.

Old and New Dreams is a lovely blend of two of jazz's key regional strains—the Southwestern blues tradition (Cherry and Haden come from Oklahoma, Redman from Texas) and the New Orleans impulse (Blackwell, a native of that city, sounds like a cross between Max Roach and Baby Dodds). So there is a lot of old here (both of those traditions go *way* back), with the newness coming from the constant melodic invention of every member of the band.

Hearing Haden again, one is reminded that of all of Coleman's associates, he was the most unprecedented. This style of bass playing, in which every note has a solemn yet joyful weight—where in the world did it come from? Nothing Haden does could be transferred to another instrument and still retain its meaning, so closely are his deep-toned, woody lines tied to the bass's unique character. But that is one reason his ideas have a transcendent grace—for by inhabiting his instrument in the way, say, that Lester Young inhabited the tenor saxophone, Haden goes beyond the bass's musical boundaries in a fashion much flashier players could never imagine.

In the last analysis—but who would want to make it?—Redman seems a shade conventional for this band. He swings in the loosey-goosey manner of trombonist Bennie Green, and his lines suggest a James Moody who has been listening to Mississippi

John Hurt. But if those honey-sweet little tunes that Redman creates are a bit too comfortable by Coleman's standards, they often are so charming that criticism is disarmed.

Cherry, on the other hand, is dangerous—never more so than when he jams a mute in his horn and produces those dense, introspective designs that seem to say, "Take that, Miles Davis!" In the past there were those who wondered how intentional Cherry's splintered lines were. But today, listening to his lace-made-out-of-barbed-wire patterns, what once might have seemed raw now stands revealed as mastery.

Blackwell's status as a master was never in doubt. The most melodic of drummers, he gives the band the richness of a string quartet—or rather a quartet in which every instrument is both a melodic and a percussive voice.

Ed Blackwell died in 1992; Don Cherry died in 1995.

[1982]

ORNETTE Coleman's music used to tell a lot of stories. In fact, Old and New Dreams, the band made up of some of his key former compatriots, was in town to tell us some of those stories just last week. Coming from them, those stories sounded as fresh as they had back in 1959, when Coleman turned jazz inside out by renouncing many previously unshakable notions of musical order so his keening melodic lines could follow a system of logic that was as "primitive" as that of a country blues singer and as sophisticated as that of a classical avant-gardist. But Coleman and his poundingly electrified band Prime Time (Bern Nix and Charles Ellerbee, guitars; Jamaaladeen Tacuma and Al McDoud, bass guitars; Denardo Coleman and Tamal, drums) have only one story to tell. It was an exhilarating, often shatteringly powerful story, and one felt grateful for the chance to hear it. But was it nostalgia alone that made one yearn for the multiplicities of the music Coleman created some twenty years ago? Or were there losses as well as gains in Coleman's decision to surround himself with Prime Time's electronic tumult?

The typical piece began with a pattern hammered out by bassist Tacuma. Soon everyone but the leader had joined in, creating a welter of sound that resembled an out-of-sync unison line, with the out-of-syncness an attempt to create useful rhythmic and harmonic friction. Then Coleman would start to soar, often beginning at a slower, semi-rubato tempo and playing off all the "noise" the others were creating.

His lines were still lyrical, though the lyricism is darker and more stern now, as though Coleman's Texas soul had been chastened by the years he has spent living in Manhattan. Climaxes came as Coleman brought his melodies into phase with the whiplash pace of the band. And here the unison concept, which always has been at the core of his music, became an almost frightening unity—as though a herd of elephants had formed a conga line, then broken into the lindy hop.

Yet Coleman's role in all of this was odd, for despite the ecstatic tone of his surroundings and the passion with which he played, there was little sense of ecstatic relief. Instead, the unity that he (but not the band) proposed was earthbound in the best sense—the music of a man who had summoned up the gods for purposes of conversation, not worship. But can a unity be restated ad infinitum and still remain intriguing? Coleman seems to think so, and I'm not about to argue with him. Yet anyone who recalls such performances as "Beauty Is a Rare Thing" is aware that Coleman once found many unities, not just one.

CECIL TAYLOR
[1978]

TUESDAY night at the Jazz Showcase, pianist Cecil Taylor, an avant-garde all by himself, presented a first set that consisted of a single solo that lasted an hour, give or take a few minutes. One hour of totally improvised music, much of it played with a two-handed percussive intensity that threatened to wreak havoc on the instrument. It was, if such a thing is possible, a disturbingly spectacular performance—a display of transcendental virtuosity that in some ways was at war with itself.

Taylor has been playing in this manner for some time now, sitting at the keyboard night after night and stunning the audience and himself with melodic thunderbolts. The goal, for the creator and his listeners, is total immersion, and amid the storm it is easy to overlook details as one is being soaked to the skin by sound. But the details are both fascinating and revealing, more revealing sometimes than I think Taylor would wish.

The pianist's debt to Duke Ellington has often been remarked on, and Taylor's music does bear some resemblance to one aspect of the Ellington universe—that blend of sophistication and sorrow that might be called the Harlem Penthouse Blues. Yet that area of Ellingtonia actually comes from Duke's longtime collaborator the late Billy Strayhorn. And Strayhorn is Cecil Taylor's real blood brother. Like the lyrics of Strayhorn's "Lush Life," Taylor's music rhymes "sadness" and "madness," with the latter word suggesting both anger and loss of control.

In other words, Taylor is a musician with a split personality who constantly sends one of his selves into combat against the other. The self one hears most of the time is the furious virtuoso who scrambles up and down the piano with such speed that his hands fly above the keyboard like quarreling blue jays. The other self—the truer, deeper one, I think—is ruminative, romantic, and almost painfully vulnerable. During Tuesday night's first set it found expression twice—once, beginning at the half-hour mark, for about ten minutes, and again at the very end of Taylor's tour de force.

At those moments, even the pianist's physical relation to his instrument seemed to change. Instead of swaying swiftly along the keyboard, he moved slowly toward and away from the piano, as though it were giving as much to him as he was taking from it. And the music that emerged under that spell had a strange, despairing sense of communion to it. If parallels to classical music can be made, it was reminiscent of Schumann's fractured lyricism.

But Taylor's exterior self—the breakneck, furious Lisztian side of him—seemingly can't abide that tenderness and feels compelled to wash it away with angry bursts of virtuosity. Nothing wrong with that, of course, except that only rarely are the shifts made in a dramatically satisfying manner—I suspect because the nature of the drama is often hidden from the man who ought to be in control of it. One result is that too much of Taylor's all-out playing is thin in ideas. He spreads leaping patterns up and down the keyboard with what sounds at first like genuine fire, but beneath the intensity seems forced and forlorn—like a man who is fleeing, not flying. Yet if Taylor is a man divided against himself, he is also a musician who lives out that conflict on a heroic scale. And for that reason, listening to him can be an enthralling experience as well as an exhausting one.

The preceding response to Cecil Taylor's music now seems wrong-headed to me. More on target, I think, is this passage on Taylor from the chapter on the avant-garde that I wrote in 2000 for *The Oxford Companion to Jazz*:

Pre–Ornette Coleman jazz was marked by a steady increase in harmonic complexity. And that took place against the backdrop of this century's western concert music, in which an increase in harmonic complexity not only had led to a drastic loosening of tonal function but also to Arnold Schoenberg's invention/discovery of a way of organizing music that did not depend on tonal function at all. Thus Taylor's early recordings . . . led composer-critic Gunther Schuller to conclude that the extremely high level of dissonance in Taylor's music meant that his work must be related to that of the "minority of jazz composer-performers" whose music "often spills over into areas so removed from any center of tonal gravity that it can be thought of as 'atonal.' " But while dissonance for Taylor would come to play almost no tonally functional role, that was not because he had a need to stretch or weaken tonal functions. Rather, what he was trying to do was collapse all elements onto the level of what might be called melodicized rhythm—into a line of leaps, attacks and their resulting/accumulating shapes in which dissonance plays an accent/dynamics/attack role, not a harmonic one. That is, the more dissonant the chord or cluster that Taylor strikes, the greater the force with which the blow has been struck, the more obliquely it has been delivered. Also put to rhythmic use are the residual directional meanings of Taylor's by now non-functional harmonic gestures, altering the rate at which the music proceeds by altering the angles at which we perceive it.

Taylor's early partner, bassist Buell Neidlinger, has said that despite its apparently formidable level of complexity, he found from the first that Taylor's music "was *clear*. I could *see* it as well as *feel* it." Consider, for instance, the accelerating burst of notes with which Taylor emerges from the ensemble on "Mixed" (1961). While the passage does not take place within the boundaries of the piece's already loose metrical framework, except in the sense that Taylor's outburst and the framework coexist, the melodic-rhythmic shape of that outburst is almost tangible—largely because Taylor's gestures at once generate and are heard against the musical equivalent of the picture plane of a non-illusionistic painting. (The "picture plane" for Taylor is the piano keyboard; and—like Earl Hines, but unlike many post-Chopin composers for the piano—he chooses to highlight rather than disguise the fact of fingers striking specific keys; every sound proclaims its actual location within space.) He reserves the right to make harmony do some work on the level of local drama, but if we listen well, it is his skein of melodicized beats that is the story.

ROSCOE MITCHELL
[1968]

*C*ONGLIPTIOUS begins with a march—the rhythm stated twice on snare drum (slightly varied the second time), then amplified by the bass saxophone and bass drum. Over this the string bass plays a melody that steps out confidently, hesitates to repeat a motif, descends in double stops, and ends with three-quarters of the initial phrase, sealed off by four unison notes from the other instruments. Pause. The sound of a bicycle horn, squeezed, held and released. Pause. Two rich notes from the bass saxophone seem as if they might begin a new melody, but, joined by the drums, they lead to a literal repeat of the march, except this time the four final notes are cut short by a percussion crescendo/decrescendo. Crashing gongs, moans from the bass saxophone, snapped-off Philly Joe Jones-like drum figures, a zooming slide from the electric bass, a siren, and gradually the drummer is left to subside with quieter snare and cymbal patterns. Pause. And now a gentle waltz, played by fluegelhorn, vibes, bass, and drums in unison. The rubato phrasing makes time as pliable as taffy. A simple, tonal melody is resolved and then its first phrase returns, subtly altered as the fluegelhorn's tone grows richer and the last note is held. Before, the phrase demanded the rest of the melody for its resolution; now it will lead to something else.

Thus the first three minutes of a twenty-minute work, which should indicate the density and variety of this music. Space prevents me from describing all the beauties of *Congliptious*, but I'd like to mention the soprano saxophone solo whose pauses convey a unique tenderness (as though the soloist, like a child, were mildly astonished by the growth of his song), the entrance of bass and drums behind this solo at the instant it becomes more assertive, the alto saxophone melody that moves from hints of Appalachian folk song (backed by bottleneck guitar) to savage swing, the trumpet passage in which half-valve effects join comedy to lyricism, and the final melody ("Old"), with its barrelhouse memories. *Congliptious* is one of the most successful large-scale jazz pieces I have ever heard—large-scale because every passage has a structural/dramatic function that gives it meaning beyond its immediate color. For example, the brief span of the opening march is, to me, a miniature drama, reminiscent of the song "Revelge" ("Reveille") from Mahler's *Des*

Knaben Wunderhorn. The abrupt turns of the melody and the dark instrumental timbres convey a mood that is both gently sad and bitter, as though the marchers were wounded or resigned to approaching death. But the relation of this march to the percussion passage, the waltz, and all that follows is impervious to verbal description (mine at least), though its emotional effect is clear. It must be heard.

What I can do is describe some of the means by which Roscoe Mitchell, Lester Bowie, Malachi Favors, and Robert Crowder create their music. First, their music arises from a deep understanding of the jazz tradition. As annotator Terry Martin points out, the ensemble has "free access to a group memory of original and borrowed themes." The entire range of jazz, and other musics too, is seen as a musical language, a historical present, which these musicians draw upon with unparalleled freedom. Delightfully, they seem to have it both ways; that is, the barrelhouse theme of "Old" and the Ornette Coleman quotes that Mitchell uses are musically valid in themselves while still retaining the force of their historical reference. I think that this attitude toward the past, along with the group's unusual empathy, is what enables them to create works of unprecedented structural unity without sacrificing any of jazz's essential spontaneity. (*Congliptious* is almost entirely improvised.)

The three solo performances on the first side present in isolation some of the qualities that are combined in *Congliptious.* They display Favors's elastic swing, huge sound (the excellent recording does not exaggerate his power), and ability to build a composition from contrasting sections; Mitchell's gift for thematic improvisation and technical innovation (at one point he plays three-note harmonics that move contrapuntally rather than in parallel); and Bowie's mastery of comic timing, both musical and verbal. This album and its predecessor under Lester Bowie's name (*Numbers 1&2*) are essential for any listener who is interested in the course of jazz and music in general. Roscoe Mitchell's music not only promises future glory, it is fully formed and beautiful now.

[1979]

Roscoe Mitchell's *L-R-G/The Maze/SII Examples* may well change the musical future. Best known today as a member of the Art Ensemble of Chicago, Mitchell has been a key figure in the jazz avant-garde ever since he recorded *Sound* for the Delmark label in 1966. His days with the Art Ensemble began soon afterwards, and he still helps that band function with some intensity. But, it has become obvious that his musical needs are leading him elsewhere, away from collective, free-association drama and into more adamantly controlled forms of creation.

The fruits of his new endeavors became visible last year with the release of his two-record Nessa album, *Nonaah,* which was highlighted by an exhaustive and exhausting solo alto saxophone performance of the title piece and another version of "Nonaah" scored for four altos. Characteristically, each of these performances began at one musical pole and traveled to an opposite position—the solo "Nonaah" imposing a stern order on seemingly ecstatic material, the quartet "Nonaah" insisting on strict repetition until the musical machine melted into calm or exploded into its component parts.

Those performances were startling enough. But the added weight of the works on Mitchell's new double album makes it clear that he is in the vanguard of all music that rewards contemplation. "SII Examples" may be the best place to start, a seventeen-minute piece for soprano saxophone that explores the myriad tones that fall between the notes of the standard scale—"quarter tones, semi-quarter tones, the same note with different timbres, that sort of thing," according to the composer. Timbre is the key element here, as Mitchell oscillates slowly through a closely bunched group of notes, creating variations that sharpen our awareness of one particular building block of music. Absorbing in detail, the piece almost becomes hallucinatory; but "SII Examples" is not "trance music," like the work of such minimalist composers as Terry Riley, Steve Reich, and Philip

Glass. Instead, as with Bach's *Well-Tempered Clavier*, one is always aware of the materials involved and the process that shapes them; no attempt is being made to seduce the listener into transcendence by shifting his attention from the matter at hand.

The next place to go is "The Maze," a twenty-two-minute percussion piece for eight players (Mitchell, Thurman Barker, Anthony Braxton, Douglas Ewart, Malachi Favors, Joseph Jarman, Don Moye, and Henry Threadgill) who perform on approximately 230 instruments—from standard drum kits to a cornucopia of bells, gongs, marimbas, and vibraphones. That layout may suggest cacophony, but "The Maze" is the calmest, most lucid percussion piece I've ever heard—a series of linked events (thirty in all) in which clearly defined percussive textures are interwoven to create a design of dense, extravagant lushness. Especially intriguing is the way "The Maze" makes one aware simultaneously of minute details and overall form, as though one were watching the creation of a Persian carpet. First, each colored thread of sound is apparent, then the middle-distance designs come into view, and finally, the completed maze solves and resolves itself.

"L-R-G" should be approached last, because it combines the timbral variations of "SII Examples" and the structural techniques of "The Maze." A thirty-six-minute trio for woodwinds, high brass, and low brass, "L-R-G" is performed by the men whose initials give the work its title—Leo Smith (trumpet, pocket trumpet, and fluegelhorn), Mitchell (piccolo, flute, oboe, clarinet, and soprano, alto, tenor, baritone, and bass saxophones), and George Lewis (sousaphone, tuba, and alto and tenor trombones). The musical events of "L-R-G" (forty-four in all if my count is accurate) are more clearly separated than the events of "The Maze." And each of these events, which range in length from about twenty to ninety seconds, is a complete multilevel structure in itself.

The degree of activity in each event is determined by how many instruments come into play, how widely separated they are in pitch, and how quickly the phrases of each instrument change shape. Functional harmony is nonexistent, as are melody and rhythm in the sense of variations from any norm outside the world of the piece. Instead, we hear timbre and the shape of phrases in space, with the space between each shape always clearly defined.

That may sound forbidding, and in a sense it is—one almost has to learn again how to listen, how to take in sounds that occur simultaneously but refuse to be integrated. But this is not the first time that music has asked that much from its audience, a fact that became apparent when I began to search through the past, hoping to come across some music that sounded like these seemingly unprecedented works. Analogies to "The Maze" were not to be found among other twentieth-century percussion pieces; by comparison Karlheinz Stockhausen's "Zyklus" seems as simple as a Gene Krupa solo. But the glacial calm of "SII Examples" pointed in the right direction, to the slowly unfolding but infinitely complex masses of the fifteenth-century French master Guillaume Dufay.

And in the fourteenth century, in the music of such composers as Grimace, Solage, and Matheus de Perusio, one can find works that resemble "L-R-G" more than any other music composed during the intervening six hundred years. Listen, for example, to de Perusio's "Le greygnour bien," which can be heard on David Munrow's recording *The Art of Courtly Love*. In the words of annotator/conductor Munrow, the composition's "three parts often appear totally unrelated," and even ears attuned to polyphonic textures are forced to hear each part as a separate entity. Such an extreme disassociation of parts was a primary goal for these fourteenth-century composers, who were working at a time when the very idea of polyphony was new and harmony was still a naked babe. Their musical world was one in which the component parts of Western music were still vigorously independent. And that independence was a quality that their music was trying to elaborate on and preserve. Because Roscoe Mitchell's music, too, is homing in on first principles, it is natural that his work should resemble compositions that were created when Western music was taking shape. And in the process, he is discovering anew that when music is truly broken down into its component parts, a new order can emerge.

What effect the discoveries of "L-R-G," "The Maze," and "SII Examples" will have on the future of music and how quickly those discoveries will take hold are questions for the future to decide. For now, all that can be said is that a different beauty has entered our world, one that demands much from us and gives much more in return.

EVAN PARKER
[1986]

THE first thing to be said about the music of English soprano and tenor saxophonist Evan Parker is that it is faster and more violent than any music previously imaginable. Performing Friday night at Link's Hall, Parker and his no-less-virtuosic partners, bassist Barry Guy and drummer Paul Lytton, strove, so it seemed, to be totally spontaneous and totally instantaneous as well—which meant that one of Parker's key goals was to produce tones that have the same abruptness one is used to hearing from an instrument that has been struck or plucked.

There are precedents for that in jazz, leaving aside the question of whether Parker's music deserves that label—particularly in the angular drum breaks of Max Roach and the electric intensity with which pianist Bud Powell leapt from one jagged peak to another. But Parker, having isolated those skittering shards of rhythm, has built an entire musical world upon them—one that differs significantly both from the tortured romanticism of bebop and the visionary ecstasies of the late John Coltrane.

Fragmentary though they may seem at first, the glittering

bits and pieces of Parker's music are not really fragments. Instead they are what used to be called quiddities: essences whose meaning resides in the fact that they are irreducible. One accepts that from Parker immediately—the sense that an absolute mental and physical barrier has been met—and realizes then that while his music has a striving quality, it does not, as Coltrane's music did, yearn toward a state of delirium or release. Once the condition of instantaneous sound production and instantaneous interaction with his partners has been reached, that is where Parker wishes to be—not only because it is, one suspects, the place that seems most real to him but also because he can make things there that can't be made anywhere else.

A good example of what is involved was Parker's fifteen-minute solo outing on soprano. Using circular breathing, in which air is constantly taken in and expelled to produce a continuous stream of sound, he skirled out countless overtones and then placed one or more of these elliptical lines in contrary motion to the others. Then, as if that weren't enough, he concluded by juggling entire blocks of overtones—as though the soprano had been transformed into a kind of atomic calliope and Parker were slamming out chords in its bass and treble registers. Before this Guy had taken a similarly astonishing solo, jamming drum mallets into his bass to produce a precisely controlled blizzard of effects. Then, in a trio performance, the group really coalesced—as Parker's initial tenor saxophone groan led to such a perfect response from Lytton's tuned cymbals and Guy's plucked bass that the three instrumentalists virtually became one during a quarter-hour's worth of free improvisation that was both absolutely lucid and furiously intense. "No ideas but in things," the poet William Carlos Williams famously wrote. If Evan Parker doesn't know that phrase, I'm sure he understands what Williams meant by it.

THE VANGUARD JAZZ ORCHESTRA
[1997]

As boldly as its title suggests, *Lickety Split: The Vanguard Jazz Orchestra Plays the Music of Jim McNeely* takes our notions of how a jazz big band can and should sound and shakes the living lickety out of them. In fact, the last time the orchestral language of jazz received such a welcome jolt may have been when the famed Miles Davis–Gil Evans album *Miles Ahead* was released—and that was way back in 1957.

The orchestral language of jazz, by the way, is not quite the same as the language of jazz as a whole. Or least it hasn't been since the mid-1940s, when the end of the Swing Era coincided with the rise of the angular music called bebop, which was made for virtuoso soloists and quicksilver small ensembles. The typical jazz big band is made up of three instrumental sections or choirs—trumpets, trombones, and reeds (commonly saxophones)—plus a rhythm section, with the number of players usually resting somewhere between fourteen and twenty. It's a setup that virtually dictates the sort of music such bands will make, one that's based on a communal, call-and-response interaction between the instrumental choirs and soloists and that builds those patterns of visceral excitement that are exemplified by terms like "flagwaver" and "shout chorus."

Of course, there's no law that says a jazz orchestra couldn't be an ensemble of any instrumentation and a certain size that plays a music that audiences agree to call "jazz." And some composers and arrangers (notably, Duke Ellington, Gil Evans, Billy Strayhorn, Tadd Dameron, Thad Jones, and Bob Brookmeyer) have wanted and managed to give us more than the standard jazz big band tends to offer—more colors, more gradations of volume, more density of texture and event, more room to build complex, long-form structures. It seems likely, though, that the style and makeup of the jazz big band will never cease to be linked to the kind of music that was played for dancing and listening in the thirties and forties by the bands of Benny Goodman, Count Basie, Artie Shaw, Ellington, Jimmie Lunceford, and others—in much the same way that, in the classical world, it's difficult to separate the concepts "symphony" and "orchestra." And this is where McNeely and friends come in, for the music on *Lickety Split* manages to extend the jazz big band tradition into remarkably adventurous directions while leaving its earthy communal roots intact.

Born in Chicago in 1949, McNeely attended Notre Dame High School in Niles and the University of Illinois and has worked as a pianist with the likes of Chet Baker, Stan Getz, Phil Woods, and the ensemble out of which the current Vanguard Orchestra evolved—the Thad Jones-Mel Lewis Orchestra, which was founded in 1965, became Mel Lewis and the Jazz Orchestra when cornetist-composer Jones left for Europe in 1979, and the Vanguard Orchestra when drummer Lewis died in 1990. (Jones died in 1986.) Made up of sixteen of New York's top freelancers, the band has remained remarkably stable—half of its current members, including the leaders of the trumpet, trombone, and reed sections, have been in place since the late 1970s. And this gives the Vanguard Orchestra the cohesiveness one might expect, plus an ability to bring off things that another band might not even attempt.

For example, on one of McNeely's pieces, "Mel"—a tribute to Lewis and a feature for the orchestra's current drummer, John Riley—there is a passage where, as the composer explains, "the band listens to Riley's four- and two-bar phrases and throws them back at him." Yes, that means that all the band's pitched instruments instantly echo the swift, skittering patterns that Riley has just improvised, giving them a melodic shape as well as a rhythmic one—a feat that is imaginable if only a single horn player were involved but one that becomes almost mind-boggling when thirteen instrumentalists must spontaneously arrive at the same musical conclusion. ("We have," says McNeely, "tried this before.")

If that passage seems a delightful stunt, rest assured that the Vanguard Orchestra has subtler, deeper effects at its command, ones that have evoked ideas of comparable subtlety and depth from the composer. The album's title piece, an up-tempo feature for baritone saxophonist Gary Smulyan, is described by McNeely as "the result of a 'What if?' proposition. What if the baritone saxophone player in James Brown's band started to OD on Woody Shaw, Sun Ra, and Witold Lutoslawski? And one night he lost it and went completely over the line." Clearly, McNeely is a man with a sense of humor, and this piece—with its half-cracked blend of R&B funk vamps, harmonically athletic brass section leaps, and exquisitely precise pointillistic textures— is at once very witty and a visionary transformation of the jazz big band tradition. While it swings like crazy and has moments of incendiary power, it's also an eight-minute-long evolving drama—one whose key moment comes after an orchestral explosion when, as McNeely puts it, "finally the baritone sax reemerges, in the way that the Apollo capsules used to reemerge from radio silence after coming around the dark side of the moon, much to mission control's relief."

A similar vein of humor runs through "Sticks," which evokes Ellington not only because the featured soloist, trombonist Ed Neumeister, has a very modern take on the "talking" plunger-muted style made famous by Ellington great Tricky Sam Nanton, but also because of its dark, shape-shifting moodiness. McNeely doesn't imitate Ellington, but he certainly knows his Duke backwards and forwards, from "Ko-Ko" to "The Mooche" to "The Mystery Song."

Most impressive of all, though, and as serious as a piece of music can get, is McNeely's "Absolution," which springs from at least two different realities: the days the young McNeely spent as an altar boy and all the years, both joyous and penitential, that he and the rest of the Vanguard Orchestra have been part of one big band or another. The featured soloist here is tenor saxophonist Rich Perry, and from the first his sound has a keening, prayerful edge to it—as though he were singing a song of woe both for himself and for unnamed others. And then the piece proceeds to name them, as an orchestral chorale is followed by what McNeely explicitly calls a "litany": a passage in which short solo statements from each horn player in the band alternate with orchestral "answers" until, the length of the solos shrinking bit by bit, the band essentially swallows its own members. It's a magical effect and a very moving one, too—as though all the trials and rewards of the big-band musician's life had taken shape right in front of us, only to be resolved into a deep communal peace. And perhaps that's the ultimate point that this lovely album has to make about the fate of the jazz orchestra— that such organizations will flourish as long as they manage to wrench communally into being a music that can be made in no other way.

PART V

Miles Davis

As the pieces that follow make clear, my feelings about Miles Davis (1926–1991) have shifted this way and that over time—largely in response to the shape-shifting aspect of Davis's music. Indeed, it would be safe to say that no jazz musician of note presented us with more different sorts of music than Davis did, though it certainly could be argued that at least one key element of Davis's personality, his will to change, remained remarkably consistent throughout his career, no matter how diverse, and at times artistically wayward, the musical results turned out to be.

MILESTONES
[1985]

I F any jazz musician deserves a full-scale biography, it is Miles Davis. A figure of major artistic importance for almost forty years, Davis also has become, in the words of fellow musician Chico Hamilton, "jazz's only superstar," a bona fide celebrity whose every move is news. And that side of Davis's career is not without meaning, both to Davis and to the public at large—a point reemphasized in 1981, when the trumpeter's emergence from five years of self-imposed retirement made waves that rippled through the world of jazz and even touched the shores of *Newsweek, Time* and *People* magazines.

But as with any celebrity who also happens to be an artist, the art is what matters most, even when the party under discussion is a figure as colorful and image-conscious as Davis is. And if the image and the art have become entangled, as they surely have in Davis's case, it is the biographer's task to separate the strands. But even though Canadian author Jack Chambers devotes more than 350,000 words to Davis's career in his *Milestones 1: The Music and Times of Miles Davis to 1960* and *Milestones 2: The Music and Times of Miles Davis Since 1960*, Chambers seldom makes contact with Davis's music—describing key performances in vague terms and refusing almost throughout to rise to the level of judgment. A particular Davis solo is said to be "bold." Another is "stunning." And when Chambers gets a bit more detailed, as in his account of "Boplicity" and "Moon Dreams" (two major recordings by Davis's late-1940s Birth of the Cool band), the results aren't very helpful. " 'Boplicity,' Chambers writes, "moves along through numerous shifts of texture as the various horns are rearranged into new alliances." And as for "Moon Dreams"—while it is "a brilliant display of inimitable talents," the piece "is a kind of musical still life, easy to admire but impossible to love." Almost meaningless in itself—why and compared to what is "Moon Dreams" "impossible to love"?—such stuff is even more annoying because the works that Chambers fails to discuss have been dealt with quite shrewdly by a number of other writers. But perhaps Chambers doesn't know genuine criticism when he sees it, for he makes little distinction between such tough-minded critics as Martin Williams and André Hodeir and the host of jazz journalists who embroider variations on "I like it" or "I don't."

Chambers's fondness for the hands-off approach is particularly worrisome because Davis's career, with its stylistic twists and turns, demands to be sorted out. But before one tries to do that, a few words about what Chambers's biography manages to accomplish. An almost day-by-day account of Davis's life, *Milestones 1* and *2* has its moments of tedium, as it delves into the many quarrels Davis has had with club owners, journalists, record company executives, and concert promoters. But Chambers does seem able to separate fact from gossip, and some of the facts are important. For instance, it is not widely known that Davis suffers from sickle-cell anemia. In his case, the side effects of this congenital disease became quite severe by the mid-1960s, leading to the deterioration of Davis's hip and wrist joints. Ever since, he has lived and played in near-constant pain. Significant, too, is the story of Davis's mid-1950s battle with heroin addiction—a period that ended when Davis kicked the habit by locking himself in a room and living through two weeks of withdrawal symptoms. But again, if a man is an artist, the art matters most—even when the life and the art are furiously intertwined.

Born in 1926 in Alton, Illinois (a satellite community of St. Louis, Missouri), Miles Dewey Davis III received his most important early lessons from trumpeter Elwood Buchanan. The models Buchanan urged upon the boy were a pair of pure-toned, graceful players, Bobby Hackett and Harold "Shorty" Baker, not the heated virtuosity of Louis Armstrong. "Play without any vibrato," Davis was told. "You're gonna get old anyway and start shaking." It was solid practical advice, and perhaps not too much should be made of it. But Buchanan's lessons may have led to the growth of two of Davis's key musical traits—his concern with sound for its own sake and his need to defeat the passage of time, his refusal to become boxed in to any way of playing that might be thought of as "old."

Davis certainly found himself in the midst of the new when he came to New York in 1944 and, within a short period of time, joined the quintet of alto saxophonist Charlie Parker—the most brilliant virtuoso of the music that had been dubbed bebop. But Davis's nascent style lacked the rhythmic and harmonic angularities of Parker and Dizzy Gillespie. And when his shaky technique improved, it became clear that Davis had been following a different path all along—one whose suave, symmetrical shapes were not that far removed from those of the better American popular songs. In fact, for all the harmonic and timbral subtleties of its arrangements (written by Gil Evans, Gerry Mulligan, and others), Davis's influential Birth of the Cool band amounted to a revamping of the pop song's aura of sophisticated romance—a way of deepening but not dispensing with prevailing notions of gracefulness and sentiment. That approach, it should be noted, was firmly linked to the world of the musical theater—a crucial point for Davis, because he was about to become the most overtly theatrical jazz artist of our time.

The theatrical side of Davis's music became more evident in 1955, when he formed his second great band—the quintet that included tenor saxophonist John Coltrane, pianist Red Garland, bassist Paul Chambers, and drummer Philly Joe Jones. The soloists were excellent, but much of the effect of the Davis quintet was built upon the dramatic contrast between, on the one hand, the leader's brooding romanticism and Garland's swinging sweetness and, on the other, the hard-edged intensity of Coltrane, Chambers, and Jones. Theatrical but still spontaneous, this approach solidified when Davis once more joined forces with arranger Gil Evans and produced three celebrated big-band albums: *Miles Ahead* (1957), *Porgy and Bess* (1958), and *Sketches of Spain* (1959–60). Here Davis became a kind of jazz Sarah Bernhardt, a "star" doing a turn in front of a mass of sumptuous scenery. And while one had to admire the results, as Davis played with exquisite taste and Evans supported him with timbral subtleties that rivaled those of Ravel, the music was very much a foreground/background affair.

Acknowledged by the late 1950s as jazz's key style-shaper, Davis now faced the first major challenge to that role, as Coltrane, Ornette Coleman, and Cecil Taylor began to move into the area that would be called "free jazz." Davis's initial response to this new and seemingly disruptive music was quite negative. "If you're talking psychologically," he said of Coleman, "the man is all screwed up inside." And as for Coleman's partner Don Cherry, whose style was a fragmented offshoot of Davis's own music, he was "not a trumpet player—it's just notes that come out." By the mid-1960s, though, Davis had formed a new band whose players (tenor saxophonist Wayne Shorter, pianist Herbie Hancock, bassist Ron Carter, and drummer Tony Williams) clearly had been affected by free-jazz styles. And in response, Davis himself began to change. Less lyrical, more fragmented, his solos at times even recalled those of Cherry, whose approach in many ways had been Davis-inspired from the first.

Especially in live performance, it now seemed that Davis's sidemen were shaping the flow of the music, leaving the leader to function as a kind of musical counterpuncher. No longer the dominant force even in his own band—"We [that is, Shorter, Hancock, Williams, and himself] had all decided on our groove before the band was formed," said Ron Carter—Davis seemed to have only two ways to go. He could continue to counterpunch, fragmenting his essential lyricism more and more. Or he could return to theatricality, abandoning the fierce interactions of the Shorter-Williams-Hancock-Carter band for the foreground/background setup of his collaborations with Evans. It was the latter course that Davis chose, in effect—at first brooding over a static backdrop of guitars and electronic keyboards on *In a Silent Way*, then adding more aggressive, rock-tinged percussion (*Bitches Brew* et al.). But always the format was that of a showcase, a kind of musical stage set that was intended to leave one in suspense about when, in what way, and if the "star" would emerge.

Since his return from retirement, Davis has followed much the same plan—fiddling here and there with the scenery (the backdrops now owe even more to the sounds of contemporary black pop music) and shunning contact with any soloist who might elbow him out of the spotlight. But even though Davis's charisma lingers on, the music no longer justifies it, as his self-cultivated image as an endlessly fruitful creator of new styles seems to have become more and more important to him. So it is the psychology of the fashion designer or the advertising man, not that of the artist, that shapes Davis's music these days. Per-

haps his career could have developed in no other way, for as
Paul Valéry once said: "It is impossible to impersonate, and at
the same time really to be, the dominant intellect."

MILES IN THE SKY
[1968]

MILES Davis has participated in one revolution in jazz and
witnessed another—which, verbally at least, he refuses to
acknowledge. When that second revolution was taking effect,
midway between Davis's 1956 quintet and his present group, it
seemed that he might be trapped in a pattern of self-imitation,
but, as this record and the recent *Miles Smiles* show, he has
triumphantly renewed himself.

Davis has always been a lyrical player with an affection for
the American popular song, and in many of his best solos (the
second *When Lights Are Low, All Blues*) he created a wonderful
tension by approaching and then withdrawing from the symmetry and sweetness of Gershwin and Richard Rodgers. In one
sense this way of playing can be called ironic; the soloist refers
to a mood of simplicity and romantic sentiment and places himself at an emotional distance from it. If that accurately describes
the Davis of '55–60, it is clear why he has been unable to accept
the essence of Coleman and Coltrane, for Coleman has never
found the popular song tradition to be relevant to his music,
while Coltrane, for all the beauty of his middle-period ballads,
finally abandoned it.

This record, one of the best that Davis has made with his
present group, shows the effect of the Coleman-Coltrane revolution even as Davis denies it, for their assault on the popular
song has pushed Davis along the only path that seems open to

him, an increasingly ironic detachment from sentiment and prettiness.

Throughout this album, Davis takes material from his earlier days and darkens its emotional tone. His opening phrase on *Country Boy* recalls a fragment from his "Summertime" solo on the *Porgy and Bess* album, but here it is delivered with a vehemence that rejects the poignancy of the earlier performance. Even on *Black Comedy*, his most straight-ahead solo here, the orderly pattern of the past is displaced and fragmented.

As Davis's playing becomes more oblique, he risks losing continuity altogether. That he doesn't is due, in large measure, to his wonderfully sympathetic group. Wayne Shorter's solos echo Davis's ironic temperament, and his tune "Paraphernalia" is a perfect example of the group's deadpan comedy. It begins with a rhythm section vamp that in the past would have led directly into the theme. Here it is presented as an object in itself, over which the horns play a gentle, seemingly unrelated melody. During the solos the rhythm section periodically rises in the sort of crescendo that McCoy Tyner and Elvin Jones employed to push Coltrane to new heights of ecstasy, but here it is followed abruptly by a return of the opening vamp. The effect is wry as the soloists ride over the crescendo, knowing that at its end the background will demand that their passion be chastened rather than released.

"Stuff" is the rhythm section's tour de force. It establishes a pattern that hints at rock, bossa nova, country and western, and even an occasional ballroom glide. Tony Williams plays a rock beat but spaces it out and diminishes its volume. Herbie Hancock does some beautiful work on electric piano, emphasizing its relationship to electric guitar and organ. Ron Carter either plays electric bass on this track or his technique on the conventional bass enables him to simulate the rumbles and slides of the electronic instrument. [The former is the case.] Over this pattern Davis and Shorter play a theme that hints at a number of the up-tempo conventions of the late fifties, but these phrases, slowed down to a walk, take on a strange grace, like a man running underwater.

On "Paraphernalia," George Benson's guitar is added, and he successfully captures the mood of the composition, subduing his bright, blues-based conception so he sounds almost like Jimmy Raney. "Country Boy" sums up the album's effect—an attempt by Davis to retain his style while pushing it to its limits. The track begins with Davis in full flight, but his first phrase (the echo of his "Summertime") sounds like the middle of something, not a beginning. He ends the track in similar fashion, letting a phrase that seems to demand a resolution stand by itself. It is as if Davis were saying, "I don't need new material. I only have to look at the old in a new way." This album indicates that, for himself at this time, he is absolutely right.

IN A SILENT WAY
[1969]

WITH the exception of *Miles Smiles* and *Miles in the Sky*, recent years have seen Miles Davis playing one kind of music on record and another kind in person. The majority of his recordings have been concerned with musical color and enforced spontaneity (as on *Kind of Blue*), and the results have been impressionistic and rather tentative. In person the group is something else altogether—an explosive band that tears into the music rather than feeling its way through it.

I prefer the in-person Miles, and I think there are objective reasons for that preference. Putting it simply, the frequency of significant musical events on this album and its stylistic predecessors (*Sorcerer, Nefertiti*, and *Filles de Kilimanjaro*) is rather low. When something does happen, it is almost always something good, but more good things happen during most in-person tunes by the quintet than on this whole album.

The new musical color this time is an intriguing rhythm section combination of electric piano and organ, but it seems as if half the album is taken up while this color is established and adjusted.

"Shh/Peaceful," which appears to have been spliced together from several takes, is the least successful performance. Davis's solo is a lukewarm elaboration of one of his favorite phrases, and there is a lengthy guitar solo that never quite emerges from the rhythm section's noodling.

Wayne Shorter's turn is brief but beautiful (the personnel listing has him on tenor, but he plays soprano saxophone throughout). He has a remarkable technical command of the instrument (this recording was reportedly the first time he ever played the soprano), and he reveals a touching, blue lyricism that rarely appears in his tenor playing.

The second side begins with Joe Zawinul's "In a Silent Way" (all the other lines are by Davis), and its hymnlike quality fits the electric piano-organ-guitar-bowed bass ensemble quite well. This segues into "It's About That Time," which finds Davis and Shorter in very good form over a striding rock rhythm.

If the performers of this music were merely good musicians the results would probably put anyone to sleep, but the skill and subtlety of the accompanists and the genius of Davis and Shorter make this album worth hearing.

THE LOST QUINTET

This is a review of Davis's so-called "lost" quintet, the band that took shape after Herbie Hancock, Ron Carter, and Tony Williams left and were replaced by Chick Corea, Dave Holland, and Jack DeJohnette. It's the "lost" quintet because, while it was electrifying in live performance, it appeared intact in the studio only twice, to record just a few pieces. Bootleg tapes of the band have circulated for years, and its July 1969 performance at the Antibes Jazz Festival has now been officially issued.

[1969]

OUTSIDE of Charlie Parker's best units, I don't think there's ever been a group so at ease at up tempos as Miles Davis's current quintet. Their relaxation at top speed enables them to move at will from the "hotness" up-tempo playing usually implies to a serene lyricism in the midst of turmoil.

This "inside-out" quality arises from the nature of human hearing, since, at a certain point, musical speed becomes slow motion or stillness (in the same way the eye reacts to a strobo-scope). Yet the group doesn't move into circular rhythms whole-sale. They generally stay right on the edge, and, when the rhythm does seem ready to spin endlessly like a Tibetan prayer wheel, one prodding note from Davis or Shorter is enough to send them hurtling into "our" time world, where speed means forward motion.

Recent changes in the group's personnel and instrumenta-tion have had important effects. Chick Corea is playing electric piano, and while this move may have been prompted by the variable nature of club pianos, Corea has made a virtue of ne-cessity, discovering many useful qualities in the instrument. In backing the horns, its ability to sustain notes and produce a wide range of sonorities frees Holland and DeJohnette from these roles. Corea is now the principal pattern maker in the rhythm section, a task to which Ron Carter and Tony Williams previously had given much attention. As a soloist, Corea has found a biting, nasal quality in the instrument that can be very propulsive. I heard a number of first sets, and each time it seemed that the rhythm section really got together for the night during Corea's solo on the first tune.

As mentioned above, Holland and DeJohnette don't often set

up the stop-and-go interludes of Carter and Williams. Instead, they burn straight ahead, creating a deep, luxurious groove for the soloists. Holland is as fast as anyone on the instrument, but it is the melodic and harmonic quality of his bass lines one remembers, as cohesive and austere as Lennie Tristano's. Shorter, in particular, responds to this kind of musical thought, because it so closely resembles his own. At times it seems as if he and Holland could improvise in unison if they wished. Tony Williams had a greater range of timbres and moods under control than DeJohnette does, but the latter is just right for this group. He sounds something like Elvin Jones with a lighter touch, and he really loves to swing in a bashing, exuberant manner.

Wayne Shorter's approach to improvisation, in which emotion is simultaneously expressed and "discussed" (i.e., spontaneously found motifs are worked out to their farthest implications with an eyes-open, conscious control), has a great appeal for me. The busyness and efficiency of a man at work can have an abstract beauty apart from the task. Of course, Shorter's playing has more overt emotional qualities of tenderness and passion which can give pleasure to the listener.

The problem with such an approach lies in keeping inspiration open and fresh, maintaining a balance between spontaneity and control. Here, Shorter's recent adoption of the soprano saxophone is interesting. A master craftsman of the tenor, he already has great technical control of the second instrument, and its newness seems to have opened areas of emotion for him on both horns. Often, while Davis solos, one can see Shorter hesitate between the soprano and tenor before deciding which to play. It's a fruitful kind of indecision. Shorter once referred to his soprano as "the baby," and I think I know what he meant.

About Davis there's not much new to say, except to note that he is to some degree responsible for every virtue of the group's members mentioned above, and that he uses all of them to achieve the effects he wants. He is the leader in the best sense of the term. Playing almost constantly at the limit of his great ability, he inspires the others by his example. There is no shucking in this band, and if Davis occasionally is less than serious in his improvising, as he was one night on "Milestones," mocking the symmetrical grace of his mid-fifties style, one soon realizes that he is serious after all.

With this version of the Miles Davis Quintet, one aspect of jazz has been brought to a degree of ripeness that has few parallels in the history of the music. Now let's hope that Davis and Columbia decide to record the group in person.

MILES RETURNS
[1981]

COULD it be that Miles Davis remained off the scene for all these years just so he could make a dramatic return to action? One might think so from the performance he gave last Friday night at the Auditorium Theater, which had as many crowd-rousing theatrical flourishes as a bullfight, along with some applause-begging effects that even Wayne Newton might have disdained, and, thank heavens, considerable proof that Davis is still a very gifted trumpeter.

To sketch in the background for all this hullabaloo, Davis, having made previous departures from playing and recording, virtually disappeared from view five years ago. The longer he remained silent, the more lurid the rumors became, helped along by news of an auto accident that reportedly left Davis a near-cripple for a time (he walks now with a noticeable limp). A number of fans began to think of him as a lost cause, while others, displeased with the fusion bands Davis led during the 1970s, assumed that even if he were to return, the results would be disappointing by his own highest standards.

Then the rumors turned positive. A new Davis album was

in the works. But when that album, *The Man With the Horn*, finally emerged, reactions were mixed. Davis came through strong and clear, but his mostly young band, which featured a blues-rock guitarist and a conga player, was no bargain. So one went to the Auditorium concert fundamentally unsure but hoping for the best. And what one got, above all, was theater.

Stalking the stage like a wounded panther while his rhythm section rumbled behind him (and, it seemed, fully aware of the suspense he was creating), Davis finally played his old "Put Your Little Right Foot Out" motif. More tightly muted trumpet blips followed, quickly cohering into Davis's dark, blues-drenched lyricism. A sudden switch to open horn, and, with a dramatic clarion blast, he brought the house down. "You see," Davis was telling us, "I still can play."

After a while one began to notice, perhaps more than ever before, what a traditionalist Davis is. Everything he plays comes down to the blues; and despite the electronic-funk trappings of his band, Davis's blues are always the jazz blues. Some of his phrases go right back to King Oliver, and during the second half of the concert he quoted from Lester Young's solo on "Taxi War Dance." But again there was that omnipresent theatricality—in Davis's physical posturings (which found him, at times, bent over until the bell of his horn almost touched the stage), and, more important, in his music as well.

The oblique, sketchlike nature of a typical Davis solo certainly has its structural and emotional meanings, which arise from his desire to make no unnecessary musical gesture. But there is a point at which implication can become coyness, as though one were expected to make no distinction between the scrawny "chic" of a high-fashion model and the gaunt intensity of a Giacometti sculpture. Less-is-more versus less-is-less— those are the twin poles of Davis's art. And Friday night, grateful that there was a good deal of the former, one was willing to accept some of the latter, including a version of "My Man's Gone Now" that began with heartbreaking poignancy and then died of a severe case of the cutes.

Harder to take, though, was the rest of the band, which

might not be a bad unit if the guitar player (Mike Stern) and the conga drummer (Mino Cinelu) were replaced. Stern's blues-rock licks were a raucous bore, and Cinelu merely seemed inept. Far better were electric bassist Marcus Miller and drummer Al Foster, who played with such urgency that it was hard to believe that they were the rhythm team on most of *The Man With the Horn.* As for the other solo voice, young reedman Bill Evans is a respectable soprano saxophonist who should grow under Davis's tutelage, though he has yet to learn the difference between being exciting and getting excited.

In typical Davis fashion, the concert was quite short—the first half lasting about thirty-five minutes, the second a little bit longer after a suddenly curtailed intermission. But relief, along with a fair amount of elation, was the final effect. Miles Davis is back; he can still do it all when he wants to; and there are signs, amidst the "superstar" turns, that he may want to do it more and more.

FILLES DE KILIMANJARO

These are the liner notes for a reissue of Davis's 1968 album *Filles de Kilimanjaro.*

[2002]

HEDGED about by constituencies, *Filles de Kilimanjaro* has come to be regarded as a place on the road from "this" to "that." Just ahead lies *In a Silent Way,* and from there it's a short trip to *Bitches Brew* and all the rest of Miles Davis's electric explorations. And in the rearview mirror one can make out the collected recordings of Davis's 1965–68 quintet—that brilliantly harried music whose patterns of fragmentation and fluidity are still a guidebook for today's jazz mainstream, if indeed jazz has a mainstream anymore.

So where you stand now, and where you stood then (if you happened to be around at the time), has a good deal to do with how you hear the music of *Filles*. To jazz traditionalists of several sorts (not to mention the jazz neo-cons of the Wyntonian era), *Filles* is a final cup of beauty laced with intimations of decay. To those who feel that jazz-rock or jazz fusion in general—and Davis's efforts there in particular—have yet to be properly understood, let alone given their due, *Filles* is an intriguing step in the right direction. To adherents of what by now might be called jazz's permanent avant-garde, *Filles* is a late-in-the-day bouquet—a gorgeous one, though a bit redolent of the hothouse. And for thousands of practicing musicians over the last thirty years it's been a key chapter in jazz's "how to do it" manual. But let's pretend for a moment that we know none of these things, for wherever *Filles* lies on whatever roadmap, it also is (counting the alternative take of "Tout de Suite") more than seventy minutes of remarkable music, made by seven remarkable musicians over the course of four days in the spring and fall of 1968.

"Except in his youth, this trumpeter was never merely a soloist," critic Max Harrison has said of Miles Davis, adding that Davis's "approach to the jazz ensemble lay near the heart of his creativity." In fact, the coming together of the Shorter-Hancock-Carter-Williams quintet might be compared to the key additions (bassist Jimmy Blanton and tenor saxophonist Ben Webster) that Duke Ellington made to his orchestra in 1939 and 1940, without which the music of "Ko-Ko," "Jack the Bear," and "Cotton Tail" might have been inconceivable. But the 1965–68 Davis quintet was not an orchestra, and not merely because of its size. Ellington's sidemen were, in effect, actors in a troupe headed by a wizardlike producer-playwright; and if Ellington asked almost every one of his sidemen to become a virtual co-creator at times, he was in charge and the play was the thing. But could the no-less-wizardlike Davis, who idolized Ellington, really be in charge, in a solo-driven quintet format, of players as volatile and virtuosic as Wayne Shorter and Tony Williams, let alone determine the shape of the things they were collectively making? In a club, on many nights, probably not—the music on the *Complete Live at the Plugged Nickel* boxed set certainly suggests that, as the sheer athleticism of Shorter and Williams and the former's infectious "fee-fi-fo-fum" quirkiness more or less wrests control of the music away from Davis, whose chops in any case were not then in good shape. But even though the trumpeter was back in fine form two and a half years later, when the first three tracks of *Filles* were recorded, it would seem that the group's musical psychodynamics were in an exceptional state of flux.

Although neither party is around to comment—not that it's likely they ever would have—the music of *Filles* suggests that Davis and Tony Williams were in each other's face and had been for some time. For one thing, just as the trumpeter was never merely a soloist, Williams was not merely a drummer. Rather, he also was a usually spontaneous orchestrator/composer, and any number of performances by the 1965–68 quintet ("Nefertiti" and "Black Comedy," for instance) were shaped and reshaped by this young percussion genius—although the sheer aggressiveness of his interventions is disguised by the fact that they almost always work. And yet there was, one suspects, something more at stake between Davis and Williams than the "this band ain't big enough for the both of us" issues that might be expected to arise. Listen, for example, to the interplay between trumpeter and drummer, and then between Shorter and Williams, on "Petits Machins" and the two takes of "Tout de Suite." At first, in terms of volume and polyrhythmic detail, Williams seems more aggressive alongside Shorter, but the byplay between them is just that—a brilliant, heady, almost puppyish joust in which both participants are always *there* but their identities are never really at stake. Not so, though, opposite Davis, where Williams often seems to be reading Miles's mind, even finishing the trumpeter's phrases before he gets a chance to play them. It is the drummer who shapes most of "Petits," and on the alternative take of "Tout," with its sibylline trumpet solo, the empathy between Williams and Davis is so complete, their taste for counterpunching foxiness so much of a piece, that a DNA test seems to be called for.

How stimulating and/or unnerving this might have been from Davis's point of view, we are not in a position to say. But beginning with the title track of *Filles* and continuing with the September 1968 date that gave us the album's last two pieces ("Mademoiselle Mabry" and "Frelon Brun," with Chick Corea and Dave Holland in place of the departed Hancock and Carter), it seems clear that the balance between background and foreground in Miles Davis's music shifts decisively. From the leader-determined lower-register hooks of "Filles" (played by Carter on electric bass) and "Mabry" (Corea on electric piano), to the ambient keyboards-and-guitar grooves of *In a Silent Way*, to the all-hands-on-deck textures of *Bitches Brew* and beyond, a common theme emerges, and perhaps it is *the* common theme: never again would another musician be allowed to interact with Miles Davis as an equal *individual*—not the way Tony Williams did.

And yet we have Davis on the master of "Tout de Suite," driving the band toward harmonic/rhythmic edges; the relaxed, shivery precision of Shorter on "Filles" and the alternative "Tout"; Williams's astonishing independence of limbs and beats behind Hancock on the "Tout" master; "Mabry" as a kind of "interval dictionary" made up of hints, winks, and shrugs; the four full, languid minutes it takes before we finally hear a solo voice on "Filles"; the way, as saxophonist/Davis aficionado Jim Sangrey points out, citing Gil Evans's role in the album, subtle "mini-motifs run throughout," while "bits of *all* the melodies and textures of every other piece emerge on the aptly titled 'Tout de Suite.'" Amazing musicians making marvelous music—on the way, to be sure, from this to that.

PART VI

Tristano-ites

The music of the men who gathered around pianist Lennie Tristano in the mid-1940s is usually regarded as crucial to the development of the jazz avant-garde because "Intuition" and "Digression"—recorded in 1949 by an ensemble that included saxophonists Lee Konitz and Warne Marsh and guitarist Billy Bauer—are reputed to be the first "free" (that is, totally improvised) jazz performances. But however challenging this haunting music was to create, the Tristano ensemble's free pieces finally sound very Tristano-like and would seem to have little or no organic connection with the music of Ornette Coleman, Albert Ayler, Cecil Taylor, et al. The deeper significance of the Tristano-ites lies in Tristano's transformation of jazz's historical self-consciousness into a rationale for making a new kind of music. The Tristano school was not just a gathering of like-minded talents but a school almost literally—one whose "curriculum" (solos by Louis Armstrong, Lester Young, Roy Eldridge, Charlie Parker, Charlie Christian, and a few other chosen masters were sung, memorized, and analyzed) traced a particular historical/critical line in order to give rise to a new one. That it did just that (Konitz and Marsh, while owing great debts to Tristano, also proved to be quite individual masters) suggests that historical self-consciousness in jazz had become both a fact and a potentially vital source of creativity.

LEE KONITZ
[1969]

A N electric spontaneity pervades this album [*Spirits*], and, on Lee Konitz's part, there seems at times a deliberate courting of risk—as though in jazz spontaneity had a meaning apart from the musical result. Perhaps for Konitz it does. The primal role the musicians associated with Lennie Tristano gave to improvisation has often appeared to be a kind of practical metaphysics (e.g., Konitz's remark in the liner notes to his *Motion* album that "I play because it's one of the few things that make sense to me"). This attitude can lead to music which is more a meditation on the fact of improvisation than the thing itself, but it can also produce an album like this—sometimes brilliant, sometimes, I think, unsuccessful, but always fascinating.

The five tracks with just Konitz and pianist Sal Mosca are quite different from the celebrated and, to me, rather bland duet between Konitz and Dick Katz on the album *Duets*. Mosca's playing is dense and aggressive and he makes few concessions to his partner. Partly because of this, and partly, I think, for reasons of his own, Konitz sounds deliberately antilyrical—as though, by fragmenting his once fluid line and throwing each burst of invention into relief, he wanted, above all, to surprise himself. Whether he did or not only Konitz can say, but he certainly surprises the listener and only rarely disappoints him. The disappointments occur when Konitz's invention falters and he must choose between remaining silent or filling the gap with something uninspired. As a result, these tracks are marked by awkward stops and starts and moments that, by Konitz's own high standards, are mere noodling. And yet there is no way, I think, to separate these flaws from the passages where Konitz is on form and he and Mosca are together. The same commitment to honesty and spontaneity—a refusal to resort to "filler" material—is at work in both cases.

The rhythmic nature of the duets, after the themes have been stated, might be called musical "prose"—a kind of recitative in which rhythm and tempo are freely varied but always present. Mosca's style is very close to Tristano's, but for me this is no drawback because the pianist is clearly responding to the material in front of him rather than to any influence. He has absorbed Tristano so completely that he is free to play like him when it's appropriate. As with Tristano, I find the rhythmic qualities of Mosca's playing the major point of interest—a strange union of asymmetrical phrases, and irregular accents within phrases, to a severely regular placement of each note right on top of the beat. (Compare the way Mosca—and Tristano—relate to the beat to the élan in this area of Earl Hines or Bud Powell, and I think you'll hear the difference.)

There are five Tristano pieces here—"Two Not One," "Wow," "Lennie-Bird," "Dreams," and "Baby." Each has that spontaneity one associates with Charlie Parker's best lines, and when they are played with the proper spirit, as they are here, they seem to have just been improvised. The four tracks with bass and drums, while not as unusual as the alto-piano duets, are very good, and "Lennie-Bird" is my choice as the album's single strongest performance. The only thing I regret is a rather aimless crash-bang quality in Mousie Alexander's drumming, especially compared to Kenny Clarke's sublime timekeeping on the original recorded performance of this piece. Alexander is energetic, however, and perhaps this is a case where a musician strikes his fellow players more favorably than he does the listener. In contrast with his playing on the duet tracks, Konitz is exquisitely lyrical through most of "Hugo's Head," his variation on "You Go to My Head."

[1981]

IN the music of Lee Konitz, silence plays a special role. Not just the rhythmically expressive silence of rests, although

Konitz, like Louis Armstrong and Charlie Parker, punctuates his lines with masterly skill, but the blank slate of nonmusic on which all sounds must be written. No matter how lyrical a Konitz solo may be and no matter how naturally it unfolds, one senses that, more than any jazz musician of comparable skill, he is often on the brink of surrendering to the impulse not to play—as though the blankness of the blank slate were so real to him that he "writes" upon it with some reluctance. And that gives his music a unique aura of honesty and strength, for what does emerge from Konitz's horn already has been subjected to tests more strenuous than those any listener is likely to apply.

What is interesting about this process, aside from the beauty and power of the music that results, is that the present-day Konitz evolved from a musician for whom self-consciousness seemed not to be an issue. The ethereal lyricism of Konitz's earliest recorded work, related though it was to Lester Young, was an essentially private affair that existed outside the mainstream of jazz history. And from that point of view, his career can be seen as one in which Konitz has tried to forge links between himself and what he saw as the central forces of jazz, without violating his personal vision. Thus the various attempts to "warm up" his music by recording with such players as Elvin Jones and Jack DeJohnette, thus the homages to Young, Parker, and Roy Eldridge that found Konitz playing some of their celebrated solos verbatim, and thus his current nonet, which often echoes the approach of the famous Miles Davis nonet in which Konitz played a prominent role. Yet all this wooing of jazz history, as necessary as it has been to Konitz's artistic well-being, also has its paradoxical side, for jazz has come to him in more ways than he has come to it.

If Konitz learned anything in the period he spent as an acolyte of the late Lennie Tristano, it was that jazz is improvisation, first and foremost. But it is, of course, much else besides— a cornucopia of timbral, harmonic, and rhythmic traditions that might be called the jazz language. And it was probably Konitz's growing awareness of that language and his desire to function within its traditions that led him to escape from Tristano's orbit.

But today, when the "language" aspect of jazz shows so many signs of stress, with revivalistic gestures becoming the norm even among supposedly "advanced" players, Konitz's ceaseless commitment to the act of improvisation is revealed to be a tradition in itself. And perhaps it is the most vital tradition remaining in jazz. Styles can be faked, and are being faked, left and right, while the truly improvised solo that does not depend on stylistic reference to make its points may be our one true link to the world of Armstrong, Young, and Parker.

There is much more to be said about Konitz's music, particularly about his lovely but often misunderstood sense of swing, which despite its relative obliqueness can be as intense as Lester Young's. But all these things become apparent as Konitz steps to center stage, decorating the blank slate with a great deal of genuine improvisation.

[1986]

WHILE jazz is supposed to be an improviser's art—"the sound of surprise," as critic Whitney Balliett once put it—not that many jazz musicians really improvise. Instead they work their way through familiar formulas and offer up their favorite licks, all of which can be satisfying at times. But then one encounters the music of alto saxophonist Lee Konitz and realizes how surprising genuine improvisation can be.

Performing through Sunday at the Jazz Showcase, Konitz began Friday night's first set with a tender but rather tentative version of "Star Eyes." A testing of motifs, his solo brought to mind an article Konitz recently wrote in which he described the ten levels of paraphrase a musician must pass through on his way from a song's original melody to a genuinely new variation upon it. So on "Star Eyes," Konitz seemed content to rest at level two or three, perhaps because that allowed his rhythm section to work its way into his conception of the music. And that proved to be a wise choice—not only because pianist Jodie Christian, bassist Steve Rodby, and drummer Wilbur Campbell began to interact with Konitz as though they could read his mind, but also because the next three tunes were sublime.

First came "Invitation," within which Konitz found a groove that is his alone—a kind of muttered-out gracefulness that seemed at first to be built upon the scattered rhythms of ordinary speech or the scuffling pace of a stroll down the street. But larger patterns soon began to take shape, and finally the whole solo stood revealed as a single unit, an event that had coalesced right in front of one's eyes. "Body and Soul" was next, taken at an unusual ambling tempo and marked by two Konitz choruses that started at about level eight and stayed right on that track. Here the lyricism was bold and openly songful; and with that to deal with, Konitz's partners rose to the challenge. Stirred by the ceaseless linearity of Konitz's playing, Christian offered up a blend of tenderness and strength that matched anything one had ever heard from this gifted player. Rodby found a similarly exalted groove, and Campbell stitched things together with accents of hair-trigger sensitivity.

Then, before a brief version of "The Theme," there was "Stella by Starlight," which had to be an example of Konitz at level ten. At once omnipresent and just out of reach, the melody of "Stella" gave birth to a seemingly endless string of variations, each of which was perfect in itself and each of which gave new meaning to what had come just before. Improvisation par excellence, this was group improvisation as well—for by this time the sharing of ideas was the norm, with each note and phrase being surrounded by so much space that the players seemed able to fully contemplate the music they made while remaining caught up in the act of producing it.

TRISTANO, KONITZ, MARSH

This essay was written for the Mosaic Records set *The Complete Atlantic Recordings of Lennie Tristano, Lee Konitz, and Warne Marsh.*

[1997]

RECORDED just past the middle of the twentieth century by pianist Lennie Tristano, alto saxophonist Lee Konitz, tenor saxophonist Warne Marsh, and friends, this remarkable music has a no less remarkable prehistory. And although the still vigorously creative sixty-nine-year-old Konitz is the only survivor of the three (Tristano died in 1978 at age fifty-nine, Marsh in 1987 at age sixty), there are signs that their music's already considerable but rather subterranean impact on the course of jazz is very much on the rise. Indeed, those of us who have known and loved these recordings for some time can only imagine how fresh they might sound, and how stimulating they might be, to the host of young musicians who are now in a position to hear them.

It will be the first and perhaps most important task of these notes to describe just what Tristano, Konitz, and Marsh were up to musically in the crucial decade or so before Lee and Lennie entered the Sing Song Room of the Confucius Restaurant in New York City on the evening of June 11, 1955, and proceeded to tape the twenty-one performances (three of them previously unissued) that lead off this set. Otherwise, the tensions and resolutions of this particular musical joust (and perhaps of all the music collected here) cannot be fully grasped. After all, while the evidence is less abundant than one might wish, it is clear that Tristano and Konitz had traveled a considerable distance from their earliest recordings (made in 1945 and 1947, respectively); that along the way their paths had diverged quite a bit;

and that the music they and Marsh would make for Atlantic is in part about the distance they traveled and the different paths they took. In a music so self-reflective in concept and deed, how could it have been otherwise?

But before we look back, I would ask the reader to stop right here and listen to two of this set's acknowledged Tristano masterpieces, "Line Up" from 1955 and "C Minor Complex" from 1960–61—the assumption being that afterwards one will know something crucial about this music that no amount of testimony or critical hectoring can replace, namely that Lennie Tristano was an improvising artist of great forcefulness, that the power of his music arises from (and to some extent is about) underlying principles striving to realize themselves, and that the various elements of this musical "complex" (the felt and expressed forcefulness; the sense that underlying principles are striving, or are being driven, to realize themselves) made it virtually inevitable that a school of some sort would coalesce around Tristano. This is not to deny that the pedagogic impulse lay deep within the man and the musician, nor to claim that his tutelage, in every case and at all times, furthered the artistic growth of those within his orbit. The point, instead, is that Tristano's music was compelling in itself, and that the reasons that two of jazz's major artists (Konitz and Marsh) and many other gifted musicians were drawn to and drew so much from Tristano are not necessarily more mysterious than the reasons such nonpedagogically inclined jazz masters as Louis Armstrong, Lester Young, and Charlie Parker spawned so many vital disciples. To paraphrase novelist Gilbert Sorrentino, people like to think that artists have complicated personal motives for doing what they do, when in fact they have complicated artistic motives.

Rhythm is the paramount issue in Tristano-related music, for a number of reasons. First, there is the immense sense of forward drive that Tristano's own improvising can create; second, there is the fact that Tristano's own playing (and perhaps even more so that of Warne Marsh) typically superimposes one or more different metrical patterns on the basic four-four pulse;

and third, there is the longstanding difficulty Tristano had with finding compatible rhythm sections in general and compatible drummers in particular. Asked about that last matter in the course of an unpublished 1973 interview with Terry Martin and John Litweiler, Marsh replied: "Lennie played in such a way that as much flexibility as possible in four-four was absolutely necessary. We had to be free to accent any way we liked. There was no 'two' and 'four' accent in the way Lennie conceived of playing. [With drummers] that was a constant problem. . . . I can get along with about the same drummers Lennie can: Jeff Morton, Kenny Clarke, those two."

Alongside this one should place bassist Bill Crow's account, in his book *From Birdland to Broadway*, of a mid-1950s jam session with Tristano and some of his students: "During [the] first tune, Lennie sat down pretty heavily on the time. He comped with dense block chords, and since he was playing a little behind the beat, I had to work hard to keep the tempo from slowing down. At the end of the first tune, I said, 'I couldn't seem to keep the tempo up where we started it.' Lennie shrugged, 'If it feels like it wants to slow down, I just go with it.' " So Tristano's music often possesses immense forward drive; it frequently has a polyrhythmic basis; and the latter quality is necessarily compatible with, and probably subservient to, the former when both are present—the outer limits being tested by the wonderful, multitracked, and perhaps subversively comic "Turkish Mambo" from 1955, with its shifts from seven-eight to seven-four, five-eight to five-four, and three-eight to four-four. We are also told what many recorded Tristano performances seem to bear out, that this living equilibrium between forward drive and polyrhythmically based accenting requires that there be no significant imposition of further rhythms on the soloist, particularly by the drummer. ("[Any] drummer that sets up counter-rhythms as part of his playing," says Marsh in the Martin-Litweiler interview, ". . . is imposing on a good horn player . . . limiting a good horn player.")

But that sort of restriction on rhythm-section activity is far from the norm in jazz, in virtually any period or style; and however much one might want to attribute Tristano and Marsh's sensitivity in this area to their sensitivity per se—that is, to their ability to hear and make rhythmic distinctions that other gifted jazz musicians do not—one need only think of Charlie Parker to realize that such a claim would be false. The answer, I think—as Bill Crow's anecdote and a good deal of other, more concrete evidence suggests—is that while rhythmic factors are indeed crucial to Tristano's music, sometimes they work within the Armstrong-Young-Parker norms of jazz rhythm with an exquisite, thrilling strictness, and sometimes they work otherwise—more loosely, one is tempted to say for the moment, as long as that does not imply a lack of attention to rhythmic detail on Tristano's part. In other words, there are at least two kinds of time at work in this music—or maybe that should be at least six kinds, because Tristano's sense of "strict" and "loose" time does not operate in quite the same way that Konitz's does, nor is either man's rhythmic manner quite the same as Marsh's.

In musician-historian Bill Kirchner's extensive notes for a never-released Tristano anthology he assembled for the Smithsonian Institution, he identifies certain flaws in the second earliest group of Tristano recordings we have, the solo piano versions of "Yesterdays," "What Is This Thing Called Love?," "Don't Blame Me," and "I Found a New Baby" that Tristano made in Chicago in mid-1946. And the same things could be said of the earliest Tristano recordings, the May 1945 date with trumpeter Marky Markowitz, trombonist Earl Swope, tenor saxophonist Emmett Carls, bassist Chubby Jackson, and drummer Don Lamond. Because Tristano "was still developing his harmonic vocabulary," Kirchner writes, "he overused certain harmonic devices that may have been 'far out' by the standards of mid-1940s jazz but that sound trite today"—and he singles out "a diminished arpeggio run that appears several times in 'Yesterdays' . . . and an over reliance on whole tone voicings and runs in 'Yesterdays' and especially 'What Is This Thing.'" Those diminished arpeggio and whole tone runs do sound dated harmonically, but in effect and perhaps in design they may be more rhythmic devices than harmonic ones—for as these runs "leap" or "skid" across the piece's underlying harmonic rhythm (that is, across the piece's prevailing rate and shape of chord change) they serve to generate arabesquelike, accelerating-decelerating rhythmic shapes, with the resulting melodic contours, at this early point in Tristano's career, being virtually dictated by the interaction between the arc of the harmonic "skid" and the arc of the rhythmic arabesque.

Art Tatum, a key Tristano influence, is one obvious reference point here. Another is the first recorded work of Lee Konitz: his solos on "Anthropology" and "Yardbird Suite" with the Claude Thornhill band (the fascinating charts are by Gil Evans), from, respectively, September 4 and December 15, 1947. Five weeks short of his twentieth birthday, when he made "Anthropology," Konitz had known Tristano for five years and "had somehow largely fashioned out of nowhere this amazingly original cool tone," as Terry Martin put it in his liner notes for *Intuition,* the album that includes the celebrated Tristano-Konitz-Marsh-Billy Bauer performances from 1949 ("Wow," "Crosscurrent," etc.). But if the alto saxophonist's tone and his ninety-degree-angle articulation was original (is it relevant that the first instrument the ten-year-old Konitz wanted to play was the accordion?), the rhythmic and melodic aspects of his solos on "Anthropology" and "Yardbird Suite" at once reveal Konitz's debt to Tristano and suggest that already he had begun to work along somewhat different lines. Melodically, Konitz's sixteen bars on "Anthropology," and, even more so, his twenty-four bars on "Yardbird Suite," are unmistakably Tristano-esque—the leaps toward harmonically oblique "target" notes on "Yardbird" might have come straight from Tristano's dazzling 1945 solo on "Blue Lou," although it's only to be expected that such essentially pianistic lines flow with much greater ease from the fingers of the virtuosic Tristano than they do from the horn of the young Konitz. But if, as noted above, Tristano's melodic shapes often seem to be the semiautomatic byproducts of his rhythmic-harmonic gestures, it's already clear that Konitz can and probably will treat virtually any sequence of notes as a nascent melody and attempt to divine its latent principles through an act of further extension. Or to put it another way, melodic material that Tristano has generated virtually secondhand will be treated by Konitz as though its angular oddities weren't secondhand at all, but a way to begin singing.

As for rhythm, the differences between Tristano and Konitz are already considerable. For Tristano, the relationship between strict and loose time is one of opposition or paradox. Tristano was far from the unemotional improviser he often was reputed to be, and when he "leaps" or "skids" across a piece's prevailing meter or harmonic rhythm, one feels that these moments are, from his point of view, both inspired and dangerous—for the ecstatic lift that takes him to and beyond the boundaries of comprehensible metrical subdivision also threatens his ability to reconnect with the four-four pulse and the prevailing harmonic rhythm, without which meaningful linear progress would be compromised. And while there is at least one Tristano solo—a 1950 nightclub performance of "Wow," from the album of the same name—where he accelerates to and maintains a tempo that is swifter than that of the rhythm section but cannot be parsed as double time, the threat to group and individual rhythmic cohesion is as obvious as the results are thrilling. Surely it's no accident, then, that Tristano's boldest loose-time adventure, a multitracked recording made in 1953, was titled "Descent Into the Maelstrom," and that by the time of these Atlantic performances he had chosen to follow the path of rhythmic strictness with, as critic Victor Schonfield once put it, "formidable exactitude."

For Konitz, however, strict and loose time do not necessarily stand in opposition to each other. If meaningful microsubdivisions of the beat come his way (and they often do), they will be welcomed and turned to advantage. But even though Warne Marsh said in the Martin-Litweiler interview that "Lee would like to have Art's [i.e., Art Pepper's] time," the music that Konitz actually makes doesn't seem to depend upon, let alone yearn for, an ability to manipulate the smallest functional rhythmic units—as Tristano's music certainly does. (By "smallest functional rhythmic units" I mean the smallest subdivisions of the beat that can be subjectively perceived as such and whose placement reinforces rather than disrupts forward movement. That Charlie Parker, forty-two years after his death, has never been surpassed in this realm, in jazz or perhaps in any other music, would seem to be a fact of some significance.)

The last of these three masters to link up was Marsh, who entered Tristano's orbit in October 1948. And if, in one sense, he never left, in another he was doing so by June 1949, when he recorded "Marshmallow" and "Fishin' Around" with Konitz, pianist Sal Mosca, bassist Arnold Fishkin, and drummer Denzil Best. If making meaningful micro-subdivisions of the beat was the goal, Marsh, at age twenty-one, was already at Tristano's level of achievement, while Parker's lay not that far ahead of him. But the partnership with Konitz, which takes place on a much more equal footing than it did on the March and May 1949 Capitol dates, reveals that at this stage in their careers, Konitz bears much the same relationship to Marsh that Tristano did to Konitz back in 1947. Then, as mentioned above, Tristano's rhythmic-harmonic gestures generated secondhand melodic shapes that Konitz proceeded to treat as though they were primary; in 1949, Konitz's by now almost uncanny, self-generated melodic flow and his lithe, ponylike tone give Marsh, the compulsive structuralist, just the sort of stimulus he needs to avoid melodic and timbral desiccation. (These were, for Marsh, virtually unavoidable problems—the former because his structuralist need to discard the nonessential could, under pressure, leave the cupboard close to bare; the latter because his fierce rhythmic acuity depended in part, as critic Don Heckman has explained, on Marsh's using his mouth, more than the instrument itself, "as an extension of the [tenor saxophone] mouthpiece's resonating chamber," which thus drastically lessened the instrument's timbral aura at times.)

One more piece of information now, before we move on to 1955 and enter the Sing Song Room. Between the 1949 Capitol date and 1955, both Tristano and Marsh made few recordings, and even fewer of those were issued at the time. But Konitz, who joined the Stan Kenton band in August 1952 and remained for more than a year as a featured soloist before forming his own quartet, had become one of the period's most prolifically recorded and influential artists. That Tristano came to regard Konitz as something of an apostate and that the breach between them eventually would became irreparable is perhaps no surprise; against that, though, one should place the fact that, musically, the dialogue between those men, and between Konitz and Marsh, has yet to cease.

"What one hears in these performances again and again," wrote Barry Ulanov, when the second batch of Sing Song Room tapes was issued in 1981, "is mutuality of feeling and closeness of thought." Well, eight of them are first-rate, but one also hears some heavy lifting here and some moments of less than mutual feeling between Konitz the soloist and Tristano the block-chordal accompanist. If one goes in search of the principles that separate the more successful tracks from the less successful ones, perhaps it would help to bear in mind that this was just one night's worth of music making and that, like most such nights, it had its ebb and flow. Of the eight tracks that seem first-rate to me—"If I Had You," "These Foolish Things," "You Go to My Head," "All the Things You Are," "Lennie-Bird," "Pennies in Minor," "A Ghost of a Chance," and the originally issued "Donna Lee"—one notes a clustering toward the middle of the evening (three tracks from set two, two of them in a row, followed by the first track of set three), which is a pattern that many club-goers will recognize. Also, Tristano probably did more than look over producer Nesuhi Ertegun's shoulder when the time came to choose which pieces to issue the first time around, because all five of them are gems—especially "You Go to My Head," with Konitz taking leave of his solo with an almost literal caress and Tristano's line coiling like an anaconda, and "A Ghost of a Chance," which Tristano dissects with a grave, Handelian eloquence.

What we will call, for the sake of convenience, the "Line Up"–"Requiem"–"C Minor Complex" sessions can profitably be considered together, for even though the earliest and the latest of these performances are separated by at least five years, one has the feeling that this and similar material was being worked over by Tristano on a near-constant basis. The best of it—the three aforementioned works, plus, I feel, "Becoming" and "Turkish Mambo"—is the summit of Tristano's art, and it is eloquently described and discussed in Barry Ulanov's original album notes. The process whereby Tristano speeded up the tapes of his piano playing on "Line Up" and "East Thirty-Second" to match the prerecorded (and also fiddled with) bass and drum work of Peter Ind and Jeff Morton inspired a fair amount of controversy at the time, and while it died away when "C Minor Complex" made clear again what ought to have been obvious from the first—that Tristano could execute at the speed of "Line Up" and "East Thirty-Second" without electronic assistance— perhaps his justification for what he did ("the result sounded good to me") ought be taken literally. That is, by recording bass-register piano lines and speeding up the tapes until the pitch of the piano lines was raised one octave, Tristano not only made the lines move faster, but he also made a new sound. The lower in register a note on the piano is, the more slowly it "speaks" and the less rapidly it decays. By forcing that effect upwards, Tristano altered the attack-decay relationship of each note— adding a tremendously propulsive, Chu Berry–like buzz or whoosh to tones that couldn't possibly have had that effect, that sound, if they actually had been played in the piano's middle register. (That Tristano, in an alternate universe, could have been one of jazz's great tenor saxophonists is a thought that more than a few people must have entertained, perhaps even Tristano himself. But, then, that probably is just another way of saying "Warne Marsh.")

Bach's name is often invoked when speaking of these performances, and Ulanov twice cites the *Chromatic Fantasy and Fugue in D Minor*. In fact, specific Bach works that sound much like Tristano are few and far between, although the ones that do—variation eleven of *The Goldberg Variations,* and number four and number ten of the *Two Part Inventions*—tell an interesting tale. In those pieces one hears with special force (though, of course, with less rhythmic heat) the trait that is so dominant in "Line Up" and "C Minor Complex"—"the use of generic motive from which everything flows and takes its shape," as Charles Rosen described it in his essay "Bach and Handel" in the book *Keyboard Music*. In fact, so much that Rosen has to say about Bach also applies to the Tristano of these performances that one must continue to quote: "It is remarkable how often Bach tries to hide [the successive entrances of a fugal theme] by tying the opening to the last note of the previous phrase, how much ingenuity he has expended . . . in keeping all aspects of the flowing movement constant. Some of the most important forces in the development—the actual movement through time—of a work by Bach are latent in its material without being audible until the moment he chose to make them so. . . . Bach's fugue themes provide their own bass, and they very often provide perfectly worked-out inner voices as well. . . . In other words, the individual voices work within a larger system of harmonic movement which transcends their integrity; and, in addition, this integrity is broken down from within by the same system. Yet the ideal of contrapuntal purity in the *Inventions* does not thereby lose its power. It gains instead a pathos—an unattainable goal that is kept alive by the pretense of achieving it."

To those of us who were around at the time, *Lee Konitz Inside Hi-Fi* was our introduction to Konitz on tenor, and his comments in the original liner notes on how his enjoyment of the new instrument might, if he played it for a while, lead him to "enjoy it too much . . . [because then] I think a lot of the neurotic relationship I have with my alto would start coming out on the tenor" instantly bring to life the man's unique, self-healing sense of humor. One might compare the role the tenor plays for Konitz to the role those speeded-up piano lines played for Tristano on "Line Up"; the effect is less dramatic, because in Konitz's hands the tenor saxophone sounds more like a tenor saxophone than the piano on "Line Up" sounds like a piano, but it's fascinating to hear the altoish core of Konitz's conception wrapped in a warmer, fuzzier, and thus more rhythmically compulsive package. In fact, one wonders whether the kick of playing tenor on the first date and the thought that he might pick it up again on "Kary's Trance" had some effect on the October 16 session, because Konitz's alto solos on "Kary's Trance" and "Cork 'n' Bib" are some of his most loosely swinging work on record.

Next we have *The Real Lee Konitz*, which, granting that Tristano's "Line Up"–"C Minor Complex" material exists in a separate realm, shares the top spot with the 1956 Konitz/Marsh album. In one sense, it's just the best work of a working band over the course of a week in a Pittsburgh club; in another, it preserves one of jazz's great but relatively little-known musical partnerships, that between Konitz and Peter Ind. The English-born bassist, a dedicated Tristano-ite, in a way absorbed the master's lessons as well as anyone, perhaps because his instrument was particularly suited to bearing the full import of Tristano's methods of harmonic-motivic propulsion. While direct influence might not have been involved, one feels that the springiness of Ind's time is akin to Oscar Pettiford's; there's the same basic centeredness with which "one" is placed, the same useful looseness with which the beat can then be attacked from either side. What security the bassist gives to Konitz on "Pennies in Minor," and what a strong, noble solo he takes on "Foolin' Myself"— which leads to an Ind-Konitz "conversation" (it's not quite public enough to be called a duet) that is one of jazz's unacknowledged and most touchingly humane masterworks.

It's hard to believe that the soaring Lee Konitz of June 15, 1955, when he and Marsh are backed by three of the most compatible rhythm section mates imaginable (Billy Bauer, Oscar Pettiford, and Kenny Clarke), is the same man who, on June 11, often had to fight to get airborne with Tristano's quartet at the Sing Song Room. Critic Alun Morgan has noted "the tremendous lift of Billy Bauer's chords," while the relaxed intensity that made the Pettiford-Clarke team one of the joys of jazz in the mid-1950s supplies Konitz and Marsh with an ideal rhythmic foundation. In fact, this classic date may be the best place to draw some further comparisons between these two great soloists—for while both Konitz and Marsh had by now reached a high level of musical maturity, the time when each man could be himself and blend wholeheartedly with the other was, oddly enough, almost at an end.

If Marsh is, as mentioned above, a compulsive structuralist, and Konitz is a compulsive melodist, the consequences are vividly evident here, against Bauer, Clarke, and Pettiford's dark, pulsating backdrop. One doesn't want to sound mystical about this, but Marsh proceeds as though silence were a kind of space, a blank, neutral medium—almost a void—that comes to life only when (and because) his lines, his living thoughts, adventurously stretch across it. For Konitz, though, silence is alive, a creature or being—each note he plays almost literally touches its flanks, and the resulting dialogue of message-bearing pressures will increasingly become one of his chief sources of inspiration. Thus, in 1961, Konitz would seek out and successfully record with the most aggressive drummer in jazz at the time, Elvin Jones, while in December 1957, Marsh will almost come to grief in the company of Paul Chambers and Philly Joe Jones.

Describing the partnership between Chambers and Jones in the liner notes to Hank Mobley's *Poppin'*, which was recorded less than two months before the first of the two dates that make up the Atlantic Marsh album, I wrote that the drummer and bassist "shared a unique concept of where 'one' is—just a hair behind the beat but rigidly so, with the result that the time has a stiff-legged, compulsive quality. The beat doesn't flow but jerks forward in a series of spasmodic leaps, creating a climate of nervous intensity that was peculiar to the era. Either the soloist jumps or he is fried to a crisp on the spot." Well, Marsh did survive the encounter, and he is a bit more at ease on the next date, in January 1958, when Paul Motian takes the place of Jones and pianist Ronnie Ball drops out. For even though Chambers's broad rhythmic impasto, so full of directional energy, still threatens to ride right over the nodes of rhythmic ambivalence that Warne must leave exposed, the absence of a chordal instrument makes just that much more space available to the soloist, who is especially fluent on "Yardbird Suite." One wonders, though, what this album would have been like if Pettiford and Clarke had been present.

If Marsh's career had ended with this date, he still would be regarded as one of jazz's great soloists, although one wonders how many people actually would have arrived at that conclusion. Tristano, Konitz, and colleagues already had, of course, and England's Alun Morgan was the first critic to give Marsh his due in a passionate, convincingly detailed *Jazz Monthly* appreciation in 1961. Then, in the mid-1960s, while Marsh himself remained virtually invisible as far as the jazz public was concerned, the stature and continuing relevance of his music received a ringing endorsement from a perhaps unlikely source, Wayne Shorter—the echoes of Marsh in Shorter's playing of this period (notably on Tony Williams's album *Spring* and on the Miles Davis Quintet's *Live at the Plugged Nickel* recordings) being evident to anyone who knew the older man's work. As it happened, though, beginning in the mid-1970s and continuing until his death, Marsh would go on to enjoy a kind of belated musical high summer—one that brings to mind the riches that another ceaselessly inventive jazz improviser, Earl Hines, managed to give us in the last decade and a half of his life. One wouldn't want to say that the best of the many recordings that Marsh made in this period—*All Music* (Nessa) and a number of his albums for the Criss Cross label—give us a more mature Warne Marsh. Once he got his feet under him in 1949, Marsh was capable of functioning at a very high level, provided the external and internal circumstances were just right. What happened, though, it seems, is that there was a little more "give" in several directions—as more rhythm sections were able to give Marsh the kind of support he needed (and record producers put him together with those players), while Marsh himself began to feel more comfortable outside the circle of Tristano-schooled accompanists. And it may be that in this period Marsh also realized that his art was as public as it needed to be—that for many others, as well as for himself, the meditative, inward strain in his music was not a sign of any withdrawal from emotion, but rather of his engagement, on the run, with an often thrilling lucidity.

PART VII

The Neo-Con Game

Most of these pieces revolve around the advent in 1980 of trum-peter/composer Wynton Marsalis and the several sorts of jazz neo-conservatism or revivalism that he and his associates began to pro-pose—first a return to a kind of classicized version of the Miles Davis Quintet of the mid-1960s, then a series of visits to chosen styles of the jazz past (New Orleans polyphony, thirties and forties Ellington, etc.). Such impulses have surfaced in jazz before, at least as far back as the late 1930s (the so-called New Orleans Revival that centered around Lu Watters and his Yerba Buena Jazz Band), and it should not be forgotten that three years prior to Marsalis's arrival on the scene, the similarly young and similarly revivalistic tenor saxophonist Scott Hamilton made his first recording. What was different about what might be called the Wyntonian Era, though, is that never before had a return to selected aspects of the jazz past been presented—and, to a remarkable degree, accepted—as an event of central aesthetic importance. That it was not such an event is the conclusion these pieces eventually reach, but that it could be regarded as one at all is significant—not quite a sign that jazz was dead or dying (although that was one thought that came to mind at the time), but evidence that the weight of the music's past, relative to its present and to its possible futures, was some-thing that jazz was grappling with as never before. A cut-and-paste, mix-and-match attitude toward the jazz past has been one result,

and that theme surfaces in the first of these pieces, "Jazz in the
Global Village," even though it deals with the nature and vicissitudes of non-American jazz and was written in 1969, when Marsalis
was eight years old.

JAZZ IN THE GLOBAL VILLAGE
[1969]

IF for no other reason than economics, the importance of non-
American jazz is likely to increase in years to come. I imagine
that for most of us the subject calls to mind one great musician
(Django Reinhardt), a number of good ones, and such slogans
as "European drummers don't swing." But what is the actual
state of jazz outside this country? Do non-American jazzmen
face different problems than their U.S. counterparts, and will
they eventually create a significantly different form of music? In
an attempt to answer these questions, I have listened to most of
the non-American jazz albums *Down Beat* has received over the
past several years (because, in general, we only review recordings that are readily available in the U.S., there was a backlog
of forty-two albums featuring musicians from England, France,
Germany, Spain, Italy, Holland, Sweden, Denmark, Norway,
Czechoslovakia, Yugoslavia, Switzerland, Brazil, Martinique,
Canada [Quebec], Belgium, India, Japan, and Indonesia). The
sample was a random one, but I think it outlined the basic situation. Many American musicians have directly carried their
message to other lands, but, on the whole, foreign jazzmen get
their information from recordings. And they get it quickly, too.
I remember my surprise when I saw the 1962 Polish film *Knife
in the Water*, directed by Roman Polanski, which had a score by
Krzysztof Komeda that precisely emulated John Coltrane's mu-

sic of the time. The gap between creation and imitation couldn't have been more than a few months. After my surprise had faded, I began to think about the musicians involved. That tenorman (Sweden's Bernt Rosengren, born in 1937) had Coltrane's current manner down pat, but where, I wondered, would he go from there? It might seem that the possibilities open to him and a talented American tenorman of the time who had listened to a lot of Coltrane—say, Joe Henderson (also born in 1937)—were similar, that their future achievements would be determined only by the degree of skill and imagination each man possessed. But it isn't that way at all, and the reasons why it isn't affect all non-American jazz.

In a sense, every work of art can be viewed as a solution to an artistic problem. Each solution bears a relation to prior solutions, and as the solutions accumulate the problem alters. For example, it is difficult to imagine Coltrane playing the way he did in 1962 if Charlie Parker, Dexter Gordon, and Don Byas had not played the way they did in 1947—and so on back to, at least, Louis Armstrong and Sidney Bechet. And Coltrane's development from 1962 on was dictated not only by his personal demon but also by a chain of linked solutions in his own music and in jazz as a whole. It is likely that our Swedish tenorman and his non-American colleagues, especially if they are young, will be familiar with only a part of that chain—less of it, probably, than their American counterparts. Thus, they can wait for the next word from the U.S., draw on some chain of artistic solutions native to their environment, or try to develop what they already have *ab ovo*. More often than not, what happens is a mixture of those approaches, but the last approach is crucial. The non-American jazzman who tries to build his music from a chosen point in American jazz is trying, consciously or not, to make one position in a chain of forms into the beginning of a new chain. The history of art contains numerous examples of such efforts (they are especially common, even unavoidable, in a colony/ mother country situation), and from these one can see that certain dangers and possibilities are involved, one that the non-American jazzman cannot avoid.

Stylistic incongruity is the most obvious pitfall—it is a rare performance in this sample that does not contain some stylistic clash in melody, harmony, or rhythm. For example, the Norwegian pianist Einar Iversen on his album *Me and My Piano* (Nordisc) chooses to interpret John Coltrane's "Spiral." But because Iversen's own style is heavily indebted to Teddy Wilson, the contrast of conceptions between Coltrane's "Giant Steps"–era theme and Iverson's Swing Era–style improvisation is rather bizarre. In a few cases, however, such incongruity can be mildly effective. The German saxophonist Hans Koller takes his inspiration from Lee Konitz on *Relax with My Horns* (Saba), but he delivers Konitz's sound and melodies with a bouncy optimism that is worlds away from Konitz's introspective manner. The result sounds rather like Cannonball Adderley playing Konitz licks, but, because Koller is a skilled executant, the music has a novelty's charm.

Fortunate accidents like Koller seem to be the exception, though. More common is the case of Danish tenorman Bent Jaedig on *Bent Jaedig* (Debut). His decent efforts at post-bop playing are marred by gawky, rhythmically corny phrases that could have come right out of the Stump Evans Songbook. Because Jaedig swings well enough at other times, it seems likely that in his case, and in those of many other non-American jazzmen, the frequent rhythmic lapses are not so much the result of lack of skill as they are of gaps in background—that is, they don't know from experience that certain kinds of time feeling don't go with (or even exclude) the use of other kinds. For example, the Italian pianist-composer Giorgio Gaslini leads an allegedly avant-garde big band on *Grido* (Durium), and though Gaslini's themes do have a passing resemblance to those of Thelonious Monk, the time feeling of the rhythm section and soloists is so stolid that the results verge on comedy.

Stylistic incongruity is, perhaps, a surface problem that can be mended by actual playing experience with good American jazzmen, but there is another, deeper problem—the non-American musician's choice of the position he wishes to develop. He may be attracted to an aspect of jazz that had little value to

begin with, or he may attempt to develop a position whose possibilities have already been exhausted. Listening to albums by
the French big band led by Jean-Claude Naude (Telerecord), the
Czech orchestra of Gustav Brom (Saba), and various Yugoslav
radio bands (Helidon), one can see the first of these dangers at
work. The execution varies from poor to adequate, but it hardly
matters, since these bands are working within a style—the neo-
Basie-Lunceford sound of the typical New York mid-fifties studio band—that was never more than a blurred carbon of an
originally vital music. The work of Belgian arranger-composer
Francy Boland is proof enough that the conservative big-band
style is still full of life, but in order to find it one must return to
the roots—you can't get there from Manny Albam and Billy
Byers.

I imagine that the music of Naude, Brom, et al. is rather
harmless, for it is doubtful that men who are occupied in making models of inferior copies could ever be capable of anything
more than that. But the other trend (the attempted development
of positions whose possibilities have been exhausted) is more
ominous—especially so since the majority of young non-
American jazzmen seem to be involved in such efforts. I have in
mind, in particular, the music of John Coltrane and Scott La-
Faro. Listening to this sample of recordings, it is apparent that
their influence abroad has been even more widespread than in
this country, and while I value the achievements of Coltrane and
LaFaro, I think their musical approaches may be poor choices
for future elaboration. From the course of Coltrane's American
disciples and from the path he himself traveled until his death,
it now seems clear that Coltrane's music was the end of one line
of development in jazz rather than a beginning, and that the
saxophonists who offer the richest possibilities for the future are
Sonny Rollins and Ornette Coleman. If a musician like Pharoah
Sanders has found that adherence to Coltrane's premises leads
to a neo-religious version of tavern tenor playing, one wonders
whether such would-be Coltranes as Norway's Jan Garbarek,
Denmark's Carsten Meinert, and literally thousands of other foreign disciples can come up with something better.

Indeed, it seems a minor tragedy that the sounds of revolt and frustration that Coltrane produced as he strove for specific musical freedoms have been seized upon, here and abroad, as the essence of his music. Interestingly, the most skilled and imaginative Coltrane-influenced reedman in this sample is Frenchman Barney Wilen, who was at one time a Lester Young disciple and then a gifted Rollins-influenced player. Wilen contributes some very good soprano and tenor work to *Jazz Meets India* (Saba), and one suspects that, in addition to his native talent, his achievements stem from the fact that he has *lived* more than one kind of jazz.

In the case of LaFaro, the problem is that his rhapsodic lyricism and slippery time conception grew in response to the special musical context of the Bill Evans Trio. LaFaro himself seemed to understand that his style needed to be modified if it were to fit other musical situations, for he played in quite a different manner rhythmically when he recorded with Ornette Coleman on *Ornette!* (Atlantic). But LaFaro's legion of disciples, especially the non-American ones, have largely missed the significance of that event, and from Sweden to Japan they ripple along in endless cadenzas no matter what the context. While the best of them (in this sample, Englishman Jeff Clyne stands out) are gifted melodists, they cripple their rhythm sections by failing to add much rhythmic impulse to the music. I don't mean that Paul Chambers and four/four swing is the only answer, but jazz without some essential rhythmic meaning seems a dubious endeavor—a kind of hip mood music. Such rhythmically powerful bass players as Wilbur Ware, Henry Grimes, Ron Carter, and Malachi Favors, who are as free as one could wish, offer alternative and more fruitful directions for the modern rhythm section. It remains to be seen whether their music, and that of Rollins and Coleman, will make significant inroads among non-American players.

So far, the picture I have presented is rather bleak, but the kind of situation in which the non-American jazzman finds himself does have its positive possibilities. The first of these might be described as creative revivalism—the attempt to present valuable aspects of the jazz past with careful authenticity. The American revivalist movement of the forties got bogged down in sentimental primitivism, and its present-day practitioners are, more often than not, playing a college-boy Dixieland even when the tune is "Grandpa's Spells." In Europe, however, the revivalist bands generally have a broader range and are of higher quality, perhaps as a result of the tradition of jazz connoisseurship among European musicians and fans. The best of these bands, such as Papa Bue's Viking Jazzband, from Denmark, have expanded the revivalist repertoire to include such forgotten gems as Duke Ellington's "Doin' the Voom Voom," and they know that revivalism does not absolve one from musicianship.

Beyond the modest craft of revivalism, there is the possibility of working within relatively conservative positions which were largely abandoned by U.S. jazzmen before all the implications had been worked out. The Yugoslavian trumpeter Dusko Gojkovic, for example, sounds a good deal like Miles Davis of the mid-fifties on "I Remember O.P." from Bent Jaedig's album, but because he really inhabits that style, his solo is of real merit. England, in particular, abounds with musicians who are producing individual music within basically conservative swing and post-bop frameworks—for example, trumpeters Jimmy Deuchar and Ian Carr, clarinetist Sandy Brown, and reedmen Bruce Turner, Ronnie Scott, and Tubby Hayes. Among the most interesting musicians in this area is Francy Boland, the co-leader of the Clarke-Boland band, whose arrangements are a real extension of the orthodox big-band tradition. His album *Out of the Background* (Saba), which features only the band's rhythm section, is a fascinating example of "arranger's piano"—a compulsively riff-driven performance such as "Dark Eyes" is a virtual blueprint for an excellent full-band setting of the piece. Perhaps the drive within jazz for constant change can be lessened or suspended in other lands, allowing honest and knowledgeable conservatives like Boland to flourish in a way that seems impossible in this country.

The final and most exciting possibility open to the non-American jazzman is true mutation—the hope that a meeting of non-American and American musical strains will yield a sturdy offspring that is significantly different from either parent. But the chances for such an event seem rather slim, for true artistic mutations require special sets of circumstances and are about as rare as biological ones. Looking at one artistic mutation that is close to home—the meeting between African and European-American ways of making music that eventually produced jazz—one can see that genuine mutation requires, among other things, that the parent strains be sufficiently different in kind for each to discover something novel and attractive in the other. But the comprehensiveness of modern communications would seem to lessen that possibility quite a bit—for there is hardly an art or folk music anywhere in the world that has not been homogenized by contact with other musics. And, without real differences in kind among musics, we get travelogue-like blending rather than true mutation.

I doubt whether jazzmen will find procedures in European art music, for example, that have not already been applied within jazz. In this sample there are several attempts to mix the two musics, and, with one exception, they are dismal failures that preserve neither music's virtues. The exception, English pianist-composer Michael Garrick's *Jazz Praises* (Airborne), is an attempt to blend a gentle post-bop idiom with the English religious-choral tradition, and it succeeds mainly because of Garrick's taste and modesty. He says that "the intention is not simply to gee-up religious music, or, belatedly, to make jazz respectable; it is, on the contrary, to draw straightforwardly on the natural resources of all participants so that there may be some emotional and musical gain." As pleasing as the results are, one doubts whether this direction will yield anything more than a few similarly modest successes.

Others have gone to non-European musics in search of a suitable mate. The principal marriage broker, German critic Joachim Berendt, has produced a series of recordings that bring jazzmen into contact with the native musics of Spain, Brazil, India, Japan, and Indonesia. And while genuine mutation does not occur, the blendings are often attractive. The Brazilian album, *Poema on Guitar* (Saba), which features guitarist Baden Powell, is charming, but it is hardly even a blending, for the bossa nova is a fully formed music that incorporated jazz elements from its beginning. The Indonesian album, *Djanger Bali* (Saba), features an exciting, eclectic pianist in Bubi Chen and a swinging drummer in Benny Mustafa, but the musicians have assimilated American forms so thoroughly that the borrowing from native sources is merely decorative.

And yet, there is Dutch reedman William Breuker. His playing on two albums by German vibraphonist Gunter Hampel—*The 8th of July 1969* (Birth) and *Wergo Jazz* (Wergo)—suggest that a true mutation may be occurring between the best of the American avant-garde and a European sensibility. Breuker is a rhythmically powerful improviser—quite different in this respect from most other European avant-gardists, who apparently feel that the end of four/four swing releases them from any rhythmic obligation. His music seems to portray the struggle of a human personality trying to assert itself within a machinelike urban environment, and it is this quality that strikes one as peculiarly European. Even though one hears echoes of Rollins, Ayler, and Coltrane in his playing, Breuker is using these influences to make his own music in a way no other non-American jazzman, to my knowledge, has done. This is not to say that he is a European Louis Armstrong, but the intelligence and vitality of his music and its real difference from its American sources are encouraging signs. Let us hope that Breuker is the first of a host of similar creators, and let us also hope that the jazz environment abroad will remain hospitable to the fruitful conservatism of such men as Francy Boland. If so, non-American jazz will give renewed strength to all of us in the years to come.

RAIDERS OF THE LOST ART

In a 1981 review of a performance by Rosemary Clooney, I wrote this about two members of her band, tenor saxophonist Scott Hamilton and cornetist Warren Vaché: "Not so gratifying [as Clooney] were Hamilton and Vaché, relatively young players who began by emulating Swing Era stylists and who have yet to find a personal manner. More disturbing than the revivalistic impulses of Hamilton and Vaché, though, are the ways in which they misunderstand and cheapen the style they profess to admire. Each man presents a surface cosmetic warmth, with Hamilton crooning à la Ben Webster, and Vaché putting a burry, Bunny Berigan–like edge on his tone. But the techniques that Hamilton and Vaché apply in such a haphazard fashion were part of a specific musical-emotional language. To hear that language being trifled with is both musically and morally disturbing."

That review led to a dialogue in *Down Beat* magazine with critic John McDonough, who saw the desire of Hamilton and Vaché (and that of other young musicians) to work within the stylistic patterns of the jazz past as a very positive development. The following was my response to McDonough's piece.

[1982]

IF we were building the ideal jazz musician, we would probably want to make him an innovator. But innovation is not the question here. Instead it is the degree of honesty and understanding with which specific players deal with the music's past.

First a distinction should be made between those jazz artists who have been inspired by their predecessors (Louis Armstrong's Swing Era disciples and the host of Lester Young acolytes of the 1940s would be good examples) and, on the other hand, those players whose approach to the jazz past is essentially revivalistic—as the music of Scott Hamilton, Warren Vaché, and many of their contemporaries seems to be. No matter how humbled he may be by his model, the disciple of the first sort doesn't wish to re-create the music of Armstrong or Young. Rather he hears something in the inspiring artist that speaks to something in him—a musical-emotional message that the disciple wishes (and needs) to expand upon and, as much as possible, make his own. The revivalist, however, regards the chunk of the jazz past that attracts him as an essentially completed act. And often he is drawn to the past of jazz in part *because* it belongs to the past—because the music speaks of values that seem to have been needlessly abandoned and that the revivalist wishes to reanimate, preserve, and inhabit. Injecting one's own personality into the music is at best a side issue, the goal instead being to accurately bring to life what is no longer as alive as it once was.

Now jazz revivalism has an intriguing, quirky history; and I would not want to be without the music of Lu Watters, Graeme and Roger Bell, or Dave Dallwitz. But revivalism works best when it deals with styles in which the soloist added color and point while the ensemble remained the dominant force; it runs into special problems when the style being re-created is one that relies on the soloist's ability to express an individual instrumental personality. Leaving aside the question of whether or not Hamilton and Vaché are self-conscious revivalists, their music certainly is based on late Swing Era styles in which individual instrumental personality was paramount. We love Ben Webster and Don Byas, Buck Clayton and Bobby Hackett, not just because their music was beautiful in the abstract sense, but also because it told *their* stories, revealing something essential about the kind of men they were. And this storytelling aspect of the music was expressed in a very precise musical-emotional language—one in which the individual artist's tonal and rhythmic inflections (the growls, smears, slides, and so forth) were both his trademark and the means he used to convey his evolving emotional messages. And this storytelling, languagelike aspect of the music has, like all languages, some specific rules of diction, grammar, and syntax.

It is there that I part company with most of today's more-or-less revivalistic players, whether their models come from the thirties and forties (as Hamilton's and Vaché's do), from the fifties (as do those of Lew Tabackin and Richie Cole), or from the quite recent past (as is the case with David Murray). To my ears, these musicians often speak the language they profess to love in a haphazard, inaccurate, even vulgar fashion, making grammatical and syntactical errors in the realm where notes are translated into emotion that are as disturbing as if they had flubbed the changes or turned the beat around. Place a typical Hamilton performance alongside a solo from such a master storyteller as Ike Quebec (or compare a Lew Tabackin effort with something by Sonny Rollins, or listen to David Murray next to Albert Ayler), and one hears countless musical-emotional gestures that have been mishandled or misunderstood, as though the perhaps unwitting emulator were wearing a tweed jacket with candy-striped pants.

So it's not just the emulative aspect of these players that is troublesome, because my knowledge (such as it is) of the music that inspired them tells me that they aren't even good emulators, let alone personal craftsmen. (A question for another day is whether one can be a craftsmanlike disciple of Albert Ayler, Eric Dolphy, or John Coltrane in the same way that one could, and perhaps still can, be a craftsmanlike disciple of Coleman Hawkins, Lester Young, or Don Byas.)

That a number of these young revivalists have been praised, and sometimes hired, by such masters as Buddy Tate, Buck Clayton, Roy Eldridge, Benny Goodman, and Earl Hines does not automatically settle the aesthetic issues in their favor. It's understandable that many older players (and those critics who have great affection for their music and may not care that much for later developments) would be cheered to find younger men paying homage to the past, for no one likes to feel lonely and most of us like to be flattered. But even if there were no trace of self-deception in the praise of Hines, Tate, et al., that praise would still be refuted by their own lastingly vital music, which remains the standard by which their would-be disciples must be judged.

While I certainly wish that there were as many personal craftsmen at work in jazz today as there were in 1935, 1945, and 1955, I believe that the craftsman approach to jazz is, for a number of reasons, becoming harder and harder to sustain. In any case, if jazz is about to turn itself into a largely revivalistic, repertory music—a kind of living museum in which everyone from Johnny Dodds to Albert Ayler is fair game—it seems all the more important to protest when one hears jazz's glorious past being reproduced in ways that are musically and emotionally inaccurate. To do otherwise would be to admit that we no longer hear the difference.

MARSALIS AT TWENTY-ONE
[1983]

A NY way you look at it Wynton Marsalis is a phenomenon. Already one heck of a jazz player at age twenty-one, Marsalis is "the crowned prince of the trumpet" according to critic Stanley Crouch—a judgment the public seems to endorse. In 1982, Marsalis won *Down Beat* magazine's Reader's Poll awards for Musician of the Year, Album of the Year, and Best Trumpeter. And in addition to his jazz prowess, Marsalis is very much at home in the classical realm. One of his two current albums on the Columbia label, *Think of One*, is a jazz date, but the other features Marsalis's performances of Haydn, Hummel, and Leopold Mozart concerti—demanding works that he handles with such ease and flair that one can understand why classical virtuoso Maurice André has hailed him as "potentially the greatest trumpet player of all time."

Also part of the Marsalis phenomenon is the zeal with which Columbia has been promoting his career. The label's efforts probably wouldn't pay off unless there were considerable musical substance to back up the human-interest side of the story (Marsalis's youth, his dual musical expertise, the fact that his father, Ellis Marsalis, is a celebrated jazz pianist, and so forth). But when a jazz musician is profiled in such mass-market publications as *People* magazine and *Newsweek* (as Marsalis has been), you can be sure that the public relations department is going all out. (In addition to the Maurice André quote and similar verbal bouquets, Columbia's latest Marsalis press release includes this gem: " 'The young man I'd like to have marry my daughter'—Bill Cosby.")

Leaving aside his qualifications as a potential son-in-law, Marsalis certainly is a remarkable young musician. But while one doesn't doubt the sincerity of those who refer to him as "the crowned prince" or "potentially the greatest trumpet player of all time," a more balanced view of Marsalis's career would seem to be called for. The first thing (and in some cases the only thing) people notice about Marsalis is his virtuoso technique. He has as much speed and range as any trumpet player who isn't into sheer trickiness, plus ideas that demand all his virtuosity for their proper execution. In jazz, however, sheer instrumental skill can be deceptive, and Marsalis, who blends a vigorous ego with a healthy sense of self-criticism, is aware of that fact.

"I know I can play fast and high," he has said, "but that's not what jazz is all about. Take Don Cherry, who is a phenomenal jazz trumpet player. He can't really play the trumpet technically, but that makes him get down to the essence of the music, whereas I have so much technique that it gets in my way. I'll just be playing stuff because I can play it, which distracts me from what I should be playing. Sure, my technique helps me get over a lot of obstacles. But in the long run, those obstacles are the stuff I have to work on—melodic phrasing, using space, developing my ear, and so forth. My biggest problem is figuring out what to play. So much stuff has been played already that it takes time to come up with something new."

Listening to the recordings he has made as a leader and as a sideman and recalling his in-person performances with Art Blakey, Herbie Hancock, and his own group, one knows what Marsalis means when he speaks of his technique getting in the way and the difficulty of coming up with something new because "so much stuff has been played already." At times, Marsalis still indulges in flurries of notes that are technically remarkable but of only momentary musical interest, and he has yet to shed his stylistic resemblances to Miles Davis and Freddie Hubbard—which is to be expected, given his youth. "I don't have enough stuff behind me to say I'm playing more than Miles and everybody," Marsalis has said. "No, man, that's not how it's done. You have to wait your turn, play and learn."

Such modesty is attractive, especially coming from a young man who is increasingly surrounded by media hype. And it's also nice to know that Marsalis thinks of his fabulous chops as both a hindrance and a help. Yet one hopes that he doesn't decide that he would be better off musically if he sobered up and slowed down. Every artist has his innate temperament, and Marsalis's is (and probably always will be) extremely flamboyant. Almost without exception, his most impressive efforts are those that are most virtuosic; and one feels certain that this fondness for musical fireworks is not just a byproduct of Marsalis's youth but an expression of his true nature. In that sense, he might be considered a modern-day counterpart of the late Charlie Shavers, a similarly fiery, technically dazzling player who quite rightly never calmed down.

As for the echoes of Miles Davis in Marsalis's music, that, too, is an aspect of his style that deserves a second look. Marsalis certainly admires Davis, but his deepest affinities are not with the trumpeter himself but with a specific Davis band—the superb mid-1960s quintet that included tenor and soprano saxophonist Wayne Shorter, pianist Herbie Hancock, bassist Ron Carter, and drummer Tony Williams. Marsalis obviously feels that the innovations of that group have yet to be superseded, because almost every performance on the two albums he has made under his own name pays homage to the style of the mid-sixties Davis quintet. But who was primarily responsible for the style of that band? Giving Davis all the credit he deserves for choosing his musical partners and maintaining esprit de corps, a case can be made that Shorter, Williams, and Hancock were at the heart of things. And it is the ideas of those men that Marsalis seems to be building upon, even though that involves some Davis references on his part. In fact, Shorter may be the most powerful influence on Marsalis's music, if one accepts the premise that Marsalis is at his best when his solos take on an aura of flamboyant fantasy and seriocomic wit.

When Shorter first emerged, he was, like Marsalis, an astonishing virtuoso, capable (as they say) of "playing around corners." Shorter could juggle notes at any tempo, and there seemed to be no harmonic possibility he couldn't hear and instantly express. Inseparable from his virtuosity, though, was the emotional tone of Shorter's playing—the way he would choose the most oblique paths and follow them to the edge of all sorts of musical cliffs with a deadpan, Buster Keaton–like logic. Inventing and then solving previously unimaginable musical puzzles, Shorter did seem to be a mordantly witty comedian at times. But his world also had a near-surrealistic aura of fantasy to it, as though his logic, humor, and superb technical command were necessary to fend off the attacks of marauding demons.

That side of Shorter's music lessened over the years, but neither Marsalis nor his older brother, saxophonist Branford Marsalis, has forgotten it—with Branford preserving the more literal aspects of Shorter's style while Wynton expands upon its core of fantasy and takes it into less haunted, more optimistic realms. (The Columbia double album *Jazz at the Opera House*, much of which pairs Marsalis and Shorter, is a perfect example of how close these two musicians are to each other, as Marsalis's flamboyant translation of early-Shorter ideas to the trumpet inspires Shorter to return to the same kind of musical thinking.) Williams's playing is vital to Marsalis as well, so much so that on the double album they made in 1981 under Hancock's leadership, *Quartet,* there are times when one feels that the normal soloist-accompanist relationship has been reversed and Marsalis is embellishing Williams percussive "melody."

As for Marsalis's recordings under his own name—*Wynton Marsalis, Think of One,* and his album of classical trumpet concerti—powerful though they are, they lack some of that feeling of gleeful fantasy and savage release that is so prominent on the *Opera House* album and on the date Marsalis made as sideman with saxophonist-composer Chico Freeman, *Destiny's Dance.* Perhaps, at twenty-one, Marsalis is still somewhat inhibited by the burdens of leadership. Perhaps, conscious as he is of how "much stuff has been played already," he finds it stimulating to bounce his ideas off his musical mentors. In any case, Wynton Marsalis definitely is a man to listen to and a man to watch—a jazz whiz kid who should live up to his already impressive credentials.

THE DEATH OF JAZZ?
[1985]

"THE old ones are going, and the young ones aren't growing." Bolstered by a few qualifications, that little rhyme pretty much sums up the state of jazz today. The most important body of music yet produced in America, jazz is a child of this century—an art whose component parts began to come together around 1900 and one that grew with such remarkable speed that in only twenty-five years it had produced at least four major figures (Louis Armstrong, Sidney Bechet, Jelly Roll Morton, and Bessie Smith) and a number of undeniable masterworks. But as we near the end of the century that gave birth to jazz, there are signs that this glorious music is about to pass away from us—

not from lack of popularity (at the moment, jazz is doing better in the marketplace than it has for some time), but because the music's artistic vitality is more and more in doubt.

Always able until now to renew itself from within, jazz seems be circling back on itself, forgoing its history of near-ceaseless invention in the name of various kinds of re-creation and revivalism. Also in the air is the related notion of a jazz fusion or blending—not so much with rock anymore (the big idea in the 1970s) but with Western concert music and/or musics from other cultures, with the result being a so-called "world music." In any case, quite a few observers believe jazz has entered its neoclassic phase, an era in which the music will devote itself, in the words of critic Sam Freedman, to producing "personally stamped recombinations of existing knowledge."

There is nothing new about the neoclassic impulse, which first surfaced in jazz in the late 1930s, when Lu Watters and Turk Murphy tried to re-create the music of such twenties figures as King Oliver and Kid Ory. And one can see the logic in these and other attempts to revive the past, for the evolution of jazz has been so swift that all sorts of fruitful positions were abandoned long before they were played out. What is new, though, is the nature and extent of the neoclassicism that runs through so much of jazz today.

The first generation of jazz revivalists were few in number and confined themselves to early styles. Now, however, almost the entire jazz past has been colonized by re-creators of one sort or another, including many who try to emulate and, in some cases, tame the music of such radical players of the 1960s as John Coltrane, Ornette Coleman, and Albert Ayler. And while these developments have produced some attractive music, one wonders about the well-being of an art that has so totally devoted itself to reexamining its past, especially when this trend coincides with a series of events that may have had much to do with inspiring it—the passing from the scene of more and more of the first-, second-, and third-generation creators who were, in effect, the music's living tradition.

"I think a lot about my buddies that left," said drummer Roy

Haynes a few years ago, and the litany of loss he was referring to has indeed become overwhelming. In the bebop era, when the use of drugs was widespread, one came to expect the early deaths that robbed us of Charlie Parker, Fats Navarro, and so many others long before their time. Then there were further shocks, as such young and middle-aged masters as Clifford Brown, Booker Little, Lee Morgan, Scott LaFaro, John Coltrane, Eric Dolphy, and Albert Ayler died when their creativity still was in full flower. But time itself has taken over now, and in recent years we have (to name only a few) said farewell to Count Basie, Thelonious Monk, Earl Hines, Erroll Garner, Charles Mingus, Vic Dickenson, Art Pepper, Sonny Stitt, Al Haig, Wilbur Ware, Kenny Clarke, Blue Mitchell, Kenny Dorham, Russell Procope, Cozy Cole, Budd Johnson, Ray Nance, Bill Coleman, Shelly Manne, Hampton Hawes, Bill Evans, Don Ellis, Paul Desmond, Red Garland, Joe Venuti, Mary Lou Williams, and Barney Bigard.

But why can't jazz continue as it always has, generating vital new artists to take the place of those who are gone? And why should there be any doubts about this neoclassic phase? Isn't paying homage to its past one of the healthiest things any art can do? To answer those questions (or at the very least to speculate about them) some historical background has to be sketched in. In its earliest days, jazz was three kinds of music in one—a folk music, an entertainment (or popular) music, and an art music. It was a folk music because it was invented by a "folk" (i.e., black Americans) and met that particular group's social needs. It was an entertainment music because it had the power to delight large numbers of people who did not belong to its original folk audience. And it was an art music because— unlike a folk or entertainment music but very much like the music of the Western classical tradition—jazz had an inherent need and ability to transform itself, to build on its own discoveries and produce works that could withstand and reward contemplation.

Almost without precedent in the history of art, this harmonious, three-way blend gave jazz a great deal of its initial thrust.

Imagine how exhilarating it must have been to work at the limits of one's artistic capacities while also fulfilling the needs of those closest to you and giving pleasure to the world at large. But this balance, epitomized by the early career of Louis Armstrong, soon began to break down. An "art for art's sake" approach first cropped up among some white jazz musicians in the 1920s. And while the relationship between black jazz artists and the black audience was mutually gratifying for at least another decade, that broad sense of agreement began to waver in the mid-1940s with the advent of bebop—a music of undeniable power but one whose aura of emotional tension and extreme rhythmic and harmonic virtuosity made it very difficult to take as entertainment (certainly it was not a music that one could easily dance to).

From that point on, then, the audience for jazz has consisted largely of "fans" of one sort or another, groups that expanded or contracted as a particular style of the music met or failed to meet their social and aesthetic needs. While it was still possible for jazz musicians of major stature to be popular too, the time when that was the norm was over. And with the advent of rock, which transformed the music industry into more of a bottom-line affair than it had ever been before, it became increasingly difficult for jazz artists of any sort to make their music available to those segments of the public that might want to hear it.

So jazz, which always had been an art music in the most positive sense, now became an art music in another sense, too. Able to address the human condition with a unique intensity and depth, jazz found itself, for that very reason, ill-equipped to survive in a marketplace that was geared toward the needs of adolescents. (Of course, the same could be said of the symphony, the opera, or the ballet, but the audience for those arts has the social standing and economic clout to subsidize its tastes.)

Meanwhile, on the creative front, jazz was passing through its most tumultuous upheaval to date with the advent in the early 1960s of the avant-garde, or so-called "free jazz," which dispensed with many of the music's most familiar harmonic and rhythmic signposts and often ventured into realms that were as abstract and sonically violent as the more extreme products of the classical avant-garde. Hailed by some and dismissed by others, the advent of the avant-garde split the jazz community as never before, and almost everything that has happened since can be seen as a response to that event.

On one hand there was what might be called the "pastoral reaction," the harmonically suave, impressionistic approach that was pioneered by pianist Bill Evans and that led to Gary Burton, Keith Jarrett, and, arguably, the aural pablum of George Winston. Embraced by a host of players who were put off by free jazz, this music allowed its practitioners to feel they were still moving forward. And in one sense they were, conquering in the name of jazz the territory that had been previously been explored by Debussy and Ravel. The implicit dreaminess of this music is a problem, though. Before this, jazz had always been art of emotional realism—a music whose most intoxicatingly joyful artists (say, Armstrong or Erroll Garner) did not take their audiences away from the actual world but instead spoke of those things in life about which one could, indeed, be joyful.

As for today's neoclassicism, it ostensibly seeks to revive the values of warmth, soul, and forthright swing that once were the hallmarks of jazz and, in the process, reach out to a wide audience in the same uncompromising way that Armstrong, Basie, and Ellington were able to do. Trumpeter Wynton Marsalis and saxophonist-composer David Murray are among the key figures in this trend, and listening to them one finds much to admire. Marsalis, in particular, is an artist of great technical and intellectual gifts, seemingly capable of realizing any idea that comes to mind. And one also has no doubt that his heart is in the right place. Lurking behind the neoclassical enterprise, though, there is a lingering sense that it is more a willed event than a natural one, despite its eagerness to restore to jazz those qualities that were, indeed, natural to the music before free jazz came along.

Warmth, soul, and swing certainly are among the hallmarks of a Ben Webster or a Dexter Gordon, but for them these things seem not be sought after in themselves. Instead they are an inevitable byproduct of the act of playing jazz, virtues that arise as a matter of course when one makes musical and emotional contact with the material at hand. And it is this sense of contact with the material that seems to be lacking in so many of today's neoclassicists, perhaps because the medium of line-against-harmony that their predecessors found so usefully resistant no longer provides them with the same kind of challenge. In David Murray's case, it is logical that this should be so, for he once was a fervent disciple of the most radical free-jazz saxophonist, Albert Ayler. As critic J. B. Figi said of another young neoclassicist, Murray "fills roles rather than playing from self," and one can hear the difference on the version of "Body and Soul" that appears on Murray's recent album *Morning Song*. Sticking to the harmonic pattern of the tune until he ends his warm-toned solo with an Ayler-like squeal, Murray leaves one with the feeling that his relative orthodoxy is very much a matter of conscious choice and that his decision to play "Body and Soul" in this way ought to be a cause for congratulation. In fact, to the degree that the solo has any emotional content, it seems to lie in that dramatized sense of choice, in Murray's eagerness to gratify his and his audience's desires to experience in the present a way of playing jazz that a short while ago seemed to belong only to the past. But aside from his need to please us in this manner, who David Murray is remains a mystery—which is odd, because the style Murray seeks to emulate was one that called upon the soloist to declare and explore his identity in every note and phrase.

There are other neoclassicists who are very aware of these problems and have come up with intriguing solutions. In particular, there are the slyly ironic Henry Threadgill and Chicagoan Edward Wilkerson Jr., a genuine romantic whose involvement with the materials at hand is never in doubt. But Threadgill and Wilkerson may only be neoclassicists in disguise, artists whose jousts with the music's past really have more to do with the specific musical issues that were raised by free jazz and that still need to be dealt with if the music is going to become something more than a museum that mounts a series of jazz-tinged puppet shows. I am afraid, though, that this is what jazz may have in store for it, as the creators for whom the making of the music is not a self-conscious act continue to pass away and the younger generation keeps trying to evoke the spirit of the past by trying on its outward forms. In the words of Igor Stravinsky, who certainly knew what neoclassicism was all about: "The borrowing of a method has nothing to do with observing a tradition. A method is replaced; a tradition is carried forward in order to produce something new. It appears as an heirloom, a heritage that one receives on condition of making it bear fruit."

"THE DEATH OF JAZZ?" REVISITED
[1986]

A little more than a year ago I raised some doubts about the present and future course of jazz, in a piece whose title alone ("The Death of Jazz?") stirred controversy. No less controversial, it seems, was the piece's basic point: that today's so-called neoclassical trend in jazz (in which a good many young players are trying to work within styles that were prevalent in other eras, particularly the mid-1960s) is not the healthy sign that many listeners and critics believe it to be.

Fueled by a desire to return to traditional jazz values, such music has an understandable appeal—not only because it sounds reassuringly familiar but also because it has arisen at a time when much of American society seems to be thinking along conservative lines. But once jazz becomes more concerned with preservation than growth, doesn't that amount to a break with one of the most fundamental aspects of the music's tradition: the need of each player to explore and express his or her personal identity? And if jazz does turn into something of a repertory art, which seems likely if the neoclassical trend continues to grow, where will that leave future generations of would-be creators who will be told, in effect, that others have felt more while they have felt less?

With those thoughts in mind, it seems like a good idea to look at the latest evidence: the music that such neoclassical young lions as trumpeters Wynton Marsalis and Jon Faddis have been making in recent months. But first a word or two should be said about the aggressively propagandistic critical prose that tends to surround this music—if only because a steady dose of it leads one to think that the journalistic fans of jazz neoclassicism are at least as interested in trend-making as they are in the music itself. *Village Voice* jazz critic Gary Giddins is the man who came up with the neoclassical label. But it is his colleague Stanley Crouch who has been the most strenuous and visible backer of the trend, thanks to the many liner notes he has written for the albums of Marsalis and friends. In that role Crouch is seldom content to celebrate the specific musical virtues of the album at hand. Instead, the technically impressive but rather straitlaced music of Marsalis and his neoclassical colleagues is played off against the supposed "decadence" and "fumbling" of the jazz avant-garde—as though jazz had careered off the tracks in the 1960s and the neoclassical trend were a kind of rebellion in reverse, an attempt to bring order and sanity back to the music.

"These young men aren't about foisting the clichés of twentieth-century European music on jazz," writes Crouch of a group called Out of the Blue, which tries very hard to sound like the clock had been turned back to 1965. "It is an ensemble luminously in tune with integrity." But if "integrity" and "foisting" are indeed the issues, it seems fair to ask how the music of Out of the Blue's eponymous first album stands up alongside a representative and stylistically similar album from the late 1960s: tenor saxophonist Tyrone Washington's *Natural Essence*, which includes trumpeter Woody Shaw and alto saxophonist James Spaulding. The two groups share the same instrumentation and the same musical techniques, as the heated rhythmic angularities of bebop are linked to free-floating modal harmonies. And even if Out of the Blue's trumpeter, Mike Mossman, and alto saxophonist, Kenny Garrett, haven't directly modeled themselves on Shaw and Spaulding, they certainly sound as though they have. But the emotional tone of the two albums is quite different. While most of the members of Out of the Blue sound as though they think of their music as a style (that is, as a series of rules one must adopt and accept), the music of Washington and his partners is fundamentally explosive, a discontented elegance that keeps zooming off in search of extreme emotional states. In fact a passionate need to exceed itself lies at the heart of Washington's music. And while stylistic patterns can be found on *Natural Essence,* they only emphasize the mood of turbulence and flux—defining the brink over which Washington constantly threatens to jump. So even though the music of Washington and his mid-sixties peers was less openly radical than that of Albert Ayler and Ornette Coleman, it was by no means a separate phenomenon. Indeed, the strains of transition that supposedly were confined to the jazz avant-garde may have been even more violently felt in the music that lay, so to speak, just to the right of it.

One wonders, then, how a music that was virtually tearing itself apart can serve as a stylistic model for today's jazz neoclassicists—for at the root of all neoclassical movements there lies a desire to transform the erratic flow of artistic change into a smooth-running, orderly process. And one wonders as well how this self-conscious return to the recent jazz past is affecting those who are actually playing the music. An example of what may be involved is Wynton Marsalis's most recent album, *Black Codes From the Underground,* which leaves one with the feeling that making a personal statement on his horn no longer is Marsalis's goal. Indeed, his otherwise admirable desire to embrace the entire jazz trumpet tradition seems to have transformed the typical Marsalis solo into a kind of musical seance—as though each phrase he plays has so many sources in the music's past that this outweighs whatever meaning those notes might have to Marsalis in the here-and-now.

Even more explicit tribute is paid to the past by another young trumpet virtuoso, Jon Faddis, on *Legacy.* A protégé of

Dizzy Gillespie, Faddis emulates Gillespie's style on "A Night in Tunisia" and "Things to Come" and then ventures back to Louis Armstrong ("West End Blues") and Roy Eldridge ("Little Jazz"). But Faddis's taste for flamboyant high-note blasts seems linked to a rhythmic and melodic rigidity that makes caricatures out of his Armstrong and Eldridge tributes. The Gillespie salutes work better, because the angularity of that master's style conceals some of Faddis's stiffness. But after listening to Faddis's handsomely austere reading of Thad Jones's "A Child Is Born," one wonders whether Faddis ought to have taken Jones, not Gillespie, as his model.

One can see the logic in what Faddis has tried to do, for it is tempting to think that the artistic past is still open to colonization, an endlessly fertile plain that will sustain new creative harvests. And at one time jazz did function in that way, as several generations of musicians were able to build directly upon the styles of Armstrong, Coleman Hawkins, and Lester Young without compromising their own musical and emotional growth. But at least as far back as the bebop era, the rate and nature of stylistic change in jazz began to accelerate; and it would be hard to think of any period in the last forty years during which the music was not urgently transforming itself. So there would seem to be something illusory in the hope that solid ground can be found in the jazz styles of the mid-1960s (particularly the music of the Miles Davis Quintet)—which is where most of today's would-be neoclassicists plant their flags—for that music was always unstable, an art of emotional and technical brinkmanship.

Perhaps today's jazz neoclassicists ought to ponder these words from composer-critic Virgil Thomson. Distinguishing between an "objective" music in which one can "represent other people's emotions" and a "music of personal lyricism" (which would seem to be the kind of art that jazz is), Thomson goes on to explain that "you can write or execute music of the most striking evocative power by objective methods, but you cannot project a personal sentiment you do not have. If you fake it knowingly, you are dramatizing that which should be transmitted directly; and if you fake it unknowingly, you are, merely by deceiving yourself, attempting to deceive your audience. Naturally, experienced persons can teach the young many things about the personalized repertory. But there is no set way it must be rendered, and any attempt to impose one on it takes the life out of it."

THE MARSALIS BROTHERS FURTHER ON
[1984]

A NY way you look at it, twenty-four-year-old saxophonist Branford Marsalis is a significant figure in contemporary jazz. One year older than his brother, trumpet whiz Wynton Marsalis, Branford exemplifies today's neo-conservative style, which tries to tame, codify, and toy with the music of the radical jazz innovators of the 1960s: John Coltrane, Sonny Rollins, Wayne Shorter, and Ornette Coleman. As one listened to Marsalis at Rick's Café Americain, it was clear that he not only has memorized almost every lick that Coltrane et al. ever produced but also possesses a technical expertise that allows him to re-shuffle these licks in some very shrewd ways. As one fan remarked, "This guy can do anything." The problem, though, is that Marsalis often seems lost in the midst of all these potential moves, unsure whether he wants to play clever, even satirically mocking games with the recent jazz past or respectfully emulate it.

Satire of some sort might be the more fruitful approach, for it fits the seemingly innate foxiness that Marsalis shares with his brother. But Rollins and Shorter already have taken that route—the former favoring Falstaffian humor, the latter indulging in near-surrealistic distortions—and that leaves Marsalis with the unenviable choice of exaggerating the already exaggerated or, on the other hand, merely toning it down. Toned-down Coltrane, which is what Marsalis offers the rest of the time, is another matter, because the implicitly romantic, and at times even desperate, aura of quest that permeates Coltrane's music would seem to call for a similar approach on the part of his disciples. What Coltrane left behind was not a "hip" style but a drive toward ecstatic transcendence; and when Marsalis fiddles with Coltrane's techniques while he holds the implicit emotion of the music at arm's length, the results can be distressing.

Within Marsalis's music, though, there is a third option, which may be the best way out for him. Given his agile mind and fingers and his basically cool temperament, Marsalis sometimes sounds like an updated Stan Getz—a musical gem cutter who would like to inhabit a world where subtlety of technique is an end in itself. From that point of view, the most satisfying piece Marsalis played Monday night was "Shadows," a moody ballad written by his pianist, Larry Willis, which allowed the leader to build a solo that relied on an exquisitely shaded purity of tone and some sly harmonic shifts. When the temperature rose, as it did most notably on "Solstice," Marsalis alternated between his neo-Coltrane manner and a close-to-the-vest version of Shorter's and Rollins's comedy. The latter style worked better for Marsalis, but even here there was little sense of emotional commitment, as though he were unsure whether he wanted to laugh with or laugh at his stylistic models.

The problems Branford Marsalis is wrestling with may be those of youth, and perhaps the passage of time will solve them. But in the midst of his often dazzling virtuosity, Marsalis seems to be playing at playing jazz instead of just playing it—as though his involvement with the music were based on a paradoxical need to fend off its emotional demands.

[1985]

WYNTON Marsalis is a remarkable trumpet player—pure of tone, long of breath, and able to juggle notes the way angels are supposed to dance on the head of a pin. But despite the passel of Grammy awards he already has won, and despite the warm reception he received Friday night, Marsalis is, at age twenty-three, not yet a remarkable jazz musician; nor do I think he will ever become one.

Why that should be so is something of a mystery, for Marsalis's commitment to the real thing would seem to be intense. He has spoken out with much forcefulness and wit against the idea of diluting jazz in any way, shape, or form, and the popularity he has won is not the result of any overt compromise on Marsalis's part. Even his recent trumpet-with-strings album was a rather sober affair; and the quintet Marsalis brought to the Vic Theater (saxophonist Branford Marsalis, pianist Kenny Kirkland, bassist Charnett Moffett, and drummer Jeff Watts) definitely was a straight-ahead outfit. But the effect of Marsalis's music is oddly and disappointingly bland—in part, I think, because of the stylistic choices he makes, but mostly because he seems to have cast himself in a role that doesn't allow his true musical personality to shine through.

Both in-person and recorded evidence (notably his early work as a sideman with Art Blakey and the album on which he appeared as part of an all-star group that included Wayne Shorter and Charlie Haden) suggests that Marsalis is at his best when he permits the more impish, fanciful side of his music to emerge. There is, one suspects, an innate foxiness to the man—a need to set off musical fireworks just for the fun of it—that is ill-served when Marsalis dons the robes of the noble young prince of the realm and plays with a solemnity that threatens to become hollow.

On "The Nearness of You," for instance, one was impressed by the sheer expertise of Marsalis's playing—the delicate thread of tone that was so lengthily and, it seemed, so effortlessly sustained. But this was a romantic ballad, after all, and despite Marsalis's apparent adherence to the mood, there was very little lyricism involved—the dominant impression, instead, being a kind of blatant tastefulness (if that isn't a contradiction in terms). On the up-tempo tunes a similar at-arm's-length feeling prevailed; and throughout the band, with the possible exception

of Kirkland's peppy but rather mechanical bluesiness, control
for its own sake seemed to be the issue—with each solo filling
in a form that, by jazz standards, felt much too predetermined.
There was, in other words, very little sense of resistance being
overcome in Marsalis's playing, aside from the resistance of the
trumpet itself; and while the latter approach holds certain
charms, they are, at best, only charming.

One problem may be that the differences between Marsalis's
music and that of Miles Davis's mid-1960s quintet aren't that
significant; indeed, Marsalis and his young partners sound as
though they are working within a tradition that is already so
familiar to them that it is almost played out. Now, perhaps as
yet unexplored and artistically useful knots and whorls still can
be found in this style of music. But if they can be uncovered,
Wynton Marsalis gives few signs that he is the man to do it.

Almost twenty years have passed since this was written, and it now
seems clear that despite the prominence that the engines of cultural
politics and publicity have given to Wynton Marsalis, his music (especially his latter-day orchestral work) is a nonissue aesthetically and
has been for some time. Such Marsalis pastiches as the oratorio
Blood on the Fields (1997), the suite *In This House, On This Morning* (1993), and the ballets *Citi Movement* (1991), *Jazz* (1993) and
Jump Start (1995) seem to come from a strange alternate universe—one in which some of the surface gestures of Duke Ellington
(Marsalis's chief model) have been filtered through the toylike sensibility of Raymond Scott.

Marsalis remains a skilled instrumentalist, but he has never
been a strikingly individual soloist. As for his orchestral works, their
relative poverty of invention becomes clear when they are placed
alongside the likes of George Russell's *Chromatic Universe* and *Living Time*, Oliver Nelson's *Afro-American Sketches*, Bill Holman's
Further Adventures, Muhal Richard Abrams's *The Hearinga Suite*,
Bob Brookmeyer's *Celebration*, John Carter's *Roots and Folklore*,
and, of course, the more successful orchestral works of Ellington
himself. A brief comparison between one of the major vocal episodes in the Pulitzer Prize–winning *Blood on the Fields*, "Will the

Sun Come Out?" (sung by Cassandra Wilson), and the opening vocal movement of Ellington's otherwise instrumental *Liberian Suite* (1947), "I Like the Sunrise" (sung by Al Hibbler), might be revealing. The works are comparable in theme—the subject of *Blood on the Fields* is slavery in America, while *Liberian Suite* was commissioned by the West African republic of Liberia, which was founded by freed American slaves in 1847—and both "Will the Sun Come Out?" (which lasts nine minutes) and "I Like the Sunrise" (half as long) are meditative semi-laments in which hope, pain, frustration, and doubt are meant to joust with one another. The melody of "I Like the Sunrise" has an equivocal, sinuous grace (climbing in pitch toward a point of harmonic release it cannot reach, it expressively stalls out on the words "raised up high, far out of sight"), while the key turn in the lyric—"I like the sunrise . . . it brings new hope, *they say*" (my emphasis)—is commented upon and deepened by a tapestry of orchestral and solo voices (particularly those of baritone saxophonist Harry Carney and clarinetist Jimmy Hamilton). By contrast, the three verses of "Will the Sun Come Out?" go almost nowhere in twice the span of time. The melody itself, despite Wilson's attempts to shape it, is hardly a melody at all, but a lumpy recitative that sounds as though it had been assembled bar by bar, while the ensemble's instrumental interventions and the solos of pianist Eric Reed merely distend things further. It could be argued that within the overall dramatic scheme of *Blood on the Fields*, "Will the Sun Come Out?" is meant to be an episode of near-paralysis, and that the music ought to mirror this. But listen to "Will the Sun Come Out?" and ask yourself how often you have heard nine minutes of music pass this uneventfully.

Why, then, the Marsalis phenomenon, such as it has been and perhaps still is? One struggles to think of another figure in the history of jazz who was a significant cultural presence but not a significant musical one. Dave Brubeck? Perhaps, but there is no counterpart in Marsalis's music to the lyrical grace of Paul Desmond or to those moments when Brubeck himself was genuinely inspired. Paul Whiteman? Yes, in terms of the ability to marshal media attention, but if we credit Whiteman with all the music that was produced under his aegis, the comparison probably would be in his favor. Think again of Whiteman and Marsalis, though, not in terms of the kinds of music they made but of the cultural roles they filled. In both the 1920s and the 1980s (when Marsalis arose) the popularity and respectability of jazz were felt to be key issues—the difference being that in the twenties some part of the culture found it necessary and/or titillating to link a popular but not yet "respectable" music to the conventions of the concert hall, while in the eighties jazz had come to be regarded as a music of fading popular appeal that needed the imprimatur of respectability in order to survive—and to be subsidized, like the opera, the symphony orchestra, and the ballet. Thus the tuxedoed Whiteman, wielding his baton like Toscanini; thus Marsalis the articulate whiz kid, equally at home with Miles Davis and Haydn and foe of rap and hip-hop. But while the byplay between notions of what is lively and what is respectable may be an unavoidable part of the cultural landscape, a music that springs from such premises, as Marsalis's so often seems to do, eventually stands revealed as a form of packaged status whose relationship to the actual making of music always was incidental.

THE SOUND-ALIKES
[1986]

A LMOST from the first, jazz has been a music of personal lyricism, a way of expressing through sound what it means to be you. And while that is not everything that jazz is, individual instrumental storytelling has been so much a part of the music for so many years that it is difficult to imagine what jazz might be like if that drive toward self-expression were not at the heart of it. But perhaps one doesn't have to imagine that anymore, because today quite a few technically adept young players sound quite a bit like one another, to the point where they seem to be working in a more-or-less generic style—the tenor saxophonists paying homage to John Coltrane and Joe Henderson, the trumpeters to Miles Davis and Freddie Hubbard, the pianists to Bill Evans and McCoy Tyner, the bass players to Scott LaFaro, and so forth. Especially distressing to those who recall the days when every good player could be identified almost from the first note, this trend toward stylistic sameness has been on the rise since the early 1960s, when the music of Coltrane, Evans, and others became profoundly influential.

But even though it might seem that dominant stylists always generate a horde of faceless imitators, in jazz that hasn't always been the case. In the mid-1930s, for instance, almost every jazz trumpeter of merit (indeed, almost every jazz instrumentalist) was profoundly affected by the music of Louis Armstrong. But so many Armstrong-influenced trumpet players went on to develop their own personal styles that a list of their names could run on for many pages: Roy Eldridge, Bunny Berigan, Cootie Williams, Buck Clayton, Bill Coleman, Rex Stewart, Bobby Stark, Red Allen, Harry James, Charlie Shavers, Joe Thomas, Frankie Newton, Shad Collins, Harold Baker, Dud Bascomb, Emmett Berry, Billy Butterfield, Doc Cheatham, Harry Edison, Bobby Hackett, Hot Lips Page, Ray Nance, and so forth. And the same is true of tenor saxophonists Coleman Hawkins and Lester Young and alto saxophonist Johnny Hodges, who came up with strikingly individual styles that still left room for their vast number of disciples to find their own tones of voice. So how did the music of Armstrong, Hawkins, Young, and Hodges manage to stimulate, rather than limit, the growth of personal jazz speech? And why does the music of today's widely influential figures seem to have the opposite effect?

Armstrong and the rest of jazz's first great role models gave their disciples a special sort of musical-emotional information, outlining possibilities that virtually begged to be filled in. First, there was the fact of swing, which Armstrong brought to life so vividly that he almost seemed to have invented it. And in the emotional realm, the intense personal feeling that Armstrong poured into every note couldn't help but encourage his disciples to strive for a similar nobility and power. Roy Eldridge summed up the whole magical procedure when he recalled his first in-person encounter with Armstrong's music, which took place in 1932. "I was a young cat, and I was very fast," Eldridge said, "but I wasn't telling any kind of story. I sat through the first show and didn't think Louis was so extraordinary, but in the second show he played 'Chinatown.' He started out like a new book, building and building, chorus after chorus, and finally reaching a full climax—right, clean, and clear. The rhythm was rocking and Louis had that sound going along with it, building the thing the whole time instead of just playing in a straight line, until everybody was standing up, including me. So I started to feel that if I could combine speed with melodic development while continuing to build, to tell a story, I could create something musical of my own that the public would like."

Notice, in particular, Eldridge's "he started out like a new book"—for even though that phrase literally refers to the zeal with which Armstrong began to play, it is easy to see how the newness of this "book" convinced Eldridge that he could create one of his own. Important, too, was what might be called the centrality of Armstrong's music, and of Hawkins's and Hodges's as well—a firmly rooted sense of emotional balance and joyful well-being that left plenty of room on all sides for further variations. For example, Eldridge's taste for bravura excitement came close to delirium at times, while off in another corner Harry Edison was able to cultivate a vein of alternately sly and slashing musical wit.

But the centrality and balance that Armstrong and the other giants of his era brought to jazz was of necessity a threatened state. The beauty of Lester Young's solos, for instance, cannot be separated from their shadowy obliqueness, from the sense that their creator was a man not quite made for this world, while alto saxophonist Charlie Parker, the key figure of the bebop era, produced a music of extreme emotional turbulence, of conjoined intensity and anguish. So even though Parker's overwhelming rhythmic and harmonic virtuosity had to be absorbed, what was one to make of Parker's emotional stance—the sense that he was dancing at the edge of an abyss, like a jazz Baude-laire or Rimbaud?

A "normalized" version of Parker's music worked well for Lou Donaldson, who blended in some of Hodges's soulful sweet-ness, while Jackie McLean found in himself a genuine echo of Parker's fragmented intensity. But for the most part, Parker's followers were less individual than those of Armstrong or Haw-kins—not only because the "on the edge" aspect of Parker's mu-sic cried out for a similarly extreme response, which few Parker disciples could supply, but also because the sheer speed and complexity of bop left less room for the personal tonal shadings that earlier stylists had used to make their mark. So after Parker the pattern of fruitful influence began to wobble a good deal, as his imposing musical achievements led to less, not more, indi-viduality in jazz. And the coming of the Coltrane-Evans gener-ation, which was followed very quickly by the rise of Ornette Coleman and the rest of the jazz avant-garde, really threw a monkey wrench into the machine.

A soloist of tremendous power and virtuosity, Coltrane, like Parker, was a man of extremes. But his music, fueled by a drive toward ecstasy and transcendence, was even less likely to meet a similar response in his disciples than Parker's was—for only a few people have genuinely ecstatic temperaments. On the other hand, Coltrane's musical techniques proved to be distress-ingly easy to imitate, provided one had a vast instrumental fa-cility. In the years since Coltrane died, in 1967, young men who can play the keys off the saxophone have been cropping up all over the place—products, for the most part, of the burgeoning jazz education movement, which also has provided the text-books that "explain" everything Coltrane has done. What has not been codified, though, is the intense emotional turmoil that lay at the heart of Coltrane's music. So, more often than not these days, one hears saxophonists who have memorized Coltrane's mannerisms but lack any sense of why those extravagant ges-tures arose.

That we now have thousands of Coltrane and Bill Evans disciples—most of them sounding much alike and few of them having a genuine personal response to the former's drive toward transcendence and the latter's introverted lyricism—is a development that cannot be separated from the rise of the jazz avant-garde. Looking back at that list of Armstrong-influenced trumpeters, one sees some undeniably major figures and a lot of middle-level players, too—men who lacked the fire of genius but who still had genuine individuality and talent. But because, in effect, the jazz avant-garde stepped away from the comforts of style—as critic John Litweiler has said, that music has as many different styles as it has major players—the last vestiges of middle-level creativity were essentially blown away.

Here, it seems, jazz is running into its own version of some of the same barriers that have bedeviled Western classical music since the turn of the nineteenth century, when composers as diverse as Debussy, Schoenberg, and Stravinsky found that their compositions could no longer refer to a seemingly stable musical language that existed outside the world of any particular new work. What was disappearing, in the words of critic Charles Rosen, "was the possibility of using large blocks of prefabricated material. To employ them, as Mozart or Haydn had been able to do, resulted immediately in pastiche [while] giving them up led to a kind of panic. It seemed as if music now had to be written note by note."

More's the pity, perhaps. But those who have flourished in the jazz avant-garde have done so only by inventing their own relatively self-contained musical languages. And the ability to do that necessarily, so it seems, has been limited to a few major figures. But what if one doesn't happen to be an Ornette Coleman, an Albert Ayler, or a Roscoe Mitchell—to name three of those avant-garde language makers? Then the need to find a style that will allow you to make a more-or-less modern, jazzlike music with some degree of ease really becomes crucial. And if the styles at hand don't leave much room for personal statement—well, what other choices do you have?

From a listener's point of view, the more-or-less generic jazz that results tends to be as limited in its satisfactions as its players are limited in their goals. In fact one critic who was involved in the formation of a jazz-repertory ensemble recently went so far as to say that what we need now are more "neutral" players, musical chameleons who can sound like Charlie Parker at one moment and Johnny Hodges at the next. Neutrality—now that's a war cry that stiffens the spine and quickens the step. But perhaps that fellow was merely being a realist, surveying the increasingly generic jazz landscape and deciding that we had better settle for second-best.

PART VIII

Singers and Songmakers

The relationship between jazz and pre–rock 'n' roll American popular song is rich, varied, and more than a little equivocal. Most obviously, perhaps, for a good deal of jazz's history the majority of its harmonic and structural frameworks were taken or borrowed from American popular songs—though "taken" and "borrowed" may imply that there was a distance between jazz and Broadway/ Tin Pan Alley when instead it was more a matter of difference than distance, and a difference that at times was not easy to detect. No less important, jazz's musical habits and its emotional atmosphere had a significant influence on the emotional tone, rhythmic traits, and melodic and harmonic flavor of a great many American popular songs—the very same songs that jazz musicians often would immediately put to fervent use. Here one need think only of George and Ira Gershwin's "I Got Rhythm" (1930)—the song itself a crystallization of, even a commentary upon, some of the musical habits and social atmosphere of jazz, while, in the words of musicologist Richard Crawford, the "classic simplicity of the song's harmonic design summoned jazz performers' inventiveness, both melodic and harmonic, to a degree matched by only one other structure in the history of jazz: the twelve-bar blues."

Simplicity summoning up inventiveness—this formula has worked, and arguably still works, in jazz, as the harmonic, formal, and metrical regularities of the popular song model serve as a near-inescapable basis for variation. But what of the ways in which jazz handles emotion, of the storytelling, "textual" aspects of the music, of the novel ways it dramatizes and tests the self? Here, too, the popular song model and its typical subject matter—the nature and vicissitudes of romantic love—are nearly inescapable, or so it would seem, and for instrumentalists as well as for vocalists. The intertwining textual/emotional/musical subtleties available to jazz singers like Billie Holiday and Sarah Vaughan, and to superior pop singers like Frank Sinatra and Tony Bennett, again make it clear that jazz as a whole has available to it a novelistic or autobiographical dimension in which the artist is at once author, enactor, and character; that his or her fate over time is always a part of the tale.

GERSHWIN MUSICALS
[1987]

IN his relatively brief life, George Gershwin made an immense contribution to the American musical theater. But in this year, the fiftieth anniversary of his death, the nature and dimensions of that contribution have become clearer than ever before— thanks to the concert performances of Gershwin's *Of Thee I Sing* and its sequel, *Let 'Em Eat Cake,* that took place in March at the Brooklyn Academy of Music under the baton of Michael Tilson-Thomas and the performances of *Primrose* and *Pardon My English* that John McGlinn conducted in May at the Library of Congress. *Of Thee I Sing*—which debuted in 1931, ran for 441 performances, and won a Pulitzer Prize (the first ever awarded to a musical)—was Gershwin's most commercially successful show and the only one of these four shows that is at all well known. Yet few of us have ever heard it, while the scores of *Let 'Em Eat Cake, Primrose,* and *Pardon My English* were virtually forgotten before their recent revivals. Now, however, we have access to half of that Gershwin bounty—a CBS Masterworks set of *Let 'Em Eat Cake* and *Of Thee I Sing*, conducted by Tilson-Thomas with the Brooklyn Academy cast. (Unfortunately, McGlinn's superb performances of *Primrose* and *Pardon My English* seem destined to live only in the memories of those who were there to hear them.)

Invaluable because it rescues from limbo some of George and Ira Gershwin's most delightful and, in the case of *Let 'Em Eat Cake*, most daring work, the CBS set also reveals that these shows are quite different in tone and style from most latter-day Broadway musicals. *Of Thee I Sing* and *Let 'Em Eat Cake* are biting political satires, with books by George S. Kaufmann and Morrie Ryskind. They focus on the same group of characters: President John P. Wintergreen; his beloved wife, Mary Turner; and Wintergreen's bumbling running mate, Alexander Throttlebottom. In *Of Thee I Sing*, candidate Wintergreen, running on a platform of love, agrees to wed the winner of a national beauty pageant, who turns out to be a Southern belle named Diana Deveraux. But Wintergreen spurns Ms. Deveraux because he has fallen in love with Mary Turner, a secretary at the pageant. Through a series of elaborate twists in plot, this almost leads to war with France and the impeachment of the newly elected president, before Mary's announcement that she is about to give birth to twins brings the show to a harmonious but madcap conclusion.

Let 'Em Eat Cake begins with the next election. Voted out of office, Wintergreen mounts a neo-Fascist "blue shirt" revolt, overthrows his successor, President Tweedledee, and sets himself up as dictator—only to find that, through further twists in plot, he and Throttlebottom are scheduled for execution, until Mary Turner has a bright idea that saves the day. *Cake*, which debuted in 1933, is much darker in tone than its predecessor ("If *Of Thee I Sing* was a satire on politics," Ira Gershwin wrote, "*Let 'Em Eat Cake* was a satire on Practically Everything"), and it is no wonder that the show ran for a mere ninety performances.

How to properly perform such musicals is not an easy question to answer—for their plots alone make it clear that *Sing* and *Cake* have little to do with any of the various kinds of "realism" that have come to dominate the Broadway stage, from the sentimental melodrama of Rodgers and Hammerstein to the tart-toned sophistication of Stephen Sondheim. Instead, *Sing* and *Cake* are deliberately artificial and artificial in a special way—as much a part of the pastoral tradition as the operettas of Gilbert and Sullivan or, for that matter, the poems of Alexander Pope. That is, both the plots and the music of these shows allude to idealized conventions of heroism and romantic love that were, from the vantage point of the early 1930s, felt to be comically outmoded—although these conventions were still familiar enough, alive enough, that references to them could be meaningfully humorous or charming.

Consider "A Kiss for Cinderella" from *Of Thee I Sing*, which Wintergreen delivers just before he and Mary Turner are married. It's a takeoff, as Ira Gershwin has written, "on the bachelor-farewell type of song, best exemplified by John Golden and Ivan Caryll's 'Goodbye Girls, I'm Through' (*Chin-Chin*, 1914)." So, at least for a 1931 audience, the meaning of "Cinderella" cannot be separated from the song's network of allusions—which places ironic quotation marks around Wintergreen's adieu to his former girlfriends, while it also permits some genuine wistfulness about his impending marriage to seep through (an emotion that would emerge in a quite different way if Wintergreen directly stated it). But such patterns of reference, which run all through *Sing* and *Cake*, would seem difficult to animate in 1987—if only because the emotional and musical conventions that the Gershwins were toying with in these scores no longer are familiar to most of us.

There is a solution, though, because if each performer understands the style of such scores and can bring it to life (as McGlinn and his cohorts did at the Library of Congress), the audience can't help but detect the special delights of early- and middle-period Gershwin and begin to grasp the delicate tendrils of reference that trail back from this music into the still more distant past. Some of that magic can be found on the CBS set, for which one must be grateful. But by no means do Tilson-Thomas and his cast always find the proper path, particularly when it comes to the question of how much, and in what way, this music ought to be characterized.

Gershwin's close associate Kay Swift—who, at age ninety, played an advisory role in these recordings—has stated that Gershwin "never had a conductor like Tilson-Thomas. Everything that's exciting in the music, he brings it right out." But Tilson-Thomas's brand of excitement veers dangerously close to artificial peppiness at times, as though the conductor felt that the music needed an extra dose of pizzazz in order to make it in today's marketplace. Tilson-Thomas takes much of *Of Thee I Sing* too quickly (faster doesn't always mean funnier), while exposed instrumental lines that have humorous connotations often are exaggerated to the point of caricature. And the same holds true for the singers—not only because some of them have voices that are a bit off for their parts, but also because, in the tricky area of characterization, they seem to have taken their cue from Tilson-Thomas's whiz-bang approach.

Of the four principals—Larry Kert (John P. Wintergreen), Maureen McGovern (Mary Turner), Jack Gilford (Alexander Throttlebottom), and Paige O'Hara (Diana Deveraux)—only Gilford is consistently "there," perhaps because he is old enough to have direct knowledge of the conventions that the other performers are attempting to re-create. Kert's voice, a bit hollow and frayed around the edges, sounds too world-weary for the role of Wintergreen—the peppiness, when it comes, is again being applied from the outside, although in both scores he handles the gentler moments with feeling and grace. McGovern's vocal equipment is in better shape, and she, too, relaxes nicely on the ballads. But McGovern has a rather brassy, "head" voice, not the light, pure soprano that Mary Turner's blend of innocence and resourcefulness requires; at times she brings Bernadette Peters to mind, turning Mary into a hardboiled mock-ingenue. O'Hara sings up a storm in her more overtly comic role, but her characterization also goes in and out of focus. Right on the mark in the bluesy recitative from *Of Thee I Sing* that begins with the words "I was the most beautiful blossom in all the Southland" (a marvelous moment that prefigures *Porgy and Bess*), elsewhere O'Hara slathers her voice with attitude—not quite killing the humor of her role but surely making it too obvious. There is, however, one performer in *Of Thee I Sing* who is ideal in every way. In the minor part of Sam Jenkins, George Dvorsky sings "Love Is Sweeping the Country" with such simple conviction that one realizes how much the other performers have been nibbling at their roles from one side or the other.

A near-flop on the stage, in musical terms *Let 'Em Eat Cake* is even better than *Of Thee I Sing*—a miniature opera of remarkable density, sophistication, and wit. And because *Cake* is a takeoff on its already satirical predecessor, the Gershwins' elaborate patterns of reference, and the conventions that underlie them, are more evident here than they are in *Sing*. Indeed, the score of *Cake* is so complex that there is less room for Tilson-Thomas and his cast to horse around with it—which may be why *Cake* receives the better, more relaxed performance. And one suspects that the chance to take a second shot at Wintergreen and Mary Turner allowed Kert and McGovern to deepen their understanding of the roles. So if CBS's *Of Thee I Sing* and *Let 'Em Eat Cake* is not the dream set one would have wished it to be, its virtues more than make up for its flaws. Besides, given the difficulties involved in mounting such a project, it seems unlikely that we will ever get another chance to find out what this music is like.

That it is wonderful music when properly performed was confirmed by the Library of Congress concert performances (musically complete, but without dialogue) of *Primrose* and *Pardon My English*. Written for the London stage, where it was a hit in 1924, but never before heard in this country, *Primrose* is a pastoral delight—an oblique tribute to the world of Gilbert and Sullivan that also is full of Gershwin magic. At least one song from *Primrose*, the slyly insinuating "Naughty Baby," has all the hallmarks of the Gershwins at their early best. But the range of the score is quite wide—encompassing the clever patter song "Mary, Queen of Scots," which is garnished with strikingly dissonant French-horn calls, and the witty "Four Little Sirens," which somehow manages to echo both "Three Little Maids from School Are We" from *The Mikado* and the Rhine maidens' song from *Das Rheingold*. And the original orchestrations (three of them written by Gershwin himself, well before he was thought to possess that skill) are a revelation, as their subtly shifting, transparent textures bathe each song in emotionally appropriate tone color.

Equally intriguing is the bolder, jazzier score for *Pardon My English*—which is set in Dresden and begins with the gaily parodistic waltz "In Three-Quarter Time" before it moves on to the more familiar delights of "Isn't It a Pity," "My Cousin in Milwaukee," and "The Lorelei." And here, as in *Primrose*, the proper mode of performance was vital. McGlinn conducted with a lilting grace, while the principal singers (Kim Criswell, Rebecca Luker, Cris Groenendaal, and George Dvorsky) found the ideal vocal middle ground that lies this side of operettalike innocence and that side of urban sophistication. Indeed, the success with which those original styles were recaptured may have been as important as the reemergence of the music itself. Heard in this way, *Primrose* and *Pardon My English* seemed to be not just precursors of the Gershwins' more famous works but a significantly different kind of musical theater—a series of fragrantly pastoral fairy-tale worlds in which a light breeze of parody animates each sweetly romantic pose.

HOAGY CARMICHAEL
[1988]

*T*HE *Classic Hoagy Carmichael*—a boxed set issued by the Indiana Historical Society and the Smithsonian Collection of

Recordings—is, for the most part, a very welcome event. Paying tribute to one of America's most appealing composers and performers, *The Classic Carmichael* contains fifty-seven recordings chosen by coproducers John Edward Hasse and Ronald Radano—including strikingly diverse interpretations of Carmichael's immortal "Stardust" by Louis Armstrong, Artie Shaw, Ella Fitzgerald, Frank Sinatra, Wynton Marsalis, and the composer himself, plus several previously unreleased Carmichael recordings. Packaged with the set is an illustrated sixty-four page booklet in which Hasse (curator of American music at the Smithsonian's National Museum of American History) tells the story of Carmichael's life, provides a critical estimate of his musical career, and discusses each recorded performance.

In his *American Popular Song*, Alec Wilder wrote that "Hoagy Carmichael has proven himself to be the most talented, inventive, sophisticated, and jazz-oriented of all the great craftsmen"—"craftsmen" being Wilder's term for those songwriters who did not write theater scores and who thus, so he felt, ranked just below the likes of Kern, Gershwin, Berlin, and Porter. The positive side of Wilder's assessment is beyond dispute, but one wonders whether his relegation of Carmichael to "craftsman" status isn't a matter of apples versus oranges—a failure to see that Carmichael's gifts were significantly different from those of Kern, Berlin, and the rest. Oddly enough, a similar unwillingness to place Carmichael within his proper musical and social context pervades Hasse's largely celebratory booklet. So even though Carmichael's music certainly speaks for itself, some course-correction seems necessary.

Born in Bloomington, Indiana, Hoagland Howard Carmichael (1899–1981) was not a figure who ever would feel at home in urban America—as Kern, Berlin, and Gershwin, all either born or reared in New York City, did as a matter of course. In fact, a dreamlike vision of the wholeness of rural or small-town life lies at the heart of Carmichael's art—just as the music of Gershwin and the rest often was pervaded by an air of urban tension, loneliness, and romantic doubt. That distinction becomes clear when one compares Carmichael's and Gershwin's approaches to the music, and the lives, of black Americans—the former's in such songs as "Washboard Blues," "Lazybones," and "Hong Kong Blues," the latter's, most notably, in *Porgy and Bess*.

As Wilfrid Mellers pointed out in his *Music in a Newfound Land*, the theme of *Porgy and Bess* is Gershwin's own experience as a displaced modern man, which he poured into the lives of his opera's passionately, though somewhat synthetically, imagined black subjects. But no such division between subject and composer exists whenever Carmichael's music touches upon black American life. Listen, for instance, to one of Hasse and Radano's most inspired choices—a marvelous 1935 recording of "Lazybones" by vocalist Fred Norman with the Claude Hopkins Orchestra. Norman, who happens to be black, sings Johnny Mercer's lyric with an irresistibly sly, slow-motion wit. Yet Hasse's booklet is eager to deprive Norman, Mercer, and Carmichael of the supple self-awareness that they and the song quite obviously possess.

"Alec Wilder has praised Mercer's 'perfect regional lyric,'" Hasse writes, "and indeed it is vivid, and together with the music, quite catchy. At the same time, it presents a stereotyped image of a lazy black person. The lyric's dialect . . . [indicates] that the lyrics are not referring to a white lad from the South." Well, maybe, up to a point. But if a finger is being aimed at anyone in "Lazybones," especially in this lovely recording, it is at the terminally lazy *deliverer* of the song's ironic lecture against laziness, not at the ostensible object of his disdain. And that—plus the song's wistful desire, evident in every phrase, to simply *be* that lazy—is the joke of "Lazybones," which all parties involved are "in" on. So it is, as they say, a sad commentary that anyone should feel the need to bring "stereotyped image" thinking to bear on artists who were, more than fifty years ago, dancing across such barriers with freedom, grace, and wit.

Quite rightly, Carmichael's songwriting and his singing are felt to be near-inseparable—especially by those who first encountered his sandy charms in such films as *To Have and Have Not* and *The Best Years of Our Lives*. But Hasse, applying rather schoolmarmish standards of musical correctness, hardly seems to care for Carmichael's voice at all. "At first," he writes, "listeners may be distracted by the flatness in much of Carmichael's singing and turned off especially by his uncertain intonation. The singer himself said, 'My native wood-note and often off-key voice is what I call "flatsy through the nose." ' But with repeated listenings one becomes accustomed to these traits and grows to appreciate and admire other qualities of his vocal performances."

Well, Carmichael was a popular recording artist for many years, which suggests that few listeners were "distracted" or "turned off" by his "flatsy" singing. Quite the contrary, because, as Carmichael said, that was his *native* wood-note"—a vital part of his expressive machinery. Or would Hasse prefer a Carmichael who sounded as smooth as Mel Torme or Vic Damone? Hasse's finicky tastes have led him to exclude performances from the 1956 Pacific Jazz album *Hoagy Sings Carmichael* because the "vocals just weren't up to snuff"—this of an album that many Carmichael admirers prize above all others, in part because of the heartfelt communion between Carmichael and alto saxophonist Art Pepper on such pieces as "Winter Moon." (Pepper's 1980 remake of "Winter Moon" is included here, but it pales alongside the original.)

Regrettable, too, is the absence of anything by Carmichael's Collegians (the quite sophisticated, rhythmically supple jazz band that Carmichael led during and after his stay at Indiana University in the mid-1920s), and the inclusion of Carmen McRae's detached, brittle version of "Skylark" instead of, say, Aretha Franklin's ecstatic reading of the song or Sylvia Syms's wise and warm interpretation. But there is a cornucopia of marvelous music here: Bix Beiderbecke and Frankie Trumbauer's "Riverboat Shuffle" ("Stardust" and "Skylark," it has often been said, are pure Beiderbecke, particularly the former song's cascading verse and the latter's bridge or release), Armstrong's "Lazy River" (with one of his most fantastic scat vocals), Benny Goodman's elegant performance of "Ballad in Blue" (in a subtle, ghostly arrangement by Spud Murphy), Mildred Bailey's glorious timbral shadings on "Small Fry" and her signature song,

"Rockin' Chair," Artie Shaw's perfect "Stardust" (with superb contributions from trumpeter Billy Butterfield and trombonist Jack Jenny), the sublime purity of Jo Stafford's "Ivy," the gliding ease of Mel Torme's "One Morning in May," Sheila Jordan's intensely hip "Baltimore Oriole," and Sarah Vaughan's sweeping recomposition of "The Nearness of You"—the music of a composer whose work still seems infinitely renewable and unfailingly fresh.

SMITHSONIAN POP
[1985]

COMPILED by J. R. Taylor, James R. Morris, and Dwight Block Bowers, the Smithsonian Institute's boxed set *American Popular Song* is a definitive piece of work, 110 shrewdly chosen recordings that outline and illuminate one of this nation's most precious cultural treasures—the body of music that was created between the turn of the century and the advent of rock 'n' roll. After listening to *American Popular Song* straight through— which is highly recommended, provided you have the time and patience—one emerges with a heart full of pleasure and a head buzzing with all sorts of discoveries and fresh ideas.

In the "discovery" category, for example, there is Marion Harris, a singer who flourished during the 1920s, only to be virtually forgotten when she emigrated to England in 1931. Represented in *American Popular Song* by three strong performances, including a superb 1927 recording of George Gershwin's "The Man I Love," Harris stands revealed as a major artist—far more rhythmically alert than most singers of her era, with a sweetly pure, "natural" voice and a depth of feeling that is timeless. Another discovery, though many listeners already will have made it, is Fred Astaire—who is, perhaps surprisingly, the anthology's most heavily featured vocalist, with nine performances. (Tony Bennett, Judy Garland, and Ella Fitzgerald are next in line with five each, followed by Frank Sinatra, Nat "King" Cole, and Bing Crosby with four.)

While Astaire's prominence may seem like special pleading on the compilers' part, it is not. Obscured to some extent by his prowess as a dancer, Astaire's vocal gifts were unique and profoundly influential; one need only listen to his 1935 recording of Irving Berlin's "Cheek to Cheek" to get the message. Astaire's spry, conversational voice never calls attention to itself but instead seems to inhabit the song—as though Berlin's words and music had proposed a world within which Astaire can move as freely as a man strolling down the street. On the other hand, that sense of freedom and space gives Astaire all the room he needs to add his own point of view, a wry inner smile that simultaneously toys with and reinforces the song's romantic sentiments. "Yes, I am in love," Astaire seems to be saying, "but I'm trying not to take it too seriously."

Romance, of course, is the chief subject of the American popular song, and if there is one key difference between this kind of music and the kinds that came before and after, it has to do with our changing attitudes toward love. "The principle shift in lyric themes," writes James R. Morris in the book that accompanies *American Popular Song*, "was from nostalgia to romantic love, as twentieth-century popular songs began to be more confrontational in their descriptions of emotion, more attuned to the protagonist's personal experience and subjective involvement. Narrative songs, and particularly third-person accounts of things that happened to other people, went into decline. Close to half the songs in this collection explore the 'you and me' vein: 'I' sing of my feelings for 'you' and 'your' response to 'me,' and both are clearly matters of great importance. But despite this concentration on a single broad topic, and the occasional lapses into fantasy, very few of these songs present a nineteenth-century fatalistic view. Instead, most of them reflect the belief—realistic or not—that experiences of the past and emotions of the present do not lock the future into place."

Moving through *American Popular Song,* it's easy to detect the changes in attitude that Morris is talking about, noticing too that these changes are linked to a series of shifts in compositional and performing style. Here, again, Astaire is a crucial figure, both in terms of the songs he sings and the way he sings them. He is sophisticated yet down-to-earth, optimistic about life and love but aware of the obstacles involved, and willing above all to talk about these matters (both to us and to himself) in a tone of voice that is very close to the one we use in normal, face-to-face conversation.

That this approach was something new becomes obvious when one places Astaire's work alongside the very first performance on *American Popular Song,* Sophie Tucker's 1910 recording of Shelton Brooks's "Some of These Days," and then moves on to Al Jolson's 1921 version of "April Showers." As Morris points out, Jolson's vocal style is "presentational, not reflective," and much the same is true of Tucker—although she sings with a driving rhythmic power that seems far more modern than Jolson's rather stiff, vaudeville manner. In both cases, though, the performances have the size and the impersonal impact of a billboard. It's impossible to imagine Tucker's "Some of These Days" or Jolson's "April Showers" being addressed to one person— their audience is a faceless multitude—and the shift from this style to the direct intimacy of Astaire or Marion Harris is almost shocking.

Such matters are relative, of course, or so we often are told. But while listening to *American Popular Song,* it's hard not to think that some genuine discoveries were being made—that the songwriting tradition of Richard Rodgers, Cole Porter, George Gershwin, Harold Arlen, et al., and the corresponding performance styles of Astaire, Sinatra, Fitzgerald, Garland, Bennett, and the rest were very real artistic and emotional advances over what had come before. But if those linked traditions are what they seem to be—a series of songs that deserve to be called "standards" and a way of performing them that heightened their virtues—then how and why did this rich body of music pass away from us?

That it has done so, no one can deny. The puppetlike flutterings of Linda Ronstadt are the latest proof that there are few young vocalists who know how to sing these songs. And it's impossible to come up with a single contemporary pop composer whose work has much to do with the tradition of songwriting that gave us "The Man I Love," "Skylark," "Stormy Weather," "Little Girl Blue," "All the Things You Are," and "I've Got You Under My Skin." To the degree that things changed for socio-economic reasons, one can date the crucial moment precisely—the week in 1956 when Elvis Presley's "Don't Be Cruel"/"Hound Dog" single first topped all three *Billboard* magazine sales charts (pop, rhythm and blues, and country). With that, as the saying goes, rock 'n' roll was here to stay, and any music that had less demographic appeal was fated, sooner or later, for the commercial scrap heap. But by the time one reaches the last two sides of *American Popular Song,* there are some hints that the great tradition also was breaking faith with itself, disrupting the delicate emotional/artistic balance that made this music possible.

While listening, for instance, to the five superb Tony Bennett recordings that come near the end of the anthology, especially his performance of Arlen's hauntingly beautiful "A Sleepin' Bee," one is overwhelmed by the sense of belief and commitment that Bennett brings to the music. Yet if Bennett's passion is compared to Astaire's cooler approach, it is clear that the two men inhabit different worlds—for there is something private, even threatened, within Bennett's emotional intensity, while the blithe Astaire seems to assume that his attitudes toward life, love, and song are so widely shared and central that he needn't press the point. But it's the rare performer who can, as Bennett still does, detect the first stages of isolation and make them a part of his art. Far more common is the approach one hears on Barbra Streisand's version of Richard Rodgers's "Quiet Night" and Leslie Uggams's reading of Frank Loesser's "Spring Will Be a Little Late This Year"—a heightening of the "presentational" nature of the performance that places the singer as singer front-and-center, deflects attention from the song itself, and breaks down the "I am speaking to you" quality that was so vital to the great tradition.

Listening to Streisand—or, for that matter, to most rock vocalists—one is right back with Sophie Tucker and Al Jolson (who was, as it happens, one of Elvis Presley's idols), responding to an art that seeks to address the audience en masse instead of quickening each individual's sense of self. From that point of view, perhaps we should be grateful that we ever had the kind of music that *American Popular Song* so handsomely celebrates, that this nation managed to give us a body of songs that blended romance and realism and a group of singers who were life-sized and humane.

BILLIE HOLIDAY
[1985]

A DMIRERS of Billie Holiday's music are legion, and they tend to fall into two camps. Those who love her fresh-voiced early work (the small-group recordings she made from 1933 to 1941, backed by such masters as pianist Teddy Wilson and tenor saxophonist Lester Young) often can't abide her later recordings, when Holiday's voice became frayed and her moods were mostly melancholic. Yet even though the strain on her vocal and emotional resources occasionally became so great that she withdrew into an uncommunicative listlessness, some listeners prefer the latter-day Holiday, feeling that the passage of time served to deepen her emotional powers almost until the very end. (She was forty-four when she died, on July 17, 1959.) Asked in the late 1950s whether he felt Holiday was in decline, Miles Davis said: "I'd rather hear her now. She's become more mature. Sometimes you can sing words every night for five years, and all of a sudden it dawns on you what the song means. So with Billie, you know she's not thinking now what she was in 1937, and she's probably learned more about different things. And she still has control, probably more control now than then."

Most of Holiday's later work has just been reissued on *Billie Holiday on Verve: 1946–1959*, a ten-record boxed set. Listening straight through these 134 performances can be a daunting experience. But it is a rewarding one, too, because when Holiday's art is encountered en masse, its most crucial aspects stand revealed as never before.

First, last, and always, Holiday was both a singer and a musician, one whose sense of swing and ability to improvise were approached only by the greatest jazz instrumentalists. In fact, when Holiday was in her early prime and surrounded by the best musicians of the day, her rhythmic ideas often were more subtle than those of her accompanists. For instance, Holiday's 1936 version of "I Cried for You" begins with a Johnny Hodges alto saxophone solo that has a bouncy charm. But when Holiday begins to sing, her stark, long-lined phrasing seems to come from a different, more rhythmically subtle world. The purely musical side of Holiday's art never ceased to develop, and *Billie Holiday on Verve* contains any number of performances (perhaps the latest being her sublime 1957 version of "Embraceable You") that are more daring than anything she attempted in her so-called golden years. But Holiday's daring was emotional, too, for all of her harmonic, melodic, and rhythmic ideas were firmly linked to the stories she told. Of course, the same might be said of any gifted jazz vocalist. But especially in Holiday's later work, her stories often ran counter to those of the songs she sang, as she took the sentimentality that pervades even the best American popular music and placed it in an acid bath of emotional realism. In some cases, a near-brutal irony was involved, as in Holiday's 1955 recording of "What's New"—where lyrics that were originally intended to be a token of wistful regret acquire such a dark, cutting edge that one feels the song might be a prelude to murder or suicide. More often, though, the emotional tone of Holiday's later work was richly complex—a blend of compassion, rage, and pathos that arose as she roamed the dream world of American popular music, aware that its romantic images were dubious or false but unable or unwilling to escape from their grip. "Pop music was her mythology," said critic Wilfrid Mellers. And as long as we believe in romantic love, it is our mythology, too—which is why the best Holiday recordings are not simply performances but acts of mutual confrontation in which both the singer and her audience are required to tell the truth.

Yet Holiday had a further truth to tell. As the shape of her later career emerges on *Billie Holiday on Verve*, it, too, becomes an essential component of her art—an account in song of who Billie Holiday really was is what one always hoped to hear from her. As her life was darkened by drug addiction, failed romances, and a host of other demons, it would have been absurd if she somehow had retained the girlish freshness of her early work. So throughout this set, one encounters unmistakable signs of vocal and emotional grief (hoarseness, darkened tone color, imprecisions of pitch, moments of tearful tremolo, and further descents in register). But these apparently insurmountable barriers to effective performance are exactly what Holiday needed to raise her art onto its final tragic plane. Unable to withstand the advance of decay and death—which is, after all, the lot of every human being—Holiday made a secret pact with defeat, one that allowed her to sing of her fate at the moment it overwhelmed her. In no way, though, should this aspect of Holiday's art be confused with the kind of morbidly melodramatic showbiz romanticism that marked the later stages of Judy Garland's career. If Holiday was an actress to some extent, she was, in critic Martin Williams's felicitous phrase, "an actress without an act."

A woman who knew the suffocating embrace of fame, Holiday never confused that world with the essentially private modes of feeling she brought to bear on her songs. In the course of *Billie Holiday on Verve*, there are times when a good many listeners will falter; for the set includes performances, and even entire recording sessions, where one feels certain that Holiday has reached a dead end. And these moments crop up as early as 1952, when she delivers the brittle lyric of "Autumn in New York" in a mood of curdled disgust. But time after time, Holiday recovers, recasting her art to fit her shrinking resources. And almost until the end, each new adjustment not only restores her to life but also inspires her to sing with passion and insight.

The glories of *Billie Holiday on Verve* begin with her famous 1946 performance at a Jazz at the Philharmonic concert (which includes her most touching version of "Travelin' Light") and a superb, previously unissued Jazz at the Philarmonic set from 1947, where she is accompanied by pianist Bobby Tucker. Then comes the studio work—two tender but rather tentative sessions from early 1952; a fine group of songs from later that year (buoyed by the presence of Freddie Green's rhythm guitar); two faltering 1954 dates; a revival in 1955 with a group under the leadership of clarinetist Tony Scott; and then a triumphant two-day, sixteen-song marathon that pairs her with trumpeter Harry Edison and alto saxophonist Benny Carter. And so it goes, in patterns impossible to predict. An August 1956 date with Edison and tenor saxophonist Ben Webster is almost unbearably grim. But Holiday's November 1956 Carnegie Hall concert is excellent, and a January 1957 reunion with Edison and Webster produces eighteen songs in less than a week, each of them a blessing. After that, though, Holiday has no more left to give, a verdict that is confirmed by a doleful date with strings and two concert performances that are best forgotten.

Commenting on some of Holiday's mid-1940s recordings, critic Glenn Coulter wrote: "A touch of self-pity might have made them less painful, but Billie Holiday does not show mercy, least of all to herself." And Holiday's closest musical associate, Lester Young (he gave her the nickname "Lady Day," and she dubbed him "Pres"), could have been speaking for both of them when he said: "It's the same all over. You fight for your life until death do you part—and then you got it made."

SARAH VAUGHAN
[1983, 1994]

L IKE Art Tatum, with whom points of comparison are fruitful and numerous, Sarah Vaughan has often been regarded as an extravagant artist—extravagantly gifted of course, for who could deny Vaughan's (or Tatum's) ear or executive abilities, but also simply extravagant, as though she (and Tatum) were musical spendthrifts who indulged in wasteful displays of virtuosity when a less flamboyant approach might have brought greater aesthetic rewards. The problem, though, if problem there be, is that we have only one Sarah Vaughan, and if the listener responds to Vaughan's undeniable virtues, how, in any real sense, can those virtues be separated from her alleged flaws? Besides, if one truly grasps the nature of Vaughan's art and makes some educated guesses about its organic interconnectedness and the emotional makeup of the person who stood behind it, are her flaws—again as with Tatum—really flaws at all? Indeed, a strong case can be made that, tempered by her humane, all-encompassing playfulness, Vaughan's fundamental themes are that darkly romantic pair trangression and rapture, and that however extravagant her means might be, they are just what is required.

Pianist Jimmy Rowles is among those who have made the Tatum-Vaughan comparison, and Rowles should know whereof he speaks, having worked with such singers as Ella Fitzgerald, Billie Holiday, Carmen McRae, and Peggy Lee. And Rowles is not the only musician who feels that way about Vaughan. Chick Corea, who once served as her accompanist, has said that playing with Vaughan was the biggest musical challenge he ever faced, "because she's so creative and never sings a song the same way twice." And no less an authority than composer-conductor-critic Gunther Schuller named Vaughan as "the greatest vocal artist of the century." "It is one thing," Schuller said, "to have a beautiful voice. It is another to be a great musician. It is still another to be a great musician with a beautiful voice who can also compose. [Vaughan's voice] is the perfect instrument, attached to a musician of superb instincts [and] capable of expressing profound human experience."

Quite a bouquet of praise. But when some of those words were relayed to Vaughan last month, the day before she was to perform an all-Gershwin program at the Ravinia Festival with the Chicago Symphony Orchestra, her response was typically irreverent; she rocked back on the couch of her hotel suite, kicked her feet up in the air, and emitted a little "he-he-he" laugh, as though she were a schoolgirl who had unexpectedly been asked to the big dance. Laughter, in fact, is Vaughan's response to a whole host of positive and not-so-positive things, and other than singing, it seems to be her main method of dealing with the world. That "he-he-he" laugh is mostly a nervous one, Vaughan's way of pushing to one side anything that doesn't quite make sense or even seems threatening to her. It's an arm's-length laugh that has a "yes, but" or a "well, maybe" built into it, and if at such moments one could read Vaughan's mind, her thoughts might go like this: "Well, maybe that 'profound human experience' stuff is how it sounds to Gunther Schuller, and I guess it's kind of nice. But it sure won't help me get through the 'The Man I Love' tomorrow night." At the other end of the spectrum there is her basso profundo guffaw, which is Vaughan's way of saying, "Hey, it *is* all right, even though I had my doubts." A vast, warm explosion of relaxation and relief, that laugh could be heard quite often during the Sunday afternoon rehearsal at Ravinia—as though each time she ran through a tune Vaughan didn't quite believe that she was going to meet her stern private standards of musical taste.

Whether or not she met those standards, only Vaughan can say. But what she did during the rehearsal certainly confirmed Corea's remark about her never singing a song the same way twice. Repeating brief sections of tunes so conductor Michael Tilson-Thomas could coordinate the orchestra with her, Vaughan varied the flow of the music even more than most jazz instrumentalists are likely to do, especially at a rehearsal. The first time through the verse of "But Not for Me," she turned the words "cheerful Pollyanna" into a startlingly baroque phrase, ending on a delicate upper-register trill that fluttered like a hummingbird. The next time she scooped into that portion of the song from the most cavernous lower reaches of her voice—rising in one unbroken swoop of sound from mock-baritone to girlish soprano and varying the density and color of her tone as she went along. The men and women of the orchestra, who must have heard almost everything in their time, looked appropriately awed, and Tilson-Thomas blew Vaughan a kiss. Her response was a laugh, the "he-he-he" one.

"About not singing a song the same way twice," says Vaughan after the rehearsal, "that's just because I can't remember what I did before. Believe me, [basso laugh] my memory's been short for a *long* time. I certainly don't do it to challenge myself or anything like that. It's just natural. I never go out there and say I'm going to do better than I did the last show, because I really don't know how good I was in the first place. Sure, there have been performances when I've done something a little different and surprised myself. But when that happens, what makes it so good is that the next bar [of the music] responds to what you've just done. Then based on what I've done, I and everybody else have an idea of where to go next. That's something you don't teach; it just happens.

"For instance, I listened to some good singers when I was coming up—Ella and Billie, Jo Stafford, and Martha Raye—and I stole from them a lot. But you don't have to steal from good singers; you can steal from a bad singer, too. Just because a bad singer sings it bad, that's got nothing to do with it. They may be singing right things and just making them sound bad. That's why if I make a mistake, I always do it again, so it won't be a mistake the next time."

Born in Newark, New Jersey, in 1924, Vaughan studied piano from age eight and sang with her mother in the choir of the Mount Zion Baptist Church, though she says (basso laugh again), "I usually played the piano. It's not that they didn't let me sing, but I never got the solos." Vaughan was familiar with jazz while still a child (her father was a guitarist who "played a little bit," and legendary trumpeter Jabbo Smith could be heard at a neighborhood bar). But a career as a hairdresser was what Vaughan had in mind when, in October 1942, a friend dared her to enter the amateur contest at Harlem's Apollo Theater.

"I played and sang 'Body and Soul,'" Vaughan recalls, "and I won first prize, which was ten dollars plus a week's engagement. What was the competition? Well, I remember this Puerto Rican who came out in a short skirt and wearing a gun. That was funny. They snatched him *right* off.

"Before that I'd tried out for Major Bowes [the popular radio amateur show], but I couldn't get on because I wasn't singing the right kind of song. Hambone, hambone—those were the only kind of people who got on Major Bowes. But I only eat ham bones, I don't sing 'em. Actually, I went to the Apollo just to get the ten dollars. I didn't think about the week, and if I hadn't won, I would have gone back home. Yeah, I might have been a hairdresser. Al-*most*."

Instead, during her prize-winning week, Vaughan was heard by Billy Eckstine, the vocal star of the Earl Hines band. Eckstine returned the next night with his boss, and, says Vaughan, "thanks to Billy I was in show business within two weeks, singing and playing the piano with Earl Hines. What kind of person was I when I joined the band? Oh, you should have seen me—very nice but very shy and very frightened and afraid to let anybody know it. You know, a real 'hip kid.' I was shocked to be there, but I was there. And I didn't stay scared for long, because I was having too much fun."

Reportedly one of the greatest jazz ensembles (though it never recorded because of the American Federation of Musicians 1942–44 recording ban), the 1943 Hines band included many musicians who were shaping the style that soon would be known as bebop, including the two most important innovators of all, alto saxophonist Charlie Parker and trumpeter Dizzy Gillespie. With her wide vocal range, deep sense of swing, and acute ear for harmonies, Vaughan fit right in with what Parker, Gillespie, and the others were doing. "Yeah, I learned a lot from those fellows," Vaughan says. "I was with 'em, and that's that, because you *know* who was there. Billy was like my father, and we all loved each other musically. I was just one of the guys, which is the best way, because I'm not happy if the musicians don't like me—especially if they're good. Charlie Parker, the Chicago Symphony—if they don't like you, you must be doing something wrong."

Vaughan and most of the other Hines beboppers left to join Eckstine's new band in 1944, which led to the first permanent evidence of what Vaughan was up to—her initial recording, "I'll Wait and Pray." After that she recorded with Parker and Gillespie and then under her own name, producing such early masterpieces as "Lover Man," "A Hundred Years From Today," "You're Not the Kind," and "Tenderly." By 1950, when Vaughan made her superb second version of "Mean to Me"—displaying, in the words of critic Martin Williams, "a sensitivity and grace worthy of the great instrumentalists"—Vaughan was out on her own, packaged as a supper-club star by her manager and first husband, trumpeter George Treadwell. Dubbed "The Divine One" by Chicago disc jockey Dave Garroway (her friends prefer "Sassy"), Vaughan began to work the fancier clubs and make pop records as well as jazz-oriented ones—a development that some of her fans considered a sellout.

Though Vaughan admits that her biggest hit, "Broken-Hearted Melody," was "a very corny song," by no means has her post-bop career been one of artistic decline. Instead, throughout Vaughan's pop period and right up to the present day, she has been deepening and refining her style. A near-ideal testing ground for notions of who Vaughan is artistically are the twenty-four tracks included on her 1956 two-LP Mercury set, *Great Songs From Hit Shows*. In the chapter Williams devoted to Vaughan in his book *The Jazz Tradition*, he pointed out that it is on *Great Songs From Hit Shows* that "all her resources began to come together and a great artist emerged." Those resources, he explained, included "an exceptional range (roughly of soprano through baritone), exceptional body, volume, a variety of vocal textures, and superb and highly personal vocal control. . . . When she first discovered her vibrato, she indulged it. But it has become a discreet ornament . . . of unusually flexible size, shape, and duration." All true, but perhaps more needs to be said about Vaughan's vibrato, which to my mind is not an "ornament," no matter how discreetly it is used, but a resource that, for Vaughan, may be the most fundamental of all.

Great Songs From Hit Shows includes at least four jazz-vocal masterpieces: "Little Girl Blue" ("the best version ever of that lovely Rodgers and Hart lament": Gary Giddins), "Bewitched, Bothered and Bewildered," "Dancing in the Dark" ("every note seems to be bursting out of the confines of that song, and it is not exactly a simple one": Williams), and "It Never Entered My Mind," where the ascending stepwise phrase that concludes the bridge is transformed by Vaughan into the musical equivalent of an Art Nouveau staircase. And there are at least three others here ("Autumn in New York," "You're My Everything," and "All the Things You Are") that are a hair's breadth below that level. All of these performances are ballads taken at slowish tempos (an almost impossibly but thrillingly slow one for "Dancing in the Dark"), with touches of rubato and/or out-of-tempo phrasing from both Vaughan and the string-laden orchestra. Yet every one of these performances is marked by a sense of swing on Vaughan's part that is quite overwhelming. Indeed, on *Great Songs From Hit Shows* she swings harder and more freely on the ballads than she does on all but one of the medium- to up-tempo tracks, where she is accompanied by a brass-and-reeds big band or a brass-and-reeds-plus-strings ensemble. In part that's because most of the big-band tracks have a rather mechanical, neo-Lunceford feel to them. But the key reason the best ballad tracks here are so rhythmically compelling is that Vaughan's sense of swing begins in her sound. That is, her shadings of vibrato, volume, and timbre are also rhythmic events (rhythm, after all, being a facet of vibration)—to the point where the degree of rhythmic activity *within* a given Vaughan note (especially at slowish tempos) can be as intense, and as precisely controlled, as that of any of her note-to-note rhythmic relationships. And one notices that so much here because, as the occasionally very sugary strings swirl around her and flutes are left hanging from the chandeliers, control of the rhythmic flow is left almost entirely in Vaughan's hands.

Of course a taste for imperceptibly shading tone-color events into rhythmic ones is not unique to Vaughan; Debussy's music, for one, is unthinkable without it, as is, for that matter, Johnny Hodges's and Johnny Dodds's. But Vaughan's overtone-rich timbre, the way it and her vibrato interact, and the seemingly spontaneous control she has over every aspect of all this are unique. As Gunther Schuller put it, Vaughan doesn't have one voice but voices, while her vibrato is a "compositional, structural . . . element." Just listen to Vaughan in full flight—say, at the very beginning of "You're My Everything." In the six seconds and five notes that it takes her to sing the title phrase, cruising out on the booming lushness she gives to "thing," it's virtually impossible to sort out whether, at any point, it is rhythmic needs that are shaping Vaughan's timbral colorations or vice versa—and that is as it should be. In fact, one way to describe Vaughan's timbre-cum-vibrato, inside-the-note rhythmic shapes would be to say that she has drums in her voice—perhaps Elvin Jones's.

"I've read that I have a four-octave or a five-octave range," Vaughan says, "but I know that's not true. If I had a five-octave range, I'd *really* be rich. But while the top has stayed about the same, the bottom has gotten much lower and richer, which I guess is an amazing thing. I know it amazes me—probably much more than it does you. And there are notes between notes, you know."

CABARET MUSIC
[1988]

WE are, so it seems, in the midst of a modest but genuine revival of cabaret music—the always sophisticated, sometimes brash and campy style of entertainment that used to prevail in the smarter nightspots of New York, London, and Paris. Essentially an American phenomenon, cabaret music took shape in the mid-1930s. And it lasted until that indeterminate point in the late 1950s or early 1960s when the notion that there was such a thing as an aristocracy of taste, let alone a literal or figurative aristocracy to support it, finally began to seem out of date. In fact, the return of cabaret music, in the hands of such earnest young interpreters as singer-pianist Michael Feinstein, is based in large part on the music's datedness. Able to evoke an era of elegance and romance that most of its current performers and fans were not around to experience firsthand, cabaret music now seems all the more attractive to some because we live in a world where such virtues are hard to come by.

But re-creations are one thing and the originals are another—which is why *The Erteguns' New York Cabaret Music*, a boxed set recently released on the Atlantic label, is a cultural-historical event of considerable importance. Produced by Atlantic's legendary chairman of the board, Ahmet Ertegun—who founded the label in 1947 and who has through the years, along with his older brother, Nesuhi, played a major role in shaping America's taste in popular music—*New York Cabaret Music* preserves some of the best work of the acknowledged heroine and hero of the cabaret style, Mabel Mercer and Bobby Short. But because, as Ahmet Ertegun explains, "we recorded this music as it showed up," the set also includes the work of a number of equally intriguing but now almost forgotten performers— among them vocalists Greta Keller and Mae Barnes, singer-pianists Ted Straeter and Hugh Shannon, and keyboard virtuosos Cy Walter and Goldie Hawkins. And it is this sense of the total scene that makes *New York Cabaret Music* so vital—for this was a style of entertainment that was so intimately tied to the emotional and social makeup of its audience that neither side of the equation can be grasped unless one has a good sense of the other.

Encountered out of context, for instance, Mabel Mercer's clipped, brittle singing can sound quite peculiar. Her "constant dignification of otherwise casual songs" (the apt phrase is composer Alec Wilder's) erects a barrier of high-toned classiness between the listener and the music, until one begins to feel that exclusion, not communication, is the goal of Mercer's art. But when the context of her work is sketched in, as it is by the rest of the performers who appear on *New York Cabaret Music*, it becomes clear that exclusion, but of a particular sort, is just what Mercer was communicating—an attitude toward popular music, and toward life in general, that only a certain group of "in the know" people were equipped to understand and share.

"In my youth," recalls Ertegun, who was very much a part of that scene, "a grand evening was to have dinner at a restaurant like Café Chambord, then go to El Morocco to dance and then travel up to Harlem or down to Greenwich Village and hear somebody like Mae Barnes. Mae's songs, I think, are among the most delightful things on the set." Indeed they are—ten cheerfully uproarious, urgently swinging performances, marked by glimmers of impish wit, from a singer-dancer who got her start in the all-black revues of the 1920s and then, in the 1940s, became a fixture at a Greenwich Village club, the Bon Soir. A favorite of the Duke and Duchess of Windsor and Elsa Maxwell, Barnes might be described as a female Fats Waller. So exuberant that it could make the whole night seem like fun, Barnes's music, like Waller's, had a definite air of the put-on and the put-down to it—a rebellious impulse that was directed in part toward her smart, sophisticated audience but one with which that audience also was able to identify. Singing Irving Berlin's "(I Ain't Gonna Be No) Topsy," a parodistic protest against the typecasting of black performers, Barnes delivers the song with a coruscating glee that borders on genuine rage at times, as Barnes plays the stereotypes that the lyric says she wishes to leave behind against her own impishly knowing "hot momma" mannerisms. But at whom was Barnes aiming this little whirlwind of wink-and-nod attitudes? Not at her fans, it would seem, though most of them belonged to the social and financial power elite. And not at herself either. Instead the joke, which she and her audience were able to share, lay in the link she drew between the song's send-up of racial servitude and her well-heeled, well-connected audience's desire to do whatever it damn well pleased (without, of course, violating the prevailing norms of good manners and good taste).

The link between Barnes's ironic Harlem uproar and Mercer's rigidly genteel restraint may seem tenuous at first, but it was, in fact, iron-clad. And its nature and strength can best be understood when one turns to yet another figure whose work is handsomely represented on *New York Cabaret Music*, singer-pianist Ted Straeter. Hired entertainers of black or racially mixed ethnic origins, Barnes and Mercer were, in several senses of the term, members of what used to be called "the servant class" or "the help." But Mercer's art depended on that role and her ability to transform it—for as she assumed a stance of such hauteur that she could look down upon anyone, she provided her admirers with an image of aristocracy that was at once more genuine than the bloodlines of the social register but not, in its fundamental gentility, at war with it.

Straeter was a hired entertainer, too—the leader of a celebrated society band of the era—but he doesn't seem like one at all. "Ted was a bit of a dandy," Ertegun recalls, "a very urbane gentleman who was always very well dressed. More than anybody, he typifies the elegant music that prevailed between the first and second world wars." That estimate is confirmed by Straeter's casual, sandy-voiced singing and his graceful yet seemingly artless piano work—which together create the feeling that he is part of the audience he has been paid to amuse and has agreed to perform only in order to amuse himself. Real or illusory, Straeter's status as a gentleman—that is, a member of the class that doesn't need to work—is evident in everything he sings and plays. And it emerges with particular force on his version of Cole Porter's "All of You," where he interprets Porter's obliquely erotic lyric with an innocent leer that couldn't be more unlike the earthy passion that marks Frank Sinatra's famous recording of the song.

There are a great many more pleasures to be found on *New York Cabaret Music*—some of the finest recordings made by Mercer, Short, and Sylvia Syms (whose version of "Tea for Two," based on a solo by tenor saxophonist Lester Young, swings like crazy); Greta Keller's medley of songs from Kurt Weill and Bertolt Brecht's *Threepenny Opera*, sung in the original German with an emotional insight that rivals the work of Lotte Lenya; the harmonic subtleties and ravishing technique of pianist Cy Walter; the almost delirious good cheer of another, very different pianist, Goldie Hawkins; the brisk, laid-back perfection with which Joe Mooney handles "The Kid's a Dreamer"; and a slow-motion Chris Connor recording of Duke Ellington and Billy Strayhorn's "Something to Live For" that sounds as though Connor had just flung herself from the balcony of the penthouse that figures in Cole Porter's "Down in the Depths on the 90th Floor" (which Syms sings to perfection earlier on in the set). But as remarkable as these and a number of other performances are, the overriding fascination of *New York Cabaret Music* lies in its ability to reveal the nature of the lost world that these artists inhabited, a world whose anxious, fragile codes of sophistication they did so much to define.

"I have always had an interest in what a lot of people call 'good music,'" says Ahmet Ertegun, "as opposed to . . . well, I think that the music that's being made today is great, but there's always a segment of the population, the older generation, that feels its music has somehow been usurped, that the new music has wiped out what they love.

"Now that's not true. Musical tastes inevitably change as history goes on. Things don't remain static; they evolve. And no music remains popular. But after its popularity is gone, the music that has been made still remains. And while the music of the cabaret era must be understood in order for it to be appreciated, that music still is, I believe, very beautiful."

CHRIS CONNOR
[1982]

C OOL, breathy, and almost barren of vibrato, Chris Connor's
voice is a haunted house. Its tone color alone would be
enough to freeze the soul, and the way each phrase seems to be
exhaled more than sung only increases the impression that in
her music Connor must contend with ghostly powers—either
that, or she herself is a spirit summoned unwillingly from beyond.

It's easy to mistake Connor's otherworldly aura for a chic,
dry-martini hipness, which is why she became a star in the
1950s, first with the Stan Kenton Orchestra and then on her
own—"the Kim Novak of the jazz set," as one writer put it. But
even though she appeared to be a second-generation disciple of
Anita O'Day and June Christy who took those singers' mannerisms to near-absurd extremes, Connor was a very different type
of artist. O'Day and Christy were her models, but Connor inhabited their detached, emotionally oblique style of singing in a
way its originators never dreamed of, transforming an attractive
show business commodity into an attitude toward life—a desperate wrestling with herself and the world. That such battles
could not be won on a nightclub stage actually contributed to
the power of Connor's music. Barely contained within the
boundaries of performance, her losses were so deeply felt and
nakedly expressed that communication seemed a paltry word for
what took place. While the pain she gave voice to (and the
numbness that followed in its wake) must have had an inner
source, to be moved by Connor's music was to recognize that
her distress was public as well as private—the advance-guard of
an emotional void that might swallow us all. In that sense the
Kim Novak comparison is perfect, for Connor, as film critic David Thomson said of Novak, has "the desperate attentiveness of
someone out of her depth but refusing to give in."

Connor now appears far more confident and optimistic than she used to be. But much of the essential Connor tension remains, the feeling that music is a dangerous medium that must be plunged into at the point of maximum threat. "The Thrill Is Gone" is one of Connor's signature tunes, and last night at Rick's Café Americain she sang it much more swiftly than in the past—perhaps because, with her vocal technique in fine shape, she needed the challenge of speed to make the emotional content come alive. On "If I Should Lose You," extreme slowness played the same role, forcing Connor into those harrowingly awkward rhythmic corners that only she dares to explore.

Impressive throughout, and altering one's image of Connor to some extent, was the sense of control she displayed on every piece. "Out of her depth" may have been an apt description of her in the past, but now the depths are entered into more out of choice than helplessness. Chris Connor's wounds apparently have healed, perhaps more than she or anyone else dared to expect. But the memory of pain still shudders through her music, creating a dialogue between self and soul, public performance and private meditation, that is as strange as it is beautiful.

TONY BENNETT
[1980, 1985]

I N popular music, it almost never pays to look for beauty in the obvious places. With singers, for example, prettiness is usually fool's gold. The voices that glitter most seductively turn out in the long run to be worthless. You get a momentary thrill, but there's nothing to take home. So forget the "poetry" of sensuous surfaces and dig down to the solid prose—music in which technique exists only to convey emotion, to tell a story and make it believable.

In that realm, Tony Bennett is a king. His voice can be a little hoarse and a shade flat, and it is by no means pretty. But Bennett's lack of vocal sheen heightens communication by lessening the distance between himself and the audience. Combine that with his uncanny sense of how to read a lyric, and the result is a musical experience of startling immediacy. In his hands, the storytelling aspect of a song becomes so prominent that he can be halfway through a familiar melody before its title comes to the listener's mind.

When Bennett talks about his craft, he likes to draw analogies to painting and tennis, his favorite pastime and his favorite sport. "I study light, how light affects nature. And I study feeling the same way. To really feel properly is an art. That's why I've always been drawn toward jazz—because the blues automatically hits the bell. By the third note any blues singer might sing, he goes right into feeling. So then in more, let's say, 'sophisticated' music, I look for songs that interest me, songs whose words represent something that I've lived. It can be simple, plaintive, complex—whatever. But if I can identify with it, I say 'yes' and include it in my repertoire.

"Jo Jones, Count Basie's drummer, told me once, 'Don't linger on any word or phrase except the word 'love.' And I've practiced that. When you get to the word 'love,' you wait a beat and then really mean it when you say it. But like a good tennis player who doesn't 'push,' every once in a while a shot comes along that you can't turn down. Like the first time the word 'fly' appears in 'Fly Me to the Moon.' You've got to whack that one. You step away from your form for half a second, and the song becomes a little different from the way anyone's ever done it before."

In the prime of his musical life at age fifty-one, Bennett has always had a taste for things that are "a little different." His influences, he explains, "have been very eccentric. I studied singing on [New York City's] 52nd Street during the days when Lester Young, Stan Getz, Erroll Garner, and Art Tatum were all playing on this one little strip. My teacher, Miriam Speir, told me, 'Instead of imitating another singer, imitate one of those instrumentalists. Try and get their sound.' The main one for me was Art Tatum. I'd listen to his records almost daily and try to phrase like him. I know it's hard to understand how a singer could be influenced that much by a pianist, but listen to his 'Without a Song' and you'll hear what I mean." And Bennett provides a demonstration, singing the song's opening bars the way Tatum played them. " 'Bah-dah-dah-*dum* (pause) *Boom*-bah-dah-duh-dah-dah-dum.' I just take his phrasing and sing it that way. If you listen to Tatum, you realize that, no matter how fast he's playing, emotion never leaves the concept."

Putting his 52nd Street lessons into practice, Bennett rose to the top in the early 1950s on the strength of his first single, "Boulevard of Broken Dreams," and a steady stream of hits followed. After a commercially fallow period, as rock 'n' roll began to take over the record industry, "I Left My Heart in San Francisco" made him a star all over again in 1962. A permanent place in the firmament seemed assured, and no less a judge than Frank Sinatra proclaimed him to be "the best—the man who gets across what the composer had in mind." But for a second time his career began to curve downward. Not because he had lost his popular appeal but because the executives at Columbia Records were determined to make him into something other than what he was.

"The profit makers," Bennett recalls, "started saying, 'Yes, you sell records, but we want you to sell a lot more.' They insisted that I start doing a lot of Top 40 material. 'Tony,' they said, 'you can sing the telephone book.' But once you start thinking that way, you can get into a big ego problem, believing that you can sing anything. Besides, why sing any old thing just to make money? How much money do you need? So we had a falling out. I left Columbia after twenty-three years and started my own label, Improv Records. The ironic thing is that now, four years after I left, I find out that I'm selling more albums for Columbia than ever before. As long as they're in the bins, people keep buying them.

"The marketing people," Bennett adds, "have some strange attitudes about what should happen to artists. Peggy, Lena, Sinatra, and myself, we never stopped selling records. No one was going to lose money putting out our music. But what the big companies did was kind of go with the overdogs. There was a period when they were taking the money they made from us and putting it into new artists, too many new artists. Every month they'd have sixteen more of them. I called it 'record roulette'—they wanted to win big so much that they put their money on every number. Finally I felt imprisoned by the big conglomerates, and not only because they kicked me around. I saw the promises they handed out to other people and how disappointed they were when the promises turned out to be false. So I just made up my mind that for the rest of my life I would do it myself, do it by hand. I'd rather have a grocery store than a big supermarket. It feels better when there's nothing to prevent me from being in touch with myself.

"But when someone says, 'I won't compromise, I will do things with care,' there comes a moment when you get very frightened and lonely. I had those feelings about two years ago, and I went to [composer-author] Alec Wilder. 'Man,' I said, 'I really feel cold up here.' He told me: 'Look, you have me, you have Mabel Mercer, you have a few people who really understand you. As long as there's a small group of believers who say you're right on course, don't worry. Just go straight ahead.' Well, somehow or other I've come out of the tunnel. The advertisers—because they have to sell their new wares—they call my music out of fashion. So long, Cole Porter, so long, Jerome Kern, so long Gershwin. But the last season and a half, I'm sold out all over the world. The whole episode forced me to make a wonderful choice—to go back to just singing. It's hard to explain, and it may even sound silly, but if you're a singer sometimes you start feeling like you just have to sing."

His escape from "the profit makers" and their philosophy of

instant obsolescence was especially gratifying to those Bennett fans who always had preferred the singer's more intimate efforts. The recordings he made for Improv—including *Life Is Beautiful* (an album of songs associated with Fred Astaire), *10 Rodgers and Hart Songs, More Great Rodgers and Hart,* and *Together Again* (with pianist Bill Evans)—presented Bennett in small-scale, jazz-tinged settings that allow the full power of his artistry to shine through. Peak performances like "Lover" on *10 Rodgers and Hart Songs* and "You Don't Know What Love Is" from *Together Again* have an emotional strength that has been rare in American popular singing since the death of Billie Holiday. But eventually Improv folded, a victim of erratic distribution, and the project Bennett looked forward to most eagerly, a sequel to the two albums he had made with pianist Bill Evans, was curtailed by Evans's death.

"That was devastating," Bennett says. "We had an album of Irving Berlin songs all worked out, and it would have been a hell of a record. We had made a commitment to each other, you know. Bill said to me, 'Don't ever record with another piano player.' And I said, 'You've got it, if you don't record with another singer.' Funny enough, he called me a few months ago in the middle of the night, which I'd never known him to do. 'Bill,' I said, 'what are you calling me for?' And all he said was, 'Tony, just think love and beauty and forget all the rest.' Hearing him say that and knowing now that he didn't have much time left to live . . . well, it's something that I really have to weigh. It may sound like an impossible or unrealistic attitude to take in this world where there's so much cynicism, but there must have been a reason for him to tell me that. Maybe it fits in with what Lena Horne says: 'As long as you sing well, then that's what you're supposed to be doing. Don't worry about anything else, because it gets too complicated.' "

When Bennett looks for new material, he usually finds himself reaching back into the store of classic pop songs from the twenties, thirties, and forties. For example, one of the loveliest moments on *Together Again* is a revival of "You're Nearer," an almost-forgotten Rodgers and Hart ballad. "It's like I've found a diamond mine," Bennett says. "There's a wealth of music that no one else is even thinking of. I find that I'm still attracted to the songs of the twenties and thirties on a daily basis. To me they're more modern than the new songs I hear. Not that I don't appreciate a Stevie Wonder or a Joni Mitchell. But the craftsmanship of Gershwin, Porter, Arlen, and so forth, you just don't find that today. For instance, take a Berlin song like 'Always.' You can do it as a march, a fox-trot, a waltz, or a disco number. Those songs will fit any style and any beat because they're written so well. But if you get, say, a 'Raindrops Keep Falling on My Head,' you can only do it in one tempo and one style, the way it was originally conceived. Very few new songs are open to interpretation. It's one version and that's all. Some contemporary songs do 'play,' but I think I'm trying to get closed-minded. I'm not going to spend that much time listening for something new that I might otherwise miss. It's damaging to the eardrums."

Bennett delivers that last remark with an ironic laugh. But when he speaks of his eardrums—and all the other physical and mental faculties that affect his music—he sounds like an athlete in training. "When my name is announced before a performance, I've prepared for that moment almost from the time I awakened that morning. Throughout the day the flow of concentration never stops. I practice with the guitar, which gets my voice in a natural, 'popular' vein. If I keep studying bel canto, the voice can get too rigid and stiff for popular singing. It's like Bing Crosby said—you just have to touch on where your voice is that day and proceed accordingly. I'd like to work on my low notes a little more. Even though I'm Italian, I'm really an Irish tenor—an Irish tenor with a baritone quality. I realize that the tenor voice is a natural, but I've always treated it cosmetically because after a while it gets too saccharine. Luckily, as I got older, I started to get those four or five lower notes. I'm trying to keep my vocal apparatus going in every way, because then the audience gets a full shot. They're not being ripped off, and I'm not just collecting my money and leaving for the next town.

"I look at it like this. When you make a recording, you just have a piece of vinyl, a hunk of scrap that could eventually become pollution. It's flat, it's unemotional when there's nothing on it. But if you're lucky enough to hear Walter Huston on 'September Song' or Fred Astaire singing with Gershwin, all of a sudden you say, 'Wow, this is something that will last forever.' And that's the attempt I make. I know it defies the law of gravity, but my ambition is to get better as I get older—like Crosby and Astaire. I'd like to keep caring, if you know what I mean. One of my favorite painters is Hokusai [the nineteenth-century Japanese master]. They used to call him 'The Old Man Mad About Painting.' I'm trying to design my career after him. I'll become 'The Old Man Mad About Singing.' "

STANDARDS AND "STANDARDS"
[1985]

T HE greatest gap in American popular music may be the one that divides rock 'n' roll from the so-called "standard" tradition of songwriting and singing—the tunes of George Gershwin, Jerome Kern, Richard Rodgers, and Cole Porter and the vocal styles of Frank Sinatra, Tony Bennett, Judy Garland, and Fred Astaire (to name just a few of the major figures). Arising after World War I, and artistically and commercially vigorous until the end of World War II and a bit beyond, this was the music that several generations of Americans grew up on. And as the "standard" tag suggests, it was a music that seemed likely to remain in the forefront for some time. But rock 'n' roll changed all that, with the crucial dates probably being 1956 (when Elvis Presley's "Don't Be Cruel"/"Hound Dog" single climbed to the top of the pop, country, and rhythm and blues charts) and 1964 (when any doubts about the staying power of rock were erased by the advent of the Beatles). Rock in its various forms is undeniably the popular music of our time, while the standard tradition is close to being a museum piece—a development that many find regrettable but one that certainly can't be denied.

Obvious, too, although time has healed some of the wounds, is the fundamental opposition between rock and the music that came before it. In fact, rock can be seen as a reaction to and a rejection of almost everything that the standard tradition represents—an attitude that a knowledgeable rock devotee summed up when she referred to the music of Gershwin, Porter, and the rest as "all those songs about women getting in and out of taxicabs." It was merely a sly dig in the ribs on her part, and at the time it made me laugh. But that remark has lingered in my mind; and the more I think about it, the more it seems to mean.

For one thing, that remark had a point to it only because its perpetrator and I both knew that the songs of the standard tradition are supposed to be "sophisticated"—a body of music about people who live in big cities, have a fair amount of cash, and work out their bittersweet romantic problems with a certain world-weary flair. But all that, my friend implied, is a crock—a set of attitudes that had nothing to do with the way she and most of the people she knew lived their lives, and that probably had little to do with the way most people lived their lives at the time those songs were written. And if there ever was a group of women who kept "getting in and out of taxicabs," my friend's first impulse would be to give them a swift kick in the shins.

What that boils down to, I think, is a belief that when most standard-tradition songs are measured against the way things happen in real life, they turn out to be false. And by the same token, a good many rock fans and rock musicians seem to believe that their music is good not only because of its visceral kick but also because it is somehow more genuine—more realistic and natural—than the music that came before it. Now there is something to be said for that way of looking at things. Place a typical Cole Porter or Lorenz Hart lyric alongside something from Bruce Springsteen or Bob Dylan, and most people would say that "Born in the U.S.A." and "It's Alright, Ma" are less artificial than "I Get a Kick Out of You" or "There's a Small Hotel." But such a judgment probably would rest on the verbal content of songs, on the kinds of stories they try to tell—which is far from the only way to measure the realism and naturalness of a piece of music.

Consider, for instance, one of the most basic questions that arises in the mind of every singer and songwriter: How do I make the words and music fit together? One way to do this, and the way that became the norm during the standard era, was to come up with a melody and a rhythmic scheme that allowed the words of the song to emerge as conversationally as possible—in the patterns of everyday, person-to-person speech. (This was, of course, a practical necessity as well as a stylistic choice, because so many standard-era songs were written for the musical stage and had to flow easily out of spoken dialogue.) So if one simply speaks the lyric of any good standard song (say, Porter's "What Is This Thing Called Love?") while trying to forget the melody and the rhythms that go along with it, there are two likely outcomes. First, the lyric can be spoken in a conversational tone of voice. And second, the words one would emphasize in normal speech are the same words that are emphasized when the song is sung. Natural, no? And while one wouldn't claim that this is true of every Cole Porter lyric, the story of "What Is This Thing Called Love?" doesn't seem very artificial either—measured against the world of 1930 (the year the song was written) or the world of today.

But when songs of the rock era are looked at in this way, one comes up with some unexpected results. Not only do the lyrics tend to be more "poetic" than speechlike, they often don't fit the music that goes along with them—that is, the words that would be emphasized if the lyrics were spoken are not the words that are emphasized when the songs are sung. For instance, in Dylan's "It's Alright, Ma," the word "return" is sung by Dylan as "*re*-turn," while in Springsteen's "Backstreets" "became" is sung as "*be*-came"—choices of emphasis that the rhythms of those songs demand but ones that run counter to the normal rhythms of speech. If you think that these are off-the-wall examples, look at the lyric sheet of your favorite rock album—first trying to speak the words in a conversational tone of voice and then listening to how they are sung. Quite often there will be a vast difference between the words you emphasized and the words the singer did. And when was the last time you heard anybody say anything the way the Beatles sing the title phrase of "Strawberry Fields Forever"?

So what is going on here? While a cranky Rodgers and Hart fan might say that lack of craft is all that is involved, that's not quite the case, despite the amateurishness of much rock—if only because the same devices crop up in the work of such undeniably slick songwriters as Burt Bacharach and Barry Manilow. No, the problem is that we're stuck with two different notions of naturalness—one that takes off from human behavior as we commonly experience it and one that believes there is a deeper, "truer" nature that is at odds with the patterns of everyday life. Follow the first path and you have songs that stick close to the texture of normal speech and singers who interpret them that way. (One of Frank Sinatra's chief virtues is his ability to make almost any lyric sound intimate and conversational.) But when the second path is followed, you have songs and singers who not only feel free to shout, mutter, swoon, and groan but also tend to twist words this way and that to fit a preexisting rhythm or melodic design. (On "Strawberry Fields Forever," for instance, the non-speechlike word emphases of the title phrase arise because at that point composer John Lennon was interested in superimposing a patch of six-eight rhythm on the song's prevailing four-four beat.)

As a child of the "standards" era, I have my preferences. But I also know that this is not a matter of right or wrong. In fact, a glance at the history of music suggests that the kind of "natural" word setting that prevailed during the era of the standard song is less common than one might think. Seemingly built into the very idea of music is the belief that it is a language in itself, a sensuously ecstatic flow of meaning whose power to move us far exceeds that of common speech, and that it also does so in a deeper, more "poetic" way. Music's desire to override the patterns of discernible speech has been constrained at times (once, in the sixteenth century, by the Roman Catholic Church, which decreed at the Council of Trent that the liturgical use of polyphonic music was permitted only if the texts of such pieces were not obscured), but that desire has never been suppressed, for in the long run both composers and listeners will resist. So perhaps no one should be surprised that we no longer live in an era when our pop songs are a kind of humane heightened conversation. What is surprising, perhaps, is that any of us grew up in a world where words and music were one thing.

PART IX

Alone Together

The men and women who make jazz are just like everyone else in any number of ways—they have to put food on the table and roofs over their heads; function as children, parents, and spouses; orient themselves toward the world as best they can along political, social, and spiritual lines, etc. But they also, however varied their individual humanity, form a group apart. What kind of group, and "apart" in what ways and for what reasons, are questions that were brilliantly explored by sociologist–jazz pianist Howard Becker in his 1951 paper "The Professional Dance Musician and His Audience" (by "dance musician" Becker meant jazz musician), which later became the basis of two chapters in his 1963 book *Outsiders: Studies in the Sociology of Deviance*. Becker's basic insight, which stemmed from his own experience as a participant/observer in the field, is that while jazz musicians by and large, and with good reason, tend to think of themselves as artists, they belong functionally to a "service occupation"—that is, one in which "the worker comes into more or less direct contact with . . . the client for whom he performs the service . . . [and one in which the client] is able to direct or attempt to direct the worker at his task and to apply sanctions of various kinds, ranging from informal pressure to the withdrawal of his patronage. . . . It seems characteristic of such occupations," he continues, "that their members consider the client unable to judge the proper worth of the service and resent . . . any attempt on his part to exercise control over the work." And, Becker dryly adds, "a good deal of conflict and hostility arises as a result." Perhaps the situation that Becker describes didn't—or doesn't, or needn't—always prevail, and certainly the nature of the lives that jazz musicians lead depends on a good many other things as well. But the social side of the music is directly shaped by the artist-for-hire and at-the-mercy-of-those-who-hire syndrome, and all the defenses, evasions, stresses, and accommodations that arise as a result. This theme is in the foreground in the first two pieces that follow, "The Jazzman as Rebel" and "Anita O'Day," and it is also prominent in the pieces devoted to Stan Getz, Art Pepper, Bill Evans, Frank Zappa, and others. "Jazz and Jack Kerouac" concerns the ways in which an influential writer tried to equate his own sense of romantic "outsideness" with that of the jazz world as he saw it. And "Jazz Goes to College" looks at the texture of what has become an increasingly common path of entry into the jazz life.

THE JAZZMAN AS REBEL
[1988]

R ENEGADES, rebels, outsiders, outlaws. In the eighty or so years that there has been such a thing as jazz, the men and women who play it have borne all of these labels. And even though the notion of the jazz musician as rebel tends to be wrapped in a rather fanciful, romantic haze, there is more than a little truth to it. Ever since the 1920s, which was, after all, dubbed the "Jazz Age," it has been common to think of the music as a kind of socially disruptive sonic hell-raising. And the musicians themselves were supposed to be either footloose, free-spirited types or tragically misunderstood "young men with horns" who were laid low by drink, drugs, commercial pressures, and a lack of recognition.

Tracing those myths back to their source, the first seems to be based on the idea that jazz is a "noble savage" phenomenon whose practitioners break all sorts of musical and social rules in order to let some fresh air into our overcivilized world. And the second resembles any number of attempts to portray the artist as a darkly romantic hero, a descendant of Shelley and Keats who wears social rejection as a badge of honor. But if the jazz musician has been a victim of such myths (and, in some cases, a beneficiary of them), where does the truth lie? Certainly he is not a "noble savage," for jazz, in the words of critic Stanley Crouch, may be "the most sophisticated performing art in Western history." And throughout the course of the music, there have been any number of gifted players who also were solid citizens. Yet it would be foolish to deny there has been a certain rebellious, outsider streak in the music itself and in the lifestyles that have surrounded it.

At no point in the history of jazz were these traits more striking than during the so-called bebop era, when a music that seemed to have rebellion built right into it was being made by musicians who often thought of themselves as being at odds with the rest of American life. Consider an anecdote that vocalist David Allyn recounts in Ira Gitler's *Swing to Bop: An Oral History of the Transition of Jazz in the 1940s*. On the road with Art Mooney's band in the early 1950s, Allyn and a busful of his bandmates are wandering through the ritzy Cleveland suburb of Shaker Heights when Allyn, strung out on heroin and in a self-pitying mood, begins to expound on the gated mansions with vast green lawns that he sees through the bus window: "Look at this. Oh, dig that pad. Oh, that's wild. . . . Oh, man, look at this. . . . So what are we? We're gypsies. We're roving and we're wandering and we're stupid. We're not hip. *They're* hip. We're square. . . . What have we got? And who listens to us? . . . We're bums. That's what we are. And nothing is right." To which saxophonist Rocky Coluccio replies: "Yeah, but wait a minute, man. . . . What do they know about Diz and Pres and Bird?" And with that everyone on the bus cracks up.

No doubt heightened in the retelling, Allyn's anecdote nonetheless captures the gist of the hipster-bohemian dream—the belief that while genuine artists are cut off from the world of material well-being, they are by the same token in contact with spiritual truths that the mainstream culture either shuns or fails to detect. But what of the sense of envy and rage that courses through Allyn's tale? That he would rather be well-off than scuffling is natural enough, but why does he think that the residents of Shaker Heights could or should care about the music of Parker and Gillespie, which Allyn and his friends value so highly?

After all, only two kinds of culture seem to exist in the modern world—highbrow, "museum" art, which grants social status to the chosen few who support it, and entertainment-oriented popular art, which provides a mass audience with immediate pleasures. But jazz doesn't quite fit into either slot. Originally a popular art, performed in dance halls and nightclubs, jazz also has all sorts of highbrow traits. Often entertaining but never merely entertainers, jazz musicians have always tried to discover and express their personal vision—one that will please the audience and, at the same time, please themselves. And the music also has been fueled by a strong "progressive" drive, as the ideas of each new wave of creators have been absorbed and zealously developed.

From that point of view, the hipster-bohemian stance of the bebop generation was based in part upon selective memories of a lost paradise, a time when it still seemed possible to reach a mass audience while remaining true to one's art. For instance, only a decade before David Allyn met the mansions of Shaker Heights, one of his heroes, Lester Young, had been the most renowned soloist in Count Basie's band, which was one of the most popular ensembles of the day. And at the same time the even more commercially successful, jazz-oriented bands led by Benny Goodman and Artie Shaw had few if any peers when it came to pleasing the public. But long before the perhaps illusory wholeness of the Swing Era was lost, leaving a generation or two of jazz musicians to divide the world into "hipsters" and "squares," the music was shaped by a more fundamental and much healthier form of rebellion.

That jazz was invented by black Americans almost goes

without saying. And whether or not that invention literally oc-curred in New Orleans, it certainly took place in an urban set-ting at some point after the end of slavery—during an era when a new sense of freedom was in the air, ready to be explored and expressed. Growing up in Oklahoma City in the 1920s, novelist Ralph Ellison was exposed to the music of quite a few young jazz masters, including guitarist Charlie Christian and singer Jimmy Rushing. And Ellison's account, in his essay "Remem-bering Jimmy," of what he felt as a boy, listening to Rushing's voice "jetting from the dance hall like a blue flame in the dark," makes it clear that he and his friends thought of jazz musicians as heroic pioneers whose art offered proof that one could sur-mount all sorts of social and cultural barriers.

"We were pushed off to what seemed the least desirable part of the city," Ellison writes, "and our system of justice was based on Texas [i.e., racially biased] law. Yet there was an optimism in the Negro community and a sense of possibility which, despite our awareness of limitation, transcended all of this. And it was this rock-bottom sense of reality, coupled with our sense of the possibility of rising above it, which sounded in Jimmy Rushing's voice."

If rebellion seems covert here, it is vivid nonetheless, in the struggle to grow up in a world of often harsh racial injustice and also in the need to define that growth on one's own terms—for, as Ellison explains, listening to and playing jazz was looked down upon as a lower-class affair by many members of Oklahoma City's "respectable" black community. But, says Elli-son of the young Charlie Christian: "He had heard the voice of jazz and would hear no other."

Hearing jazz's voice and recognizing what it meant was, of course, something that white musicians and their fans were do-ing as well. And while it is tricky to generalize about such things, it seems that in their case the struggle against "respectable" at-titudes and behavior almost became a value in itself—a way of separating oneself from the stuffiness of middle-class culture. According to critic Francis Newton, "the white jazz musician in America has been an outsider-type practically from the start."

And while many such players chose the music first and then chose or accepted (or were even stuck with) the "life" second, more than a few went at things the other way around. Consider, for instance, the testimony of saxophonist-bandleader Charlie Barnet. Born into a wealthy family (his grandfather was a bank president and an official of the New York Central Railroad), Barnet says in his autobiography, *Those Swinging Years*, that "it's hard to say what attracted me more at this period [the late 1920s], the music or the life. I had been brought up comfortably, but now I thought it was just the greatest thing to have a room of my own at the Chesterfield Hotel. Guys in traveling bands would come in, and I found the idea of life on the road very intriguing. I wanted that experience, too, and I took a romantic view of the whole scene. And as it unfolded, it was even better than I had imagined. So I think I probably was more enthralled with the life than the music—at first. There seemed to be a free spirit in it all."

A cheerfully forthright libertine, Barnet managed to survive a hard-drinking ("in that era just about everybody was a lush"), marijuana-using, "burning the candle at both ends" lifestyle. But others, who lacked Barnet's rugged constitution and his fund of ready cash, were not as fortunate. Trumpeter Jack Purvis ("one of the wildest men I've ever met," says Barnet), finally found himself "in prison for what could have been any of several reasons." And cornetist Don McCarter, "always in rebellion against society," ended up "under a subway train, although we never knew whether he jumped or was pushed."

Of course a good deal of the social rule-breaking that has been associated with jazz has less to do with the music than it does with the rootless, vagabond life that potentially separates entertainers of most sorts from the rest of the population. But if the notion of the hip insider who looks down on the rubes isn't the exclusive property of the jazz world, it certainly became a key part of it—especially during the bebop era, when drug use became so prevalent that an entire generation of players seemed to be trying to wall themselves off from a society they no longer wished to contemplate.

"The musicians were so good," says trumpeter Red Rodney in *Swing to Bop*. "Yet we were so screwed up. It was a period of being very bugged. Why, I'll never know, but we were. And it [drug use] became the thing. That was our badge. It was the thing that made us different from the rest of the world. It was the thing that said, 'We know, you don't know.' . . . But [drug use] had a great deal to do with the music, especially the intellectual part of it. When a guy is loaded and at peace, he shuts everything out except what he's interested in. Being interested in music, he could tune out the honking of the world."

One doesn't want to describe bebop as more of a social than a musical event. But no matter how striking the music that emerged in the 1940s, and despite its roots in previous jazz styles, the emotional tone of the music had changed. The forthright quest for freedom that Ellison had found in the jazz of the twenties and thirties was transformed into a rebellion of romantic despair, an attempt to evade or tune out the "honking" of the world. And when that need to escape was combined with drugs, a great many players destroyed themselves. "We were pilgrims," said pianist Hampton Hawes, "the freaks of the forties and fifties—playing bebop, going through a lot of changes and getting strung out in the process. And our rebellion was a lonely thing."

Obviously there had been a shift in values—in the music and in the society, too. And among those who prefer the orderliness and optimism of older jazz styles to the hectic beauties of bebop, one often hears the complaint that none of this needed to occur. At one time, so the argument goes, jazz musicians were content to think of themselves as entertainers, not self-conscious artists. If the practitioner of modern jazz wants to please himself and his peers first and the audience second, if at all, he must endure the consequences of this unrealistic, willful act.

The problem with that argument, though, as British saxophonist Bruce Turner says in his whimsically titled autobiography, *Hot Air, Cool Music*, "is that scarcely any jazz musicians are able to recognize this picture of themselves. There are some jazzmen who are great entertainers. Louis Armstrong, Fats Waller, and Lionel Hampton come immediately to mind. But they are the exception, not the rule. For the most part those of us who play jazz for a living do not know any way of entertaining an audience other than by making the best music we are capable of. . . . The 'jazz is entertainment' theory is only about money, when you boil it down. Jazz finds itself sponsored by the entertainment industry, and in return the latter feels entitled to demand its pound of flesh. Fair enough, but why in heaven's name confuse the issue? The distinction between what is done for love and what is done for quick cash is an obvious one."

Obvious, yes. But Turner's "distinction between what is done for love and what is done for quick cash" points to an even more fundamental issue. If it seems logical to think of jazz as a music that can and should be played *con amore,* that is because it is this century's most humanistic art—a music whose goal (the discovery and expression of one's personal identity) can be reached only when musicians speak openly and honestly to those who are willing to respond in kind. But the belief that such transactions can take place rests on a faith that individual human beings still care to make that response—a faith that is seldom found in the elaborately coded messages of this century's highbrow art and is even less prevalent in the mass-market products of our popular art. So the jazz musician, whose rebelliousness has ranged from bold cultural pioneering to romantic despair, now finds himself cast in the role of the loneliest rebel of them all—an artist who is unable to speak with evasion or artifice in an age that seems to demand little else.

ANITA O'DAY
[1981]

HOWEVER you define truth, an autobiography is supposed to tell it. The factual truth about the author's life, of course, but also the truth about the meaning of that life, which is at least as important and far more difficult to tell. And from both points of view, vocalist Anita O'Day's *High Times, Hard Times* is a remarkably truthful book. An innovative, talented musician, a former drug addict, and a Caucasian working in a predominantly black art form, O'Day is also a person for whom the choice of jazz as a means of expression was just that, a choice. And the story of how and why O'Day chose jazz and the jazz life is the essential story of her book—one whose significance extends far beyond the human-interest boundaries of her undeniably colorful career.

Born in Chicago on October 18, 1919, six months after her parents' marriage, Anita Belle Colton (O'Day's given name) was at best a partially wanted child. Her hard-living, free-spirited father soon abandoned his family (eventually he would be married ten times before he reached the age of fifty), leaving O'Day to grow up pretty much on her own, a weed pushing through the sidewalks of Chicago's Uptown neighborhood. School was a bore and a burden for her, but music was a readily available blessing, since Uptown was one of the city's entertainment centers in the twenties and thirties.

O'Day had innate musical gifts, which might have led her to jazz no matter what. But her choice was shaped by other factors, too—a need to escape from the passive, put-upon, self-pitying image of femininity supplied by her mother and a corresponding desire to be, like her father, "where the action was." Having had a taste of the action before her teens, when she and an adult partner participated in lindy-hop contests, casually smoking marijuana before they went on, O'Day left home at age fourteen to make a living in the Walkathons—the Depression-era endurance trials in which young men and women danced until they dropped. But the Walkathons provided room for entertainment, too, and O'Day soon realized that she wanted to become a singer—not one of those "peaches-and-cream chicks" who were little more than "trinkets to decorate the bandstand" but an "uncompromising swing singer" who would be "part of the gang." That "gang," of course, was composed of jazz musicians. And as O'Day tells how she worked her way up as a singer until she

made it big with Gene Krupa's band in 1941, it becomes clear
that belonging to the masculine, sardonically unsentimental, in-
group world of jazz had become very important to her. "I was
my own woman," O'Day says, comparing herself to a female
friend who was "a lovebug, in and out of love every week." But
to be her "own woman," to totally disassociate femininity from
any hint of weakness, O'Day had to make herself "as tough as
any man that came down the pike."

That hardboiled image, heightened by her decision to wear
a band jacket ("just like the guys") instead of the gowns that
were the norm for female singers at the time, led to rumors
about O'Day's sexual orientation, which *High Times, Hard Times*
certainly refutes. When her type of man came along, a fellow
with "curly blond hair, blue eyes with a devilish glint, and a good
physique," O'Day could be a lovebug indeed. But as she tells it,
there was little tenderness in those romantic episodes. Or rather
what tenderness there was seemed reserved for moments in
which she and her partner could relate to each other as sister
and brother. And that brings us to the oddest part of *High Times,
Hard Times,* the story of her intense, complicated twenty-seven-
year relationship with drummer John Poole, her closest friend
and, not so incidentally, the man who turned her on to heroin.

"Everyone assumed we were lovers," O'Day writes. "Carl
[O'Day's second husband] even called me 'Mrs. Poole.' He was
wrong. John and I were hype [hypodermic needle] friends. Nobody thought of that. What could we do? Explain it was dope
instead of sex?" When she and Poole crossed paths in 1954,
O'Day had just been released from prison, having been framed
on a dope charge. Not yet an addict, though she had sniffed
heroin, O'Day was in what might be called a pre-addictive
state—unhappy, down on her luck, almost constantly drunk, and
working in an environment where pushers and users were common. "I was," she writes, "fascinated by John Poole. Not because
he was tall, slim, and good-looking or was a terrific drummer.
What interested me was that he never took alcohol of any kind.
I guessed he had a secret I wanted to be let in on."

Formerly a student of the ministry, Poole began by pressing

the Bible on O'Day. But faced with her demands, he finally revealed the other source of his inner peace. "I don't like anything you smoke or drink," he said. "If I can't shoot it, it doesn't interest me." Unable to talk her out of shooting heroin, Poole gave in at last, explaining that "the way you're coming on, if I don't, somebody else will." And from then on they became a brother-sister team of drug users, with Poole protecting O'Day whenever possible by personally administering her injections. That aspect of their relationship finally ended with both of them off drugs, though not before O'Day (momentarily out of Poole's tender care) almost died of an overdose. But for all their dangerous and, in the eyes of the law, criminal behavior, Poole and O'Day are a perfectly matched pair of pals, the Tom Sawyer and Huck Finn of heroin.

Having found within the subculture of jazz the further subculture of drug addiction, O'Day was finally able to draw away from those aspects of the world that disturbed her. And her drug use was also a logical outgrowth of her desire to be "part of the gang." (As the poet Edward Dorn once wrote, "Junkies must be the tightest little group of how-to-live-ers since the days of Brook Farm.") So if *High Times, Hard Times* is an exemplary tale, its message amounts to this: Jazz has been both a music and a subculture, one that has always attracted people who were at odds with the mainstream of American life. And with varying degrees of success, they used the jazz life to define themselves, to find a way to live that did not force them to submit to values they found unacceptable. For O'Day, much was unacceptable, including the more commercial aspects of show business ("You can't buy what I do," she writes, "but you can pay me, and I'll do it") and the passive, suffering image of femininity exemplified by her mother. And she traded those things in for the camaraderie of the jazz life, adding to that the camaraderie of drug use.

Of course, O'Day's membership in the latter fraternity almost led to her death. But when all is said and done, there is an appealing forthrightness to her search for the place "where the action was," which she sums up by comparing herself to vocalist Johnny Desmond, who sang alongside her in the Krupa band. "A straight cat in every way," O'Day writes, "Johnny didn't smoke, drink, or do dope, and, as far as I know, he was true to the pretty wife he had at home. It paid off. He's still out there, doing his thing. But come to think of it, I did all the things he didn't do, had a lot of fun, and I'm still out there too."

JAZZ AND JACK KEROUAC
[1983]

WHAT can jazz tell us about Jack Kerouac? That would seem to be the obvious question, but it's one that can't (or shouldn't) be answered until it's been turned the other way around. Jazz was part of the furniture of Kerouac's fiction, perhaps as much so as anything this side of Neal Cassady. But jazz, as Kerouac seemed to know from time to time, was not quite raw material, waiting there to be rearranged as the novelist saw fit. Instead, jazz has its own thingness, makes its own demands, and is likely to turn on anyone who would merely use it. Which is not to say that jazz can't be put to fictional use or that Kerouac didn't use it in more-or-less valuable ways—as subject matter, as the trappings of his personal myth, and as a guide to prose technique. But there has been so much loose romantic talk about Kerouac and jazz, some of it Kerouac's own doing—as in his cry "I'm the bop writer!" from *The Subterraneans*, or "The Great Jazz Singer / was Jolson the Vaudeville Singer? / No, and not Miles, me," from the 116th Chorus of *Mexico City Blues*— that it's time to look at the role of jazz in Kerouac's fiction and give the music equal weight.

A good place to begin is at a level that might not seem very important at first—the quasi-journalistic, jazz-tinged vignettes that Kerouac sometimes used as scenic backdrops. Here, in *The*

Subterraneans, is Roger Beloit (a character based on tenor saxophonist Allen Eager): ". . . listening [on the radio] to Stan Kenton talk about the music of tomorrow and we hear a new young
tenor man come on, Ricci Comucca, Roger Beloit says, moving
back thin expressive purple lips, 'This is the music of tomorrow?' "

The actual name of the musician involved is Richie Kamuca,
not Ricci Comucca, but leave that be. What matters is the way
Kerouac has captured a small yet essential twitch of the jazz
sensibility. Beloit-Eager, "that great poet I'd revered in my
youth," as Leo Percepied says to us and to himself a few pages
later on, was a first-generation disciple of Lester Young and, of
all those players, the one best able to modify Young's style to fit
the more rhythmically and harmonically angular world of bebop; while Kamuca, coming along a half-generation or so behind Eager, was also inspired by Lester Young (and perhaps by
Eager as well). Eager was at his peak in the mid- to late 1940s,
but "now it is no longer 1948 but 1953 with cool generations
and I [i.e., Percepied-Kerouac] five years older." So the joke, if
that's the way to put it, is that Beloit-Eager's "This is the music
of tomorrow?" remark is steeped in mordant irony, as though
he were saying, though he's too "hip" to be this explicit, "Hey, I
was ahead of this guy five years ago."

Hearing that actual tone of voice (and, just as important,
putting it on the page), Kerouac is as far as can be from the
romantic posing he falls into elsewhere. Even though the point
of this brief passage now may be lost on many readers (and may
have been obscure even then), it has an irreducible grittiness to
it that gives strength to the surrounding fictional enterprise in
any number of ways, even if one doesn't know a thing about
Allen Eager or Richie Kamuca. Kerouac did know, and the point
of that knowledge was not lost on him, for as a novelist who
chose to work close to the autobiographical bone, he could
never be sure, as he transformed fact into fiction, which bits of
factual "grit" might be essential. Thus the widely acknowledged
brilliance of Kerouac's naming ("Lorenzo Monsanto" for
Lawrence Ferlinghetti, "Bull Hubbard" for William S. Bur-

roughs, and, of course, "Cody Pomeroy" and "Jack Duluoz" for Neal Cassady and himself), which surely arose from a need to place the actual at just the right distance from his created, fictional world. And thus the weakness at the heart of *The Subterraneans,* in which events that took place in New York were transferred to San Francisco—a shift in scene that might have given no problems to a different kind of novelist but one that seemed to disrupt Kerouac's fictional machinery, in the same way Proust might have been thrown off if he hadn't been able to use César Franck's Piano Quintet as a model for the "Vinteuil Septet" in *The Search for Lost Time.*

In Kerouac's fiction there are a number of other moments like the Beloit-Eager passage—brief, seemingly casual glimpses that take the reader and the narrator into the heart of what Kerouac chose to call, at various times, "Jazz America" (*On the Road*) or the "Jazz Century" (*Book of Dreams*). But these glimpses are only glimpses. The narrator happens to be there, and what he sees or overhears doesn't bring him into direct contact with what he has perceived.

A good example, no less shrewd than the Beloit-Eager vignette, is the narrator's reminiscence, in *Desolation Angels,* of Stan Getz sitting in a toilet stall in Birdland, "blowing his horn quietly to the music of Lennie Tristano's group out front, when I realized he could do anything—(Warne Marsh me no Warne Marsh! his music said)," Marsh being Tristano's tenor saxophonist of the time. Again, this has meaning within Kerouac's self-referential fictional world; it's a thought that ought to occur to Jack Duluoz at the time. But "Warne Marsh me no Warne Marsh!" is also, one suspects, exactly what Getz was saying to himself as he sat there in that actual toilet stall.

It would be nice to linger over these precise, attractive insights, but now it's time to look at the painful stuff, the yearning Kerouac's heroes have to be part of something they can't really belong to. At times there is (at least one hopes there is) a deliberate edge of farce to the program, for how can one do anything but gag at stuff like "I am the blood brother of a Negro Hero!" (*Visions of Cody*), "good oldfashioned jitterbugs that really used to lose themselves unashamed in jazz halls" (*Visions of Cody*), and "wishing I could exchange worlds with the happy, true-hearted, ecstatic Negroes of America" (*On the Road*). As Jack Duluoz says in *Visions of Cody*, referring, perhaps, to Sherwood Anderson's novel: "Dark laughter has come again!"

Of course this is fiction, and it's fair, especially in the "true-hearted, ecstatic Negroes" case, to put some distance between Kerouac and his narrator, who at that point in *On the Road* ought to be half a fool. But common sense finally says that this not only is fiction but is also, more often than not, exactly what it seems to be—a moonstruck desire to turn jazz into some imaginary black earth-mother and, in the process, shed all sorts of inhibitions, just like those "unashamed . . . good oldfashioned jitterbugs." And Kerouac pushes it even further at times. "You and I," writes Jack Duluoz to Cody Pomeroy in *Visions of Cody*, "could be great jazz musicians *among* jazz musicians"—a vision that again raises the question of how much distance there is between the narrator and his words, for if "You and I could be great jazz musicians *among* jazz musicians" is to be taken at anything close to face value (and I can see little reason not to take it that way), it is the self-delusion of a naive tourist. Jazz has, and always will have, its romantic component, but surely this is a music of overriding emotional realism. So if anyone thinks that there is some intrinsic bond between the music of Charlie Parker or Lester Young and a "weekend climaxed by bringing colored guitarist and pianist and colored gal and all three women took off tops while we blew two hours me on bop-chords piano . . . and Mac fucked J. on bed, then I switched to bongo and for one hour we really had a jungle (as you can imagine) feeling running and after all there I was with my brand new FINAL bongo or rather really conga beat and looked up from my work which was lifting the whole group . . ." (this from *Visions of Cody*)—well, James Dean played the bongos, too.

But what of the "jazz" texture of Kerouac's prose and verse, for which some grandiose claims have been made (Kerouac himself saying of *Mexico City Blues*: "I want to be considered a

jazz poet blowing a long blues in a jam session on Sunday")?
The "spontaneous prose" business isn't worth bothering about
in any literal sense, because the "no pause to think of proper
word . . . if possible write without consciousness" aspects of the
program apparently were not adhered to very often. How "the
object is set before the mind" is the point; and in any case it's
the results that matter—that is, do the words, labored over or
not, manage to capture the feel of spontaneity?

To a remarkable degree they do, less so in the raggle-taggle
verse (the *Book of Dreams* being much superior to the otherwise
comparable *Mexico City Blues*) than in the best of the prose,
where Kerouac does at least two things: he captures the sound
of all kinds of jazz-related talk, from the hip, ingrown-toenail
language of his Subterraneans to Cody Pomeroy's manic,
carnival-barker monologues. And having a wonderful ear for the
speech of others, Kerouac also could hear himself, which is
where his wish "to be considered a jazz poet" really rests.

What kind of a jazz poet? That brings us back to Roger
Beloit–Allen Eager and the other white Lester Young–influenced
tenor saxophonist Kerouac seemed most fond of, the late Brew
Moore (or, as Kerouac always spelled the name, "Brue" Moore).
Moore figures most prominently in Chapter 97 of *Desolation Angels*, which has its moments of fanlike, romantic presumption
("Brue has nevertheless to carry the message along for several
chorus-chapters, his ideas get tireder than at first, he does give
up at the right time—besides he wants to play a new tune—I do
just that, tap him on the shoe-top to acknowledge he's right").
But this dream of participating in the magical "IT" of jazz, "the
big moment of rapport all around" (words given to Cody Pomeroy in *Visions of Cody*) seems small alongside Kerouac's ability
to sustain the rhythm of a paragraph or a chapter on a series of
long, swinging, almost literal breaths. Here Kerouac achieved
his dream of a prose that shadows the chorus structure of an
improvising jazz soloist. And it is the sound of men like Moore
and Eager, not the heated brilliance of Charlie Parker or the
adamant strength of Thelonious Monk, that he managed to capture.

"I wish Allen [Eager] would play louder and more distinct," Kerouac writes in *Book of Dreams*, "but I recognize his greatness and his prophetic humility of quietness." Listening to Eager or Moore, one knows what Kerouac meant, a meditative, inward-turning linear impulse that combines compulsive swing with an underlying resignation—as though at the end of each phrase the shape of the line drooped into a melancholy "Ah, me," which would border on passivity if it weren't for the need to move on, to keep the line going.

Of course there are other precedents for this, which Kerouac must have had in mind, notably Whitman's long line and Thomas Wolfe's garrulous flow. And I wouldn't insist that Kerouac's prose was shaped more by his jazz contemporaries than by his literary forebears. But that isn't the point. For all his moments of softness and romantic overreaching—his "holy flowers floating . . . in the dawn of Jazz America" and "great tenormen shooting junk by broken windows and staring at their horns" stuff—Kerouac's desire to be part of "the Jazz Century" led to a prose that was, at its best, jazzlike from the inside out, whether jazz was in the foreground (as in much of *Visions of Cody*) or nowhere to be seen (as in *Big Sur*). And perhaps none of this could have come without the softness and the romanticism, the sheer boyishness of Kerouac's vision.

"These are men!" wrote William Carlos Williams of Bunk Johnson's band, and he certainly was right, as he would have been if he had said that of Louis Armstrong or Coleman Hawkins, Benny Carter or Thelonious Monk. But there is something boyish in the music of Allen Eager and Brew Moore—and in the music of Bix Beiderbecke and Frank Teschemacher, for that matter—a sense of loss in the act of achievement, the pathos of being doubly outside. That is an essential part of their story; and when he was on his game, Jack Kerouac knew that it was an essential part of his story, too.

JAZZ GOES TO COLLEGE
[1986]

What is jazz? The rhythm—the feeling. And it can be taught.
Or at least its mechanical aspects can be.

—COLEMAN HAWKINS

If you have to ask, you'll never know.

—VARIOUSLY ATTRIBUTED TO LOUIS ARMSTRONG AND
FATS WALLER

THE students straggle in, looking much like any batch of college kids on a school day at 10 a.m.—their as-yet unformed
faces still pasty from too little sleep, while their outfits, which
run to T-shirts and blue jeans, seem to have been snatched at
random from whatever was lying near the top of the clothes
hamper that morning. But instead of notepads, textbooks, and
ballpoint pens, these would-be scholars come to class carrying,
among other things, a tenor saxophone, a handful of drumsticks,
and an electric guitar. Their teacher peers up at them from a
page of score paper as he absentmindedly fiddles with his slide
trombone.

"OK," he says, when everyone is finally present and in place,
"let's start with one of mine—'Robotic Love.' " And he counts off
the tune, twisting his shoulders to suggest the kind of funky,
rhythm-and-blues, stop-and-go groove he feels the piece requires. It's a rhythmic scheme that can be found in a lot of contemporary pop music, but the rest of the tune is different—
bristling with swiftly changing harmonic patterns that would, so
it seems, give pause to the most accomplished professional jazz
soloist. So after the theme of "Robotic Love" is run through, one
feels a moment of doubt as the tenor saxophonist rises from his
chair to give it his best shot—only to relax with pleasure as he
spits out a quote from "Johnny One Note" and digs into a swinging solo that betrays the near-universal influence of John Col-

trane but also shows genuinely individual traits. Meanwhile the rhythm section is hard at work, the drummer's accents reverberating like gunshots; and by the time the teacher-trombonist takes his solo turn, one has lost all sense that he and his students exist on different levels of musical accomplishment. And that is saying something, because the teacher is no less a figure than forty-nine-year-old Phil Wilson, a much-recorded, poll-winning virtuoso on his instrument, while the students are young enough to be Wilson's sons. Indeed the most precocious players in the band—tenor saxophonist Donny McCaslin from Santa Cruz, California, and drummer Ben Perowsky from Manhattan—are still one year away from losing their status as teenagers.

But precociousness is the name of the game at Boston's Berklee College of Music, which has, since it was founded in 1945 by Lawrence Berk, produced a remarkable number of celebrated musicians—including such jazz and pop notables as vibraphonist Gary Burton, pianists Keith Jarrett and Makoto Ozone, guitarists Al DiMeola and John Scofield, keyboardists Joe Zawinul and Jan Hammer, and composers Toshiko Akiyoshi and Quincy Jones. Offering courses that range from "Harmonic Considerations in Improvisation" to "Modern Audio Recording," Berklee is the most prominent school devoted exclusively to what its administration prefers to call "contemporary American music." And with a student population of twenty-five hundred, it is also the largest. But Berklee is far from alone in the field, even in the Boston area. A short walk from Berklee through the Back Bay neighborhood and one is at the door of the venerable New England Conservatory of Music—which concentrates on training classical musicians but also has a relatively small but prestigious jazz department (this year it has 83 jazz students out of the NEC's total enrollment of 750).

Founded in 1969 by composer Gunther Schuller, New England's jazz department is currently chaired by bassist Miroslav Vitous. But Schuller's legacy lives on—in the school's uncompromising focus on jazz as an art music and in the faculty members who continue to share Schuller's vision. They include such men as composers George Russell and Tom McKinley, pianists

Ran Blake, Fred Hersch, and Jaki Byard, trumpeter John Mc-
Neil, drummer Bob Moses, and sixty-five-year-old saxophonist-
clarinetist-composer Jimmy Giuffre—who is, on the morning after Phil Wilson's Berklee students played "Robotic Love,"
guiding his class through Wayne Shorter's "Footprints." Giuffre's
tenor saxophone is the only horn, and his graceful, Lester
Young–influenced improvising automatically raises the performance to a high level. (Later on, the band's drummer, eighteen-
year-old Scott Mitchell, would say: "Jimmy sounds so good.
When I heard him warming up today, the reality of his playing
was just shattering.") But in the midst of "Footprints," Giuffre
detects some room for improvement. "Let's make it more compositional," he whispers to bassist Wesley Wirth—suggesting
that from time to time Wirth could bring back under the soloists
the haunting vamp that underlies Shorter's theme.

Then "Footprints" fades out, and it's time for some amiable
but serious group criticism. "Norm, your solo was really loud,"
says Wirth to guitarist Norm Zocher—whose playing indeed had
threatened to alter the architecture of the practice room. "Yeah,"
Zocher says, with a half-proud, half-sheepish grin, "I'm getting
deaf, I guess"—to which drummer Mitchell replies: "You mean
you can't tell?" And now it's Zocher's turn to hand out advice,
an idea about how to deal with the ethereal double-time groove
that makes "Footprints" so tricky to perform. But Mitchell isn't
ready for any of that right now. "Don't talk to me, Norm," he
says, shadow-drumming his way through a potential variation.
"I sort of know what I'm doing."

Yes, jazz (or "contemporary American music") can be, and
is being, taught—at Berklee, at the New England Conservatory's
jazz department, and at a host of other colleges and high schools
around the country. But if, as Coleman Hawkins said, the mechanical aspects of the music can be taught, is its nonmechan-
ical side also open to instruction? And speaking of matters of
the spirit, what about the musical marketplace that every Berklee and New England student will have to deal with once he or
she leaves school? While administrations and faculties have to
take account of the world beyond the classroom, does that mean

they should adopt a trade-school approach and teach whatever kinds of music are currently saleable? Or should they take a purist view and devote themselves to producing would-be creative artists, even though the marketplace may have little or no use for them?

"Over the years," says Berklee's dean of students, Lawrence Bethune, "we have gotten the reputation of being a jazz school, although I don't think [founder] Larry Berk ever looked at it that way. He thought of it as a school that would teach contemporary popular music; and it just so happened that what he was teaching in 1945 was big-band music, because that was the music that was popular. Nowadays contemporary music moves very quickly, so we have to adapt very quickly, too. What we're teaching this year we may not be teaching five years from now. So in some ways we do respond to the marketplace. We try to explain what's going on there, and then it's up to our students to utilize it—either commercially or in a purely creative manner.

"What happens here is that a student will get a great bebop tenor sax player as a teacher—a guy who's obviously going to put his aesthetic and musical beliefs into his course work—and that same semester the student may be studying pop songwriting with a teacher who has a very commercial outlook. Now the first guy would starve to play his music and would never do anything that was, in his mind, for the market, while the second guy is saying, 'Follow the market—if you try to be a maverick, you probably won't make it.' And it's up to the student to make the choice that's right for him. One hopes the student will come to see that art and craft are not mutually exclusive. Some people would argue with that, of course, but that's how most of us think around here."

A different but not entirely opposite view is espoused by Tom McKinley, who teaches composition and jazz piano at the New England Conservatory. "Boy, that's a tough one," McKinley says, when asked how he prepares his students to face the outside world. "I guess it boils down to the difference between a pedagogical and a spiritual education, if you want to make that distinction. 'Be strong,' that's what I always try to tell my stu-

dents—'be strong and realize that you're not going to succeed
unless you put your art on the line.' Those who have succeeded
will always tell you the same story—that they lived and breathed
what they believed in, even if they had to go through some pretty
hard times. I hate to be metaphysical, but it's like Schopen-
hauer—"The Will as Idea." Very few go right to the top; but if
your will is strong enough, and it's commensurate with your
talent, which often is the case, sooner or later the talent and the
will do it for you.

"There is no pedagogy, no system of scales or finger technique, that's going to make it any better for you in the real
world. You just have to sit down and play. And the students who
say, 'Teach me these scales and these modes and these tunes,'
they're the ones who are going to go out and make their little
six-nights-a-week livings. I'm not saying they're bad people or
they're wrong; but they aren't the people who are going to make
the real statements in music. And I think you'll find that in any
school, whether the subject is music or painting or whatever.
Now I'm a stickler for craft in composition. When it comes to
making something presentable for other musicians to play, the
ABCs are essential. But that's not creativity. Here we talk about
craft only when it's necessary to communicate the message,
whereas most schools talk about craft all the time."

If by "most schools," McKinley has Berklee in mind, he
would find some evidence to support his view and some that
would not. For one thing, such Berklee courses as "Advanced
Digital Synthesis Techniques," "Technique for Programmatic
Film Music," and "Location Recording and Sound Reinforce-
ment Systems" simply cannot be taught without devoting a great
deal of time to nuts-and-bolts matters. But Gary Burton's course
in "The Music Business," which might seem dry as dust, turns
out to be a remarkable blend of inspiration and common
sense—as Burton (a 1963 Berklee grad and now the school's
dean of curriculum) shrewdly zeroes in on the doubts that are
eating at his students and offers reassurance whenever possible.

"What you're going through, I went through," is the gist of
what Burton has to say. And one feels certain that the infor-

mation is really sinking in, as Burton explains in lucid detail what does and doesn't run through his mind as he improvises a solo—how when things are going well his unconscious mind seems to speak directly to his hands; how the times when he thinks everything he plays is terrible are always followed by times when he thinks he sounds pretty good, even though that wheel of despair and elation tends to spin more swiftly at age twenty-one than it does at age forty-one.

"The jazz musician," Burton explains later on, "leads a very divided existence. On the one hand you have to practice an incredible amount of hours and build up an incredible self-discipline in order to perform well on your instrument and learn all the repertoire that's needed. Dedication and self-control— you have to be almost fanatical about those things if you're going to make it in a big way. But you also want to be unfettered creatively, spontaneous and uncontrolled—which is the exact opposite mindset. So musicians traditionally do eccentric things in order to keep themselves loose and slightly crazy, while at the same time they're very strict with themselves in other areas. You end up balancing those things all through your life."

"This is almost our last session," says George Russell to three of his New England students—pianist Ben Schwendener, saxophonist Rob Schoeps, and trombonist Scott Matalon. "So what did we do?" That seems to be a rhetorical question, because Russell quickly moves on to some answers. "Scott," he says, "you should work on your vertical playing"—meaning that the twenty-two-year-old trombonist, whose melodic ideas are quite striking, needs to concentrate more on harmonic structure. "Rob, think about planning. And give your enormous wit a rest." Schoeps—whose wit, musical and otherwise, does seems irrepressible—looks as though he's thought of a snappy retort and then decided to swallow it. "Ben . . ." But by now everyone, Russell included, has begun to grin a bit at the thought of how formal things have become after a year of freewheeling give-and-take—either that or what Schwendener ought to do is so obvious that it needn't be stated. Laughter. Class dismissed.

"The main reason I came to Berklee," says tenor saxophonist

McCaslin, "was because I really wanted to get a chance to play with new people in a lot of different settings, from studio work to salsa to jazz or whatever. I come from the beach in Santa Cruz, California, and to play with a guy from New York like Ben [Perowsky]—it's been a real treat. Of course a lot of times I really want to get out into the world, but . . . like, I got an offer to go with the Buddy Rich band, which is a great gig. But I'm really young and still at the point where I don't know what I want to do. If I don't have to, I don't want to get into the GB circuit [i.e., "general business," the Boston-area term for playing weddings, private parties, and so forth]. That's great in some ways, and there's a lot of money there. But right now I don't just want to be a musician, a player. I want to work on becoming an artist."

"The biggest major around here," Perowsky adds, "is musical production and engineering, and that's mostly pop. And if you walk past the ensemble rooms, you'll hear a lot of heavy metal and not so much jazz. But I think that's the way Berklee might prepare you for the real world—not because of the administration or anything but just because the majority of the musicians who come here now are pop-rock oriented. It's just like it is outside." And what path does Perowsky hope to follow once he gets out? "Well," he says, nodding toward McCaslin, "I look to be playing with this guy here."

Both Donny McCaslin and Ben Perowsky are now New York City–based jazz musicians who have recorded under their own names and as sidemen.